UNTO THE UTTERMOST

Missions in the Christian Churches / Churches of Christ

edited by
Doug Priest Jr.

William Carey Library
P.O. BOX 40129
PASADENA, CALIFORNIA 91104

William Carey Library
P.O. Box 40129
Pasadena, California 91104

© 1984 by Doug Priest, Jr.
All Rights Reserved. No part of this book may be used or reproduced in any manner whatsoever without written permission, except in the case of brief quotations embodied in critical articles and reviews.

Printed in the United States of America

Chapter 14, "Toward the Symbiotic Ministry" by Tetsunao Yamamori, from *Missiology: An International Review*, Vol. V, #3, 1977, pp. 265-274, used by permission.

Library of Congress Cataloging in Publication Data

Main entry under title:

Unto the uttermost.

    Includes index.
    1. Christian Churches and Churches of Christ--Missions--Addresses, essays, lecturing. 2. Missions--Addresses, essays, lectures. 3. Missions--Theory--Addresses, essays, lectures. I. Priest, Doug, 1952-
BV2525.2.U57   1984   266'.66   84-11386
ISBN 0-87808-197-6

In accord with some of the most recent thinking in the academic press, the William Carey Library is pleased to present this book which has been prepared from an author-edited and author-prepared camera ready copy.

Contents

List of Contributors   iii

Preface   ix

Introduction: Missions in the Restoration Movement   1
          by Woodrow Phillips

Part One: Theology of Missions

1. Covenant and Mission   21
      by Mont W. Smith

2. The Concept of Discipling in Mission   38
      by Harry R. Baird

3. God and the Gods: Expect Footprints   55
      by Frederick A. Norris

4. Missions in Revelation: Research in Progress   70
      by James C. Smith

Part Two: History of Missions

5. Alexander Campbell's Conception of Mission   95
      by William J. Richardson

6. Revival and the Restoration Movement   116
      by Max Ward Randall

7. Unity and Mission in the Restoration Movement   136
      by C. Robert Wetzel

Part Three: Missionary Anthropology

8. Culture, Ideology and Christian Mission 155
   by Charles R. Taber

9. The Mexican Middle Class Family 176
   by Rex R. Jones

10. A Maasai Purification Ceremony 199
    by Doug Priest Jr.

11. An Eye-Opener for the Rural Javanese 216
    by W. Michael Smith

Part Four: Theory of Missions

12. Donald A. McGavran: The Development of a Legacy 231
    by Herbert M. Works, Jr.

13. Ten Emphases in the Church Growth Movement 248
    by Donald A. McGavran

14. Toward the Symbiotic Ministry 260
    by Tetsunao Yamamori

15. Inter-Cultural Leadership Development 270
    by Edgar J. Elliston

Conclusion: To Fulfill the Task 293
   by Ray A. Giles

Index 309

Contributors

Dr. Woodrow Phillips is currently the Minister of Missions for the Overlake Christian Church located in Kirkland, Washington. His entire life has been dedicated to missions, serving as a minister, a missionary to Jamaica and Eastern Europe, a professor of missions and a Bible College President, serving on various missionary boards, and as a father to missionary sons. His educational background includes the Ph.D degree from the California Graduate School of Theology. He has authored several books and articles on missions related subjects.

Dr. Mont W. Smith was the pioneer missionary for the Christian Churches in the country of Ethiopia. After his return he completed the D. Miss. degree from Fuller Theological Seminary. He began teaching at Pacific Christian College in the fields of church growth and missions. He is currently Chairman of the Bible faculty at that college. He has written several books, including What the Bible Says About Covenant. Every year he lectures and conducts seminars on missions subjects both at home and abroad.

Dr. Harry R. Baird received his D. Miss. degree from Fuller Theological Seminary following a lengthy experience in missionary endeavors. Besides being a minister in the United States he has served as a long-term missionary in Brazil and as a professor of missions at Manhattan Christian College. He is currently teaching missions and also serves as a board member for the Christian Missionary Fellowship.

Dr. Frederick A. Norris served as director for the Institute of Christian Origins in Tuebingen, West Germany prior to accepting his current teaching post as professor of Christian Doctrine at Emmanuel School of Religion. His Ph.D degree was taken at Yale University. He is the author of numerous articles in the areas of church history, theology and missiology and is currently serving as editor of the review **Patristics**.

Dr. James C. Smith has for over fifteen years served as the General Director of the Christian Missionary Fellowship. His work with CMF has taken him around the world numerous times, and under his leadership the CMF has grown dramatically. He received his D. Miss. from Fuller Theological Seminary. Besides being an ordained minister, he is an elder at a local church, an author and editor, and a popular missions speaker.

Dr. William J. Richardson wrote the important book Social Action vs. Evangelism: An Essay on the Current Crisis and served as editor of Christian Doctrine: The Faith Once Delivered. He received his Ph.D degree from the University or Oregon. He taught thirty-one years at Northwest Christian College and is currently professor of Church History at Emmanuel School of Religion.

Dr. Max Ward Randall earned his D. Miss. degree from Fuller Theological Seminary following a missionary career in South Africa and Zambia. Several countries were opened to mission work for the Christian Churches/Churches of Christ due to Randall's survey work and assistance, such as Zimbabwe, Zambia, Ghana, Indonesia and New Guinea. He authored Profiles for Victory in Zambia and a book on the influence of revivals in the Restoration movement. He serves on numerous missions boards and currently teaches missions at Lincoln Christian College and Seminary.

Dr. C. Robert Wetzel is the Principal of Springdale College and Director of the Institute for the Study of Religion and Culture in Birmingham, England. In his latter capacity he is a recognized lecturer in the Department of Theology at the Univeristy of Birmingham. He is the editor of Essays on New Testament Christianity. He received his Ph.D degree in philosophy from the University of Nebraska.

CONTRIBUTORS

Dr. Charles R. Taber is a respected scholar and has a long career in missionary service. He has served as a missionary in the Central African Republic, as a missions professor, as a translation consultant for the United Bible Society, as editor of both Practical Anthropology and Gospel in Context, and has authored several books. His current position is professor of World Missions at Emmanuel School of Religion. His Ph.D was received from the Hartford Seminary Foundation.

Dr. Rex. R. Jones served as a minister before working in Ethiopia for five years as a missionary. He has taught as a professor of both missions and practical ministries. After a term of pioneering urban missions among the middle class in Mexico City he received his Doctor of Ministry degree from Fuller Theological Seminary.

Doug Priest Jr. is the son of missionary parents. He spent his high school years in Ethiopia and then returned to Africa to serve as a missionary with the Maasai tribe in Kenya. He is currently pursuing his Ph. D degree in missiology from Fuller Theological Seminary while serving as a missionary in Tanzania.

W. Michael Smith has served as a missionary in Ethiopia and presently in Indonesia. He took his M.Div. degree from Emmanuel School of Religion and numerous courses from Fuller Theological Seminary. Between field assignments he served as Director of Church Relations for the Christian Missionary Fellowship.

Dr. Herbert W. Works for many years taught missions at Northwest Christian College before moving to his current position in recruiting, fields and church relations with the Christian Missionary Fellowship. He took his D. Miss. from the School of World Mission at Fuller Theological Seminary and has traveled throughout the world assisting and observing mission efforts.

Dr. Donald A. McGavran has been called the foremost missionary statesman of our century. His grandparents were missionaries in India where he was born and served as a missionary for some thirty years. The "Apostle of Church Growth" earned his Ph.D. from Columbia University and then following an illustrious career started the Institute of Church Growth at Northwest Christian College which became the School of World Missions at Fuller Theological Seminary. He has authored dozens of books and articles on missions. He is an ordained minister with the Christian Church/Disciples of Christ.

Dr. Tetsunao Yamamori is President of Food for the Hungry International. After receiving his Ph.D degree from Duke University he taught and served in adminisrative capacities at several colleges, besides authoring numerous books and articles on missions subjects, including <u>Church Growth in Japan</u> and <u>Introducing Church Growth</u>. He has traveled extensively throughout Asia, Africa and Latin America.

Dr. Edgar J. Elliston has served as a missionary in Ethiopia and Kenya. His Ph.D was taken from Michigan State University in the field of education. Besides studying leadership development and literacy, he has completed numerous research projects and served as a missions professor in both Kenya and the United States.

Ray A. Giles is Co-Director of Personnel with the Christian Missionary Fellowship, with responsibilities in recruiting and field visitation. He earned his M.Div. degree from Southern Baptist Theological Seminary and has studied linguistics and missiology. He has served as a missionary in Ethiopia, and has conducted extensive research in East Africa.

Preface

Unto the Uttermost was an idea that came to me just over a year ago while wrapping up my first term of missionary service with the Maasai tribe in Kenya. After having thought little of "academia" for some four years I found myself preparing to return to the United States to go back to school among other things. Pondering further graduate study led me back to my Bible college and seminary days when I prepared for missionary service. One of the lacks that I had felt was that I was not able to read many missionary books coming out of the Restoration movement.

The movement has a fairly good missionary history, though the current plateau in the total number of missionaries working in cross-cultural situations is distressing. We have many field missionaries who have also earned their stripes in the classroom. I thought, "Why not solicit articles from some of these people and have them published as a volume?"

The intended audiences for such a book would be: Bible college and seminary students taking courses on mission subjects; ministers, elders and members of missions committees; and church members interested in missions.

After conceiving the idea and discussing it with several colleagues, I decided to take on the project as editor and solicit articles. My criteria for selecting authors was that they had been missionaries or involved with mission work as well as being academically qualified since the book was to serve primarily as a college and seminary textbook. All of the authors chosen replied that they would be happy to contribute an article on the theme that I suggested to them. A publisher was found, the articles were written and edited, and the printing commenced.

The format of this book is derived from the academic discipline of missiology -- the study or science of missions. That discipline is as old as Creation and will last until our Lord's return, but as a classroom discipline is only fairly recent. Missiology is divided into various fields: theology of missions, history of missions, missionary anthropology, theory and practice of missions, comparative religion, area studies, etc. Of course, each of these fields can be studied apart from the mission dynamic, simply as a classroom exercise. But for Christians, it is the mission element that brings life and purpose to these disciplines.

In April, 1974, Milligan College in Tennessee hosted a symposium with the imposing title "The Adaptation/Syncretism Axis." At the symposium a committee of renowned missiologists were appointed to examine the question of guidelines for a curriculum suitable for the training of missionaries in cross-cultural understanding. The committee did its work and a short report was issued in the **Milligan Missiogram** (Tippett, 1974:1-3). Since we have moved beyond the days of simply sending out missionaries with little or no training in missiology, portions of that report are reproduced here in the hopes that the work of that select committee will serve as a guideline for our missionary training and curriculum planning.

The Statement

1. The training of cross-cultural missionaries for the changing times and conditions of the mission fields of the world in our day requires more and more understanding and empathy. For many years the discipline of anthropology (especially such aspects as social and applied anthropology, acculturation, cultural dynamics, the phenomenology of religion and ethnolinguistics) has been inadequately utilized in the majority of educational institutions where missionaries are trained. With the availability of this kind of education in our day, the sending forth of missionaries untrained in anthropology is no longer justified.

PREFACE

2. We recognize that the missionary situation in the world has changed dramatically since World War II, and that the old methods need revision, and the training provided for missionaries needs to be more relevant to the new situations. This requires a re-evaluation of missionary methods and a reconsideration of fields of concentration in any missionary training curriculum.

We recognize that as long as missionaries do go forth they need to be trained within a well developed and relevant cross-cultural curriculum.

3. The following model is recommended for consideration by an institution planning or adjusting its curriculum for the training of missionaries. It is meant to serve as a basis for discussion and not in any way to limit or control the field -- merely to assure that all these emphases receive serious consideration.

It is assumed that each missionary will have received his general education, together with his or her theological and biblical training. The fields set out in this model are related to **preparation** for service in Christian cross-cultural mission, not the home ministry.

We do not say that all these subjects should be taught before the candidate leaves the institution: e.g. Language Learning might be taken in a special institution or on the field -- but it should be taken somewhere.

The model is set into two columns, the left column being a simplified training and the right column being a more developed training that may require a larger faculty or a training program for a wider range of mission fields.

The Model for Missionary Training

I. Simplified	II. More Developed
1. History of Missions	Hist. of Missions to the Reformation. Hist. of Missions from the Reformation
2. Theology of Mission	Theo. of Mission - Gospels Theo. of Mission - New Testament Church
3. Principles and Practice of Missions	Prin. and Practice of Missions Indigenous Church
4. Cultural Anthropology	Cultural Anthropology Social Structure and Authority Patterns
5. Comparative Religion	Hinduism and Buddhism Islam
6. Applied Anthropology	Applied Anthropology Theory of Anthropology
7. Traditional Religions	Phenomenology of Traditional Religions Traditional Religious Practitioners and Practices
8. Church Growth Case Studies	Ch. Growth Case St. - Africa Ch. Growth Case St. - Asia and Latin America
9. Language Learning	Language Learning Language and Culture
10. Missionary Internship	Missionary Internship Mission Project
11. Global Awareness and World Affairs	Global Awareness and World Affairs Cultural Dynamics
12. Spiritual Growth of the Missionary	Spiritual Growth of the Missionary

PREFACE

Several others have shared in the production of this book: those who contributed funds so that the book could be printed; those who shared in the artwork and the proofreading; and the staff of the William Carey Library whose technical advise was appreciated. So to Charles Kizer, Wayne Wertz, Kim Osness, Gene Sonnenberg, Robyn Priest, Chuck Hammond, Doug and Marge Priest, Trina Crockett, the Koinonia class from Eastside Christian Church and the authors, my profound thanks.

Doug Priest Jr.
Fullerton, California
1984

BIBLIOGRAPHY

Tippett, Alan R.
    1974   "Report of the Curriculum Committee on the Training of Missionaries." <u>Milligan</u> <u>Missiogram</u>. 1:3:1-3.

Introduction

Missions in the Restoration Movement

by Woodrow Phillips

In writing of the Restoration Movement, the continuing fragmentation of a people conceptually committed to unity poses expanding difficulties. In missions this fragmentation has produced serious and long lasting consequences that continue to this moment. It is not my purpose to dwell on these, but their existence must be noted to place in perspective the mission thrust of the churches.

Even on the mission field the fragmentation has continued when many other church bodies seem to be able to transcend differences in realizing the unity in basic doctrines that send men and women forth to fulfill Christ's commission. It is my prayer that this unity can be achieved among all mission heirs of the restoration ideal.

From their early writings, it is evident that the world wide implications of the gospel were apparent to Restoration leaders although this movement was slow in developing a means by which mission could be achieved (DeGroot, 1963:20-21).

On October 23, 1849, Alexander Campbell became president of the newly formed American Christian Missionary Society despite his protest against all organizations other than the local congregation. In accepting this position he tacitly admitted that individual congregations needed to share together in promoting and funding the Bible cause or Bible publication, the missionary cause and the educational cause (Campbell, 1849:476).

The example begun in forming a missionary para-church organization through which local congregations could share in missions ministry and financial responsibility set the pattern for Restoration missions for the next 75 years and continues as a major force in the mission thrust today. Missionary societies are part of our historic fabric although only one segment of the movement ever attempted a "churchwide" or representative denominational mission agency. This decision that produced the formation of the United Christian Missionary Society of the Disciples of Christ further divided the Restoration heirs. It also confused the issues of extra-congregational cooperation by the charges of liberalism and irresponsibility toward brotherhood decisions leveled against the U.C.M.S.

Once the Restoration leaders followed Alexander Campbell in his approval of the American Christian Missionary Society the pattern was continued. Campbell was its president until the year of his death in 1866.

The A.C.M.S. sent J. T. Barclay, a medical doctor, to Jerusalem in 1850. Finding a more open door six miles south he established a school and hospital in Bethlehem. Barclay returned home in 1854. A year earlier the society had sent Alexander Cross to Liberia. Cross was a slave who had purchased his freedom. Unfortunately, he died a few weeks after entering Africa and no work was continued there. In 1854 the A.C.M.S. sent J.O. Beardslee to Jamaica. This effort resulted in 13 churches and 640 converts and continues to the present (Carr, 1946:3).

By 1859 the anti-slavery advocates in the Restoration ranks were very strong. At Indianapolis they formed their own Christian Missionary Society. It was an opposition move to Dr. Barclay's reappointment in 1859 by the A.C.M.S. to return to Jerusalem because Barclay was a slave owner. Their organizing business meeting recorded this statement:

> The true policy of the Christian Church is to encourage the formation within the role of her communion of as many missionary societies as by reason of the convenience of locality and facilities of social and religious intercourse, may be deemed necessary to call out the full liberality of the brethren, and interest and engage them all, as far as practical in missionary work (Vandergrift, 1945:46).

Even with such lofty ambitions the Christian Missionary Society ceased to function in 1863.

From its inception many brethren questioned the Biblical validity of the A.C.M.S. or any organization except the local church to fulfill the missionary mandate. Among these Tolbert Fanning and William Liscomb voiced their opposition in the pages of the **Gospel Advocate** (West, 1950:205).

In spite of such views the majority of the brotherhood moved ahead in forming organizations for spreading the gospel. Most of these were state missionary societies whose goal was to evangelize the American frontier. These societies spread rapidly into most states where the Restoration movement was strong, such as Ohio and Missouri. By 1929 forty of these societies had been formed. Most grew out of earlier informal state or regional conventions. They became the backbone of Restoration mission efforts, particularly in evangelizing the American West.

As a result of the growth of these state societies, the influence of the A.C.M.S. and the commitment to foreign missions declined. By 1874 very little foreign effort was being attempted, so in 1875, due to the efforts of W. T. Moore and others, the Foreign Christian Missionary Society was formed in Louisville. That same year Carolyn Neville Pearce of Iowa led 75 women at the General Missionary Convention in founding the Christian Women's Board of Missions.

Isaac Errett of the **Christian Standard** was alone among Restoration editors of that day in strongly advocating the missionary societies. These societies succeeded in placing missionaries on the field. The Christian Women's Board of Missions did an outstanding work in organizing youth of the churches for mission support and interest. Both societies gave the Restoration movement increased missionary outreach and influence. By the close of this period these agencies had placed missionaries in 21 foreign countries (Filbeck, 1980:25):

Argentina	France	Mexico
Belgian Congo	Hawaii	Panama
Canada	India	Paraguay
China	Italy	Philippines
Cuba	Jamaica	Puerto Rico
Denmark	Japan	Tibet
England	Liberia	Turkey

The Growth of Church of Christ (non-instrumental) Missions

The opponents to the method of congregational cooperation through the state conventions and agencies saw in the rise of these para-church structures a departure from original Restorational principles. They believed the local church was God's missionary society and was ordained within the framework of its own structure to evangelize the world. They concluded that use of these societies was a violation of God's New Testament plan. Hence the next step was to declare missionary societies heretical and divisive.

The **Christian Evangelist** now took up the society cause along with the **Christian Standard**. Their chief argument for the societies was their expediency. They also appealed to the opposition to demonstrate that their idea of single church responsibility for missions could reach the world (Errett, 1866:20).

Soon this debate spilled over from the journals into the churches with resulting congregational disunity. A brotherhood-wide division was on the way. On August 18, 1889, the Sand Creek Address and Declaration asked for this division by declaring:

> We state that we are impelled from a sense of duty to say that all such as are guilty of teaching or allowing and practicing the many innovations and corruptions to which we have referred...if they will not turn away from such abominations -- we cannot and will not regard them as brethren (West, 1950:432).

In 1906 the anti-society churches withdrew to form the Churches of Christ (non-instrumental). The issue was not just the missionary society, but the whole realm of church life and action unauthorized by explicit Biblical example or command. Beginning with 2,649 congregations in 1906 and a membership of some 160,000 this separating group had growth that peaked in 1960 with 16,500 churches having a membership of 2,025,000. They outstripped both the Disciples and the independent churches in the Restoration movement.

For many years these churches did little in the area of foreign missions. In 1880 the Jamesville, Texas congregation sent R. W. Officer to the American Indians. In that same year Jules DeLannay was sent to France. In 1889 Azariah Paul went to Armenia. The first missionary effort of the Churches of Christ was to Japan. W. K. Azbill and J. M. McCaleb were the missionaries. Azbell later joined the Disciples but McCaleb laid the foundation for the work in Quika, Japan.

At the present time the Churches of Christ have more than 200 families working in 70 nations. Exact figures are difficult to obtain because of complete congregational autonomy and because there exists no reporting system for the whole group of congregations. They have developed a large and successful foreign missions ministry using local churches as the sponsoring, sending and supporting agencies. Two missionary magazines keep the churches informed of Church of Christ world outreach and progress; **World Vision** and **Christian Chronicle**. Among the countries where Church of Christ missionaries serve are:

Australia	Holland	Scotland
Austria	Hong Kong	Singapore
Belgium	Italy	South Africa
Canada	Korea	Sweden
Cuba	Nigeria	Tanzania
Denmark	Norway	West Germany
England	Philippines	Zimbabwe

While full figures cannot be easily obtained for the mission work of the Churches of Christ (non-instrumental), they can no longer be called anti-missionary, which was a charge against them in their early history. It is estimated that these churches now give over fifty million dollars per year for missionary, educational and benevolent purposes (Murch, 1962:319).

The Growth of Restoration Missions from Non-U.S.A. Churches

While their strength and witness cannot be adequately dealt with in this introduction, it must be noted that Churches of Christ in Great Britain, Australia, New Zealand and Canada have also produced missionary personnel and funding for overseas work. These churches, with the exception of the Churches of Christ non-instrumental among them, are organized into national church bodies with foreign mission departments. They are all at least loosely associated with the Disciples of Christ, although theological shifts in recent years have produced some divisions among them. The arguments that led to the 1906 separation in the American churches have not touched these churches to any large degree. Their mission efforts are done through cooperative church-wide agencies similar to the pre-1906 practice of the Restoration churches in the United States.

Individual heroic mission workers are well known from their ministries -- especially in India and East Africa. Statistics showing fields, missionary personnel, dates of entry, churches established and number of converts can be obtained from the missionary departments of the sending countries.

Changing Mission Patterns in the Restoration Movement

Another significant branch of Restoration thought and life began to emerge at the beginnings of the 20th. century. Deeply committed to biblical Christianity and opposed to the influence of liberal theology, these people were part of the Disciples of Christ. They felt the "Divine Silence" of the scriptures was not **prohibitive** but **permissive**. They believed that the churches were free to write into this silence congregational and intra-congregational practice as long as it did not invade or violate scriptural commandments. They believed the New Testament is the guide for personal and corporate Christian life but freely used agencies, organizations, conventions, associations, etc. for missions, benevolence, education and other activities that the single congregation could not easily assume.

Even so, there has been a reluctance to utilize church-wide missionary societies by some within the movement. This stems, not so much from a conviction that such organizations are prohibited, but from experiences of the World War I to 1926 years and the futile attempts to have their conservative views represented in the existing missionary societies.

As early as 1867 Isaac Errett expressed their views:

> The **Standard** is the only weekly paper among us now that advocates missionary societies... But we have no idolatrous attachment to the General Missionary Society. If it can do the work proposed, we will encourage it. If it fails to command sufficient confidence and sympathy to enable it to do its work wisely and well, we shall go in for whatever form of associated effort the general wisdom of the brotherhood may approve (Errett, 1867:68).

Many began to feel that the existing mission societies were no longer doing their work either wisely or well. They were convinced that essentials to the gospel were being ignored and violated. For many years voices of protest were raised but no overt act of sufficient impact to produce sharp controversy or division arose. One group sought to strengthen, enlarge and depend for church life on the organizations. The others saw the organizations as expediencies to accomplish the work but were ready to discard any agency no longer fulfilling local congregational aims and purposes. With such a dichotomy eventual embroilment and finally separation were almost inevitable.

Theological liberalism on the mission field became the focus for distress and division. This form of thought, applied to the mission situations, produced divergent methods of ministry. Liberalism saw persons needing to be taught, but not persuaded to accept Christianity since it was not part of their culture. The conservative missionary, on the other hand, sought to convert non-Christians and would not accept persons into church fellowship who had not become believers. Liberal theology saw Christianity as a cultural product while biblical theology saw Christianity as the Revelation to be brought to all nations. Liberalism embraced Rationalism while biblical theology held to authoritative revelation and evangelism. Liberalism first entered Restoration ranks in colleges and universities where Disciple students were studying for ministry and missions.

The Development and Mission Outreach of the United Christian Missionary Society Among Disciples

Unfortunately, the growing influence of liberalism coincided with the call for uniting the missionary societies of the Disciples of Christ so that there would be a greater unity in missions outreach and funding from the churches. J. H. Garrison began to promote this unification as early as 1892 in the pages of the **Christian Evangelist.** Boards for missions, benevolence and education continued to grow and the many appeals to the churches for financial aid increased proportionately. Many churches wanted relief from these constant demands for presentation of good causes. Other persons desired a unification of Disciple agencies to solidify their witness to other denominations regarding unity, as there was a growing sentiment among Protestant denominations for closer consolidation on the mission field and in seeking funding at home.

The fear of many concerning a church-wide society was two-fold. J. A. Lord, editor of the **Christian Standard**, expressed the fears that the societies would be diverted from their original purpose of evangelizing, and that they might also become dictatorial (1906:1202-1203). His fears were realized in the opinion of many conservative Disciples two decades later. In 1919 after much debate, writing and controversy, the United Christian Missionary Society was born in Cincinnati during the meeting of the International Convention. The existing missionary societies, benevolent organizations and other Disciple cooperative ministries were brought together under one organization and leadership. The six boards and societies that merged were: 1) the American Christian Missionary Society; 2) the Christian Women's Board of Missions; 3) the Foreign Christian Missionary Society; 4) the Board of Church Extension; 5) the National Benevolent Association; and 6) the Board of Ministerial Relief. From these organizations the U.C.M.S. inherited

> the administration of ten mission fields, 275 missionaries, and 23,711 church members on foreign soil. From the Christian Women's Board of Mission, the UCMS inherited mission fields in Jamaica, India, Mexico, the Belgian Congo, Argentina, and Paraguay. From the Foreign Christian Missionary Society, the UCMS assumed control over mission work in India, China, Japan, the Philippines, and Puerto Rico (Carr, 1946:11).

The formation of the missionary society and the subsequent battle over open membership, liberalism, interdenominational cooperation, funding of non-missionary ventures and other concerns became the focus from which the "independent missions" movement among the Disciples gained its impetus and growth.

The Disciples of Christ continued through the U.C.M.S. to send missionaries to the foreign field. Increasing involvement in social schemes reduced their evangelistic missionary personnel however. In 1919 the U.C.M.S. reported 300 missionaries, 1700 national workers, 230 church organizations, 560 schools and colleges, 18 hospitals and 20 dispensaries.

The foreign arm of the U.C.M.S. later became the Division of Overseas Ministries of the Disciples of Christ (Christian Church). Present figures for foreign ministry include work in twelve different lands:

Argentina
India
Jamaica
Japan
Mexico
Nepal

Paraguay
Philippines
Puerto Rico
South Africa
Thailand
Zaire

An impressive journal, **The Disciple**, formerly **World Call**, is published and informs the constituency of mission work and new developments in thinking and strategy. The Disciples of Christ are sponsoring in cooperation with varying agencies 240 missionaries, 2200 national workers, 267 churches, 1430 meeting places, 130,500 members, 336 schools, 13 hospitals and 23 dispensaries. Its work force has declined in the past decade as a movement of its funds and personnel has gone into ecumenical ministries. Evangelism in the Great Commission context seems to be no longer a priority in their ministry.

Emergence and Growth of Independent Missions in the Restoration Movement

The independent missions movement among the Disciples began before the break of 1926 in the Restoration movement. By 1895 there were 21 independent missionaries receiving support in various ways who were not under the auspices of any of the Disciples' missionary societies. There were others besides these 21, but their disassociation from any missionary society relationship makes their discovery difficult.

In 1926 the actions of the U.C.M.S. and the issue of open membership divided the already fragmented Restoration movement. From these earlier independent beginnings, and from the thought and writing of W. K. Azbill, the foundations for an expanding missionary force was born. The first of this new wave of Christian Church missionaries were in a sense accidental. Azbill and others serving overseas, for various reasons, were sponsored independently or resigned from the existing societies to become part of the vanguard of the independent missionary movement among Christian Churches. In the same year the Leslie Wolfe family, who were serving in the Philippines, were dismissed from the U.C.M.S. As a result of their dismissal it was felt by many that the church-wide board of the Disciples was no longer interested in appointing conservative missionary personnel.

This independent missions movement, then, flowed from two streams: the early mission agencies and the pre- 20th. century independent missionaries. Filbeck illustrates this movement:

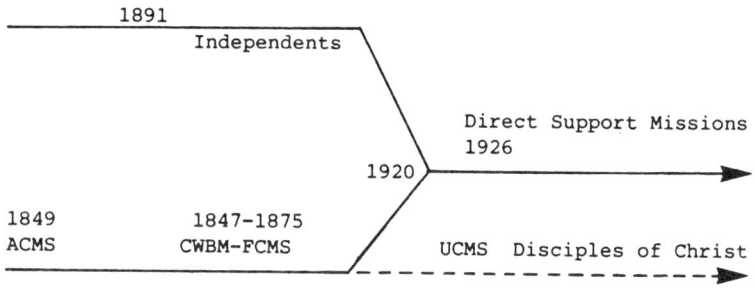

(borrowed from Filbeck, 1980:175).

"Independency" and "direct support" are two missions concepts that became intertwined in the early days of the new independent missions movement[1]. As used in Restoration thought, independent meant simply that a missionary was not sponsored or supported through existing brotherhood recognized agencies. Direct support referred to the practice of sending funds directly to the missionary without the use of an agent to supervise or disperse the funds. With modifications this model of missionary support was widely adopted by the newly emerging independent missionaries.

Not all independent missionaries continue to follow this support pattern. Many have organized independent mission boards, corporations, advisory boards and forwarding agents into their concept of this model. In the past few decades an increasing number of missionary personnel are being sent out under the sponsorship and guidance of missionary organizations somewhat similar to the early Restoration societies. Among these missionary sending organizations could be included the Christian Missionary Fellowship, Brazil Christian Mission (now defunct as a sponsoring organization), Pioneer Bible Translators, TCM International (formerly Toronto Christian Mission), Jamaica Christian Mission, the Continuing Christian Church in India and many field organizations that provide guidance and promote cooperation on the foreign field. Few of these organizations are broader in scope than one particular country or mission field, the Christian Missionary Fellowship and Pioneer Bible Translators being notable exceptions.

These organized efforts at missions are modifications of the independent direct support method used in the conservative Christian Church mission enterprise. All share a deep commitment to the Word of God, the New Testament church and the Great Commission mandate. Almost all require recruits to raise their own support which is then forwarded to them on the field. Perhaps in this modification the best of two ideologies can be attained. Cooperation on the field and missionary accountability are badly needed; and independency helps preserve personal initiative and ministry.

No matter from what precise position in this spectrum the independent missionary operates, it is apparent that this movement unleashed a new wave of cross-cultural missions among Christian Churches and Churches of Christ. However, we have gotten ahead of ourselves. Let us return to the post World War I situation.

The Rothermels in India; the J. Russel Morses in China; and the Harry Schaefer Srs. in India were among early independent mission leaders who withdrew from the United Christian Missionary Society to begin new evangelistic works. To support themselves, ideally each would have a "living link" church sponsoring and supporting their work. In reality, the missionaries often needed many living links to survive and meet their ministry needs. The living link concept gained ground over the earlier "clearing house" free agency offer of the Christian Restoration Association. This agency had generously volunteered to receive and dispense funds directly to any missionary approved by the churches.

The depression of the early 30's and World War II were harsh barriers for all foreign mission work in the Restoration movement. Societies and independents alike suffered loss of personnel and fields in the changing political, economic and cultural revolutions. Several direct support missionaries were held in the Philippines as prisoners of the Japanese. The Schaefer family and some from the Morse mission in China remained in India. Epic stories of heroism and evangelism remain a legacy from these world disasters.

By 1945, ninety independent missionaries were known and listed. Some 3000 baptisms per year were being reported in the same year (Carr, 1946:158). In 1976 the number of missionaries had grown to almost two-thousand, serving in forty-five nations in 300 different missions.

Without doubt the Faith-Promise concept of church involvement in support of world evangelism has contributed greatly to the ability of independent Christian Churches to support this growing number of missionaries. The Faith-promise concept in essence says that a congregation trusts God to supply a certain financial amount which, when supplied, is given to the mission program of the church. Most of the congregations that have used this approach to fund-raising for missions have found that they have been able to give much more than they previously gave with the typical "percentage of the budget given for missions" approach.

Along with this unprecedented growth has come a plethora of para-church agencies to provide service support, materials, resource persons and missions strategy for the front-line missionaries. Some of these service organizations include:

>Christian Military Fellowship
>Christian Missionary Fellowship
>Fellowship and Association of Medical Evangelists
>Good News Productions
>Hungry Children, U.S.A.
>International Disaster Emergency Service
>Operation Evangelistic Ministries
>Pioneer Bible Translators
>South Pacific Evangelizing Fellowship
>Specialized Christian Services

The growth of these agencies showed that direct-support missions were becoming more structured and organizational in their orientation. This trend, which has continued and even grown into the present, poses an interesting dilemma for direct support missionaries among conservative Christian Churches. The issue is this: How can these churches preserve the best of direct support and independent vitality, personal initiative and church-to-missionary relationship and responsibility and still meet the demands of the changing and chaotic international political scene, as well as deal effectively with the mounting economic demands of sending and supporting a family on the field. Hopefully, the same genius for practicality and biblical authority that has characterized the rapid growth of this third segment of Restoration mission life will supply adequate solutions.

It does seem inevitable from the trends already in progress that the extreme independency of the first 50 years of direct support missions, 1926-1976, is ending and a new dynamic and thrust is developing. While some may decry this change, it may well be the leading of God into even more missionary outreach.

The recent awareness of "people groups," especially **hidden** people groups, passed over or unknown in the Protestant missions wave of the 19th. and 20th. centuries, can only be penetrated by more cooperative efforts. This is already happening in Chile, Kenya, Indonesia and the Philippines among other areas where people groups must be reached. The methodology varies from field organizations composed of families of the direct support procedure to small mission societies, also independent, but administering funds in corporate fashion. In at least one of these fields, Indonesia, both of these independent methodologies have banded together in the work of evangelism. This seems to indicate a breaking down of old barriers against cooperation among missionaries of Restoration heritage in recognition of the enormity of the task before us.

The creation of the National Missionary Convention was a significant move to report and promote the growing direct support missionary enterprise. The first meeting was a one-day rally preceding the meeting of the North American Christian Convention in 1948. Another meeting was held two years later in Indiana. From this meeting the determination to hold a missionary convention separate from the North American Christian Convention was decided. It was reported that:

> two decisions were reached which have served
> to build a strong (missionary) convention:
> 1) By popular demand, it was decided to include
> home missionaries on the program, instead of
> making it strictly a foreign meeting; and 2) It
> was decided to make the meeting a separate con-
> vention (McFarland, 1955:109:2).

The formation of Mission Services as a serving agency for direct support missionaries also played a significant role in the life of the independent missions movement.

> Another agency created in the years immediately
> after World War II was Mission Services...
> The purpose for establishing Mission Services
> was twofold: 1) to publish news and reports of
> missionaries and their work for churches and

individuals in the USA; and 2) to serve as a purchasing service for missionaries through which missionaries could buy equipment more cheaply than otherwise (Filbeck, 1980:216).

Mission Services, after several moves, continues its ministry from Tennessee. Its influence among direct support missionaries is waning as other means of advertizing and competing agencies continue to be organized and developed.

The Bible Colleges and Mission Recruitment

When World War II came to an end, mission work among Christian Churches was in a shambles. But the seeds for new growth were present. Four Bible colleges from among these churches supplied most of the missionary personnel: Cincinnati Bible Seminary; Northwest Christian College; Johnson Bible College; and Minnesota Bible College. Several of the newer colleges were beginning to catch a vision for world evangelism. Among these were San Jose Bible College, Lincoln Christian College, Ozark Bible College and Manhattan Christian College.

Returning World War II veterans enrolled in these schools and told of world need and began to volunteer for foreign missions. Several military chaplains from these schools also determined to return as missionaries where they had served in the armed forces.

From these seeds an enlarging flow of volunteers began to go to the field. The schools, sensing the need for better programming in missionary preparation, began to invite missionaries to serve as faculty members. Among these were Max Randall at Lincoln, Woodrow Phillips at Ozark, and Laverne Morse at Cincinnati. Soon permanent mission's curriculum staff, supplemented by furloughing missionaries, became the norm for most of these schools.

The fortuitous opening of the Institute of Church Growth by Dr. Donald McGavran at Northwest Christian College (which later moved to Fuller Theological Seminary in California and became the School of World Mission) coincided with this new outpouring of recruits and provided graduate study opportunities in missions for many of these new volunteers as well as for trained professors eager to learn more about mission principles.

The Bible colleges have played a significant role in the growth of Restoration missions since World War II. They have helped produce the rapid field entry and personal expansion of missions in the last 30 years. Hopefully, they will continue to expand their training and recruiting potential.

At this writing, in early 1984, the Bible colleges are suffering severe financial and enrollment problems. This has caused a cut-back in missions emphasis in some schools. It will be to the advantage of both the Bible colleges and missions in the Restoration movement to see this trend quickly reversed.

The Church Growth Movement

Another factor in the development of Restoration missions has been the Church Growth movement. These concepts from the New Testament were given new life in our century by Roland Allen, a missionary to China. His books, written and distributed in the 1920's, were decades ahead of their time. Their central theme was to establish "self-propagating, self-supporting, and self-governing churches," after the New Testament model.

It remained for Dr. Donald McGavran and his School of World Mission faculty to develop these principles and others into a systematic mission methodology. He helped to provide the spark that made the Church Growth movement a dominant ideal in the 25 years of post-World War II missions expansion. McGavran's writings, years of field experience in India, brotherly spirit and tenacity to biblical authority gave him a hearing as the senior missionary statesman of our age.

The good achieved from the Church Growth movement has tended towards some dilution as disciples of this methodology have continued to expand its application into situations not originally in Allen's and McGavran's thought. In time the abuses may be corrected, or they may result in discrediting what is without doubt one of the foremost factors in the advance of world missions in this century.

CONCLUSION

Some summary of this brief historical overview of missions in the Restoration movement should offer insight into their future in world missions in this day. The trend toward rapid missionary expansion among the Churches of Christ (non-instrumental) and the independent direct support missions paralleled the growth in Christian missions of evangelical persuasion for a similar period (Winter, 1970). The relatively stagnant outreach of the Disciples and their turning from evangelistic, church planting strategy toward social service and ecumenical priorities also followed the general movement of a world ecumenical and national councils of churches ideal. This has resulted in a decline of evangelistic missionaries and overall personnel in this segment of Restoration church life.

The present purposes of these three groups in the Restoration movement may be most clearly reflected in their various practices. The Churches of Christ (non-instrumental) appear to be committed to world evangelism. Though slow and late in accepting the missionary implications of the Gospel, they have grown in both number of missionary personnel and countries entered. Their strategy is church planting. In general they do not believe the Gospel or the Church is biblically represented until they arrive and establish a congregation in a community. This tends to separate them from the main stream of evangelical Protestant missions.

The Disciples pre-occupation with structural union to create unity has dulled their sense of world missions from soul winning and church planting so that their main force is expended in national church movements for union with increasing disengagement from direct evangelism. While commendable in concept, this removes the Disciples from the arena of world missions as mandated in the commission of Jesus Christ. Their gradual merger into a broader union movement is signaling their withdrawl from evangelistic missions.

The independent or centralist portion of Restoration life may be in the position to continue not only to increase their own missionary numbers both in personnel and fields, but recognizing that the larger brotherhood of faith can work cooperatively in any biblically based Christian effort without abandoning or ignoring the distinctives that mark their churchmanship. In benevolent, emergency relief needs, Bible translation, moral movements and education this is already being done.

The great gulf between pagan and non-Christian peoples brings Christian representatives of different theological interpretation closer together in view of the task to be done. Where a common foundation of faith based on biblical authority and life are evidenced, cooperation can be achieved.

Because of the "middle ground" mentality, the independent Christian Churches have bridged many deficiencies within their group to cooperatively create colleges, evangelistic associations, camps, benevolent agencies, mission societies, mission field organizations and new state conventions for sharing ministries they could not accomplish individually. They have also reached out to other Christian groups to utilize their skills and commitment to world need and evangelism. All of this indicates that vibrant life and witness could be ahead for the independent movement.

In missions, the decade of the 1980's will reveal the response to these trends that will either signal the peak of their missions thrust or a continuing pattern of growth and service. Voices are being raised in sharp protest to any change from independent direct support methodology within recognized limitations in the changing world scene. These voices may prevail or evan cause another division in the Restoration movement. The dynamics are present for several different groups to emerge.

More hopefully the desire for unity on the basis of biblical authority without using the "divine silence" in a prohibitive but a permissive way may guide this group into renewed evangelism and church planting at home and a continuing growth and expansion in missions outreach abroad.

It is my prayer that this second course of action will prevail.

NOTES

[1] It is uncertain who first tied these two ideas together to form the model for most independent missionaries from Christian Churches and Churches of Christ.

BIBLIOGRAPHY

Campbell, Alexander
   1849   "Convention." Millennial Harbinger. 476.

Carr, James B.
   1946   The Foreign Missionary Works of the Christian Church. Manhattan: Manhattan Bible College.

DeGroot, A. T.
   1963   New Possibilities for Disciples and Independents. St. Louis: Bethany Press.

Errett, Isaac
   1866   "Missionary Effort." Christian Standard. 4:21:20.

   1867   "Tell It as It Is." Christian Standard. 3:2:68.

Filbeck, David
   1980   The First Fifty Years. Joplin: College Press Publishing Company.

Lord. J. A.
   1906   "The Nature and Limits of Our Missionary Societies." Christian Standard. 8:22:1202-1203.

McFarland, Harrold
   1955   "Convention Fills Need." Horizons. 109:2.

Murch, James D.
   1962   Christians Only. Cincinnati: Standard Pub. Co.

West, Earl Irvin
   1950   The Search for the Ancient Order. Indianapolis: Religious Book Service. (2 vols.).

Winter, Ralph
   1970   The 25 Unbelievable Years: 1945-1969. South Pasadena: William Carey Library.

Vandergrift, Eileen Borden
   1945   The Christian Missionary Society: A Study in the Influence of Slavery in the Disciples of Christ. Unpublished M.A. thesis, Butler University.

Part One

THEOLOGY OF MISSION

"God desires all to be saved."

I Tim. 2:4

1

Covenant and Mission

by Mont W. Smith

It is the proposition of this study that keeping the New Covenant is the execution of the Great Commission. That is, the winning of the ethnics to Jesus Christ, integrating them into the church and equipping them for further world mission is the administration of the terms of the New Covenant.

The above stated proposition includes several assumptions. It is assumed, for instance, that biblical religion is essentially covenantal religion. It is further assumed that covenants are to be understood as treaties having different parties, terms and promises. A competent Bible scholar can easily establish the keeping of the terms of a covenant as the entire duty of the encovenanted, and that failure to execute the terms of a covenant is by definition sin. Since God always benefits the keepers of the covenant, the ethical response to God's grace takes the form of administering the revealed word or will of God. One who has accepted the benefits given by God and has entered a covenant with Him but does not return good to God in the form of administrating His covenant will is unethical. If the covenant will of Christ is the execution of the Great Commission, then one not engaged in that work is in rebellion and is seriously unethical.

In this chapter a rather direct effort will be made to define covenant duty generally, identify New Covenant duty and then relate both to world mission.

BIBLICAL COVENANT

The word covenant translated the Hebrew word berith, which meant treaty. Recent discoveries in the Near East have proven conclusively that the understanding of covenant in the Old Testament meant that Israel had a political type treaty with the Creator of the world. The religious language of the Old Testament was found to be full of diplomatic phrases. The implication of such language is simply that the Hebrews understood they had a valid treaty with Jehovah and that relationship should be taken as seriously as any pact made with clan, king or empire.

Various ancient treaties followed similar formulations or had similar components. No treaty had fewer than three parts: the parties, the terms and the promises. The parties referred to those who had been offered a treaty. Since most ancient pacts were imposed treaties, the word "elect" or "chosen" became a synonym for "party to a covenant." This usage was true in the Old Testament, the Inter-Testamental period and in the New Testament: "Therefore, brethren, be the more zealous to confirm your call and election..." (II Pet. 1:10). Just as the nations surrounding Israel were not members of the Old Covenant, the pagans of today are not members of the church unless they have become parties to the New Covenant.

The terms of a covenant referred to the obligations of the weaker party of the covenant. The vassal would be loyal to the king who agreed to protect him for such loyalty. When a vassal accepted the role of the elect he also agreed to carry out the will of the lord. In the Old Covenant Israel had certain obligations due to her covenant with God; love, faithfulness, obedience, loyalty, sonship, brotherhood, living at peace. The Old Covenant was not a one-sided undertaking by God. It involved the mutual commitment by both parties.

The promises of a covenant were the obligations of the stronger party of the covenant. His promises amounted to moral obligation, yet the weaker member would hesitate to refer to them as duty. In treaties and in the Biblical covenants the obligation of the Lord were called promises. A continued failure to keep the terms of the covenant resulted in the cessation of the promises of the covenant. Consistent breach of the agreement or utter disregard for the welfare of the other made free the partner from his sworn obligation.

God's covenant promises were for a group. An individual Israelite participated in both the promises and the curses of a covenant based upon the group's behavior before God. For instance, God was true to His promise to lead Israel out of the Egyptian captivity and into a promised land, but an entire generation of sinners left their bones in the desert. Similarly God has promised the churches success and eternal life in Heaven. But He did not thereby insure individuals against failure or expulsion from covenant (Rev. 3:15).

It is proper for Christians to emphasize the benefits received because they are under the New Covenant. Confidence in God means confidence in His promises (Heb. 11:6). The mission of Christ will not fail for the simple reason that He has promised it eventual success. That is the major motivation that sends missionaries to foreign lands.

Oath of Covenant

One accepted or entered a covenant by means of an oath swearing procedure. It was called "passing between the halves" (Jer. 34:18-20). In such a ceremony an animal was slain, cut into two halves from head to foot and laid so that the two contracting parties could walk between the halves (Gen. 15:17ff). As each party passed between the halves he uttered, "This is covenant blood." When the slightest element of blood touched him, he had formally signed the covenant (Heb. 9:20). The act of passing between the halves pictures the two as becoming one body. The covenant commitment made their futures one. They now shared a common blood, life, property and fate.

When Christ went to the cross He invoked formal covenant making words, "This is my blood of the New Covenant." The resurrection was referred to as an "oath offering" (Acts 17:34). The death and resurrection is to be understood as God's pledge to mankind that He would do all that Jesus had promised. God signed the New Covenant at Calvary in the blood of Jesus.

Oath Renewal Sacrifices

God provided a way, as part of the treaty itself, for Israel to renew her covenant. The Day of Atonement was a reminder of the original oath swearing at Sinai. Blood sacrifices were the way an individual could cleanse his conscience and obtain a right relationship to God again. They were blood sacrifices because they were designed to remind all of the occasion when their fathers had "cut the covenant" with God. Each year the individual Israelite made that historic event at Sinai his own. While it was a covenant renewal, it was also a remaking, in all good faith, of the vows given originally. When an animal on the altar died, it was understood to stand in the place of the sinner. He, the sinner, ought to have been slain for he had indeed broken the treaty. God was generous to allow the innocent animal to take the place of the Israelite.

In addition to the Day of Atonement sacrifice the scapegoat ceremony pictured atonement. A goat was brought to the high priest. He laid one hand on the animal's head, raised the other hand to heaven, symbolizing the transfer of the sin and guilt from the man to the animal. Then he confessed to God all his own sins and then the sins of all the people. The now guilty animal was then driven out of the camp into the wilderness, bearing the sins of the people with him. When the one animal died and the other was driven out, the Lord had promised He would withhold the punishment due the sinner for another year. If the individual participated in the sacrifice in good faith, his sins were rolled away for a year.

The Levitical Priesthood

The priests administered the entire sacrificial system. In the New Testament scriptures there were several references to the administration of Old Testament sacrifices with a "shadow and substance" fulfillment. Whatever the duties of the New Testament Levites might prove to be, it would constitute the essence of priestly and thus covenantal duty. Paul made several references to sacrificial and priestly duty under the new era. A very consistent theme ran through them. It will be of special interest to see what those activities were. If it can be shown that activities relating to winning the ethnics were linked theologically to priestly duty under the New Covenant, it will almost certainly establish the proposition of this chapter: the evangelization of the nations or peoples is the keeping of the new covenant.

Covenant and Ethic

In the Old Testament ethical words were related to covenant keeping. For instance, chesed was used most frequently in parallel with covenant keeping: "Know therefore that the Lord your God is God, a faithful God who keeps covenant and chesed with those..." (Deut. 7:9). Faithfulness is a word associated by parallelism to chesed: "My faithfulness and my chesed will be with him forever..." (Ps. 89:2). The word chesed was used most frequently to describe the character of God. Chesedness was therefore godliness. The primary aspect of godly behavior would be faithfulness to commitments made or demands associated with the treaty.

A second major ethical term of the Old Testament was righteousness. It was defined by Moses as conforming to the statutes of the Code (Deut. 6:25). Later the Apostle John would hold the same definition, although the commandment had changed (I Jn. 3:7).

The Hebrew word for hear or harken was shema. The word for commandment was mishemarette. To listen to God or to obey Him was to do what He had commanded. What He had commanded was the Torah. Hearing the Lord, walking with Him, loving the Lord and cleaving to Him were all used in parallel with keeping the Law of Moses, administering the duty of the pact (Deut. 30:15-20).

The Hebrew word for justice was mishpat. The words judge, justice and judgments all come from the same original Hebrew stem and share the same root meaning. The judgments of the Lord were the commandments, laws, judgments and statutes of the Code. To be just meant living according to the Torah. To execute judgment meant to live and make decisions according to the known will of God. Giving justice in the courts by a Levite was rendering verdicts using the Code as the standard.

This same procedure, defining Old Testament words by context and parallelism can be applied to such terms as integrity, true to, knowing God, being without fault, being faithful to and walking before God with a pure heart. None of these words have any real meaning apart from a relationship to the terms of the covenant.

It is axiomatic that New Testament words have the same meaning as the Old Testament unless they are clearly redefined by the apostles. If it can be shown in the apostolic writings that ethical terms such as Christlikeness, righteousness, keeping faith with, being true to, hearing Christ and being a good steward were associated with keeping the Great Commission, the proposition of this study is certainly established.

To conclude this section, we have affirmed that morality it covenant keeping behavior. It would be difficult for a Christian or a church to claim to be moral but have no immediate and helpful relationship to world mission. New Testament morality is, by definition, winning the world to Jesus Christ by the gospel and in a Christlike manner.

CHRIST AND COVENANT

Jesus taught that the Hebrew scriptures pointed to Him and specifically to the atonement:

> Then He opened their minds so they could understand the scriptures. This is what is written: the Christ will suffer and rise on the third day and repentance and remission of sin will be preached to all nations (Lk. 24:25-27).

Jesus frequently used the idea of parallel prophesy to relate the scriptures to Himself. Paul referred to the same procedure as "shadow and substance." There was first the example from the Old Testament and then an event or person in the New Testament. Generally speaking, Christ was the anti-type for most previous types. Thus He was at the same time Isaac, true priest, altar, sacrifice, blood and tabernacle. His baptism was the new Red Sea crossing. He was the rock that Moses tapped to supply water in the wilderness. He was the second Adam, second Moses and the true son of David.

The issue before us in this study is whether the idea of covenant remained the essential frame of reference in the New Testament or whether the idea of covenant was itself discarded as an aspect of ceremonial religion. That is, did the very concept of covenant come down into the new age as a new treaty, a formal pact, but with different parties, terms and promises? Did the new elect take a covenant oath?

Five models shall be used for affirming that the New Covenant was a new treaty, with new parties, new obligations and new promises. If it can be determined that the obligations or terms of the New Covenant were centered in the winning of the ethnics to Christ, then the basic proposition of this study is proven.

Model One: Covenant Formulary Itself

In this model it will be shown that the word covenant was used in the New Testament scriptures in direct reference to the categories of parties, terms and promises. There was a new group of the elect: the followers of the Lord Jesus Christ became the people of God (Gal. 3:27-29). The church of Christ was called the Israel of God (Gal. 6:16) and the elect (II Pet. 1:10). The word covenant was directly associated with the idea of parties in the Pauline metaphor (Gal. 4:21-31). In the former dispensation the parties of the covenant viewed themselves as servants of the Lord. The Apostles saw themselves as "servants of the new covenant" (II Cor. 3:6).

The word elect in the New Testament had reference to all in Christ. Christ was elect (I Pet. 2:4), the prototype of all believers. When one joined Christ he too became elect (I Pet. 2:9). The Pauline phrase "in Christ" referred to all who had affirmed allegiance to Christ in baptism and had thus been united with Jesus in His oath at Calvary (Rom. 6:3-6).

The terms of the New Covenant referred to the duties agreed to in the oath taking act. Such duty was called Law under the Old Treaty. It was also called Law under the New (Heb. 7:12). Paul referred to the entire era of Moses as the Law. He identified the new law in two ways: the new covenant and the covenant of the Spirit (II Cor. 3:6). He contrasted the two covenants and called the new one the law of the Spirit (Rom. 8:1). The new covenant set one free from the old covenant.

The member of the pact with Christ agreed to do whatever the Lord Jesus commanded him to do. A disciple tried to be like Christ (Lk. 6:40). To be like Christ meant not only to share Jesus' lifestyle and ethics but to share His goals as well. It is obvious from the scriptures that Christ's goal in coming to the earth was "to seek and to save the lost" (Lk. 19:10). He also came so that He could in turn send others (Jn. 17:18).

Paul summarized the promises gained by those who are in covenantal relation with Christ. Along with the blessings came the anticipated glory of the end. He also added the types of sufferings the believer might expect because he was a member of Christ. He said, "We shall share all things with Him provided that we suffer with Him" (Rom. 8:35).

Jesus summarized the parties, terms and promises of the new era in the Great Commission:

> All authority in heaven and on earth has been given to me. Go therefore and make disciples of all nations, baptizing them in the name of the Father and of the Son and of the Holy Spirit, teaching them to observe all that I have commanded you; and lo, I am with you always, to the close of the age (Mt. 28:18-20).

Model Two: The Sacrifice of Christ

The entire sacrificial system was to provide atonement or forgiveness for erring Hebrews. The benefit of such grace went to the Jews alone. The ethnics of the world, called Gentiles, were not part of the treaty and were not responsible for keeping it (Rom. 1:18-32). It was impossible for all nations to have kept the law of Moses. For instance, all Hebrews were required to "appear before the Lord" at Jerusalem three times a year (Ex. 34:23). The trip from Rome took months.

The Exiles could not possibly have met the requirements of the Code of Moses regarding sacrifices. Sacrifices had to be offered in the Temple on certain days. The Jews of the Diaspora could not meet the demands of the Torah about Temple sacrifices, which meant that they could not have clear consciences because of such failure.

The atonement of Christ swept away the problems of the failure to sacrifice properly. Christ became the last sacrifice under the old code (Heb. 10:8-18). The sins of generations of past Israelites were utterly forgiven in Christ. It was no longer necessary for the Hebrew living in exile to come to the Temple. The church, Christ's body, became the new temple. That good news went out from the holy city first to the Jewish exiles according to the commands given by Jesus.

Included in the blessings of the last great sacrifice were all the ethnics of the world. The entire world was forgiven by God at the Cross (II Cor. 5:14).

There were but two ways a human adult could be sinless. He must have lived all his life without error or he had to be forgiven. It seemed an existential reality that only in being forgiven could any man be declared to be without sin.

But if mankind were utterly forgiven at the Cross, could not all mankind be saved without further ado? If at the moment Christ died all mankind were forgiven then all would be saved and go to Heaven. That reasoning is a kind of universalism and is not apostolic. The apostles taught that Christ's death alone purchased man's redemption. But Paul was not so poor a thinker that he understood one was unconditionally forgiven at Calvary. A sinner was undeservedly forgiven but he had to participate in Christ's death and resurrection to be saved. That participation was sometimes referred to as "calling on the name of the Lord" (Rom. 10).

It was the intent of God that all mankind participate in that last sacrifice and be incorporated into the new emerging Israel (Rom. 9:24-26). That new Israel was called the body of Christ. The apostles made it very clear the ethnics must become part of the church to be saved. Being in the church and being in Christ were but two ways of saying the same thing. Christ's death alone saved but one must get into Christ at His death to participate in it. That was the heart and soul of apostolic theology.

There was another factor added to the atonement. The presence of that factor created the core of apostolic thinking. The ethnics were a matter of serious concern to the apostles as they had been to the prophets of the Messiah:

> Behold my servant whom I uphold, my chosen in whom my soul delights; I have put my Spirit upon Him and He will bring forth justice to the nations... (Is. 42:1).
>
> I have given you as a covenant to the people, a light to the nations... (Is. 42:6).

The entire Old Testament is full of references pointing to the Gentiles or ethnic groups as being part of the concern of God's redemptive purpose.

The sacrifice of Christ was the best news mankind had ever heard. The message of that sacrifice need to be heard around the world or that death was in vain. God could have continued indefinitely to require the blood of bulls and goats if it were only Israel that concerned Him. The entire world needed to be included in God's grace in Christ. World mission made that possible.

God ended the first covenant that He might establish the second and by that covenant He provided for the salvation of all mankind. The new covenant centered in the atonement. Atonement meant forgiveness for the purpose of reconciliation. Was the new covenant simply an agreement between God and Jesus wherein Christ agreed to die for sins and God agreed to forgive all mankind? In such a case man was merely a third party beneficiary of the pact, not a party to it. No, the atonement was an offer by God to forgive all who actually joined Christ at the Cross. Apostolic preaching pointed to the need for man to believe and repent and become united with Christ as a part of the covenant relation. The new covenant without the Gospel and the church was nothing more than transactional universalism -- salvation apart from actually joining Christ as presented in the Gospel. If the saved were, in turn, the ministers of the Gospel then the church became part of the covenant. It was an empty covenant unless it were communicated to pagans and unless they could be persuaded to unite with Christ. The new covenant became, because of the Gospel, a pact between God, Christ and the church. Christ was spoken of as the mediator of covenant. Christ mediated between God and estranged mankind and continued as mediator between God and the church as Moses had between God and Israel. The new covenant was between God and man (Jer. 31:31).

All who accepted Christ's mediation became parties to the new covenant. As a party they were responsible for carrying out the stated will of the Lord. Just as Jesus had said, "Lo, I have come to do Thy will, O Lord," the one in Christ became God's servant. Any servant executed the will of his master. It was the will of his master that none should perish, but that all should come to repentance (II Pet. 3:9).

Model Three: The Royal Priesthood

Every member of the new Israel was a part of the new priesthood (I Pet. 2:9). The new priesthood offered a new type of sacrifice, as Jesus had foretold: "the true worshippers will worship the Father in spirit and in truth" (Jn. 4:23).

There were at least three separate words used in the Greek text that have been rendered "worship" in English. The two main ones were <u>proskunaiseis</u> from which the word prostrate came. Another word, <u>latreuseis</u>, meant an official or covenantal service. The English work "liturgical" came from this word. The two words were often used in parallel:

> You shall worship (proskunaiseis) the Lord your
> God and Him only shall you serve (letourgon)
> (Mt. 4:10).

We must conclude that <u>latreuseis</u> meant worship in the minds of the Biblical writers. The noun form of the same verb was <u>letourgon</u>. Paul used the word in the following passage:

> To be a minister (letourgon) of Jesus Christ
> with the priestly duty of proclaiming the
> Gospel of God, so that the Gentiles might become
> an offering acceptable to God, sanctified by
> the Spirit (Rom. 15:16).

The context clearly showed that ministry meant the temple service of the sacrificial system. Paul departed from his usual typology in this passage. For Paul, usually Christ was the altar, sacrifice, priesthood and temple. In this passage Paul used a different application. He made the preacher the priest, the preaching of the Gospel to the Gentiles the service at the altar. He then added to the picture making the sacrificial animal a Gentile convert.

Peter had said the new priesthood was to "declare the praises of Him who called us out of darkness" (I Pet. 2:9). Preaching the Gospel was declaring God's praises and His grace. One was forbidden to come before the Lord empty-handed under the old covenant. The new covenanter was to bring a convert as a gift of God. Such was worshipping the Father in spirit and in truth. That was the kind of worship the Holy Spirit led the churches to perform (Acts 13:1-3). To use up one's life in the service of the Gospel, "preaching the word," was part of the oblation offering of the new covenant (II Tim. 4:1-6).

Paul alluded to worship practices and sacrifices when writing his letter to the Philippian church (Phil. 4:18). The administration of the duties identified in the treaty as the terms included in a major way the sacrificial system. It is the unescapable conclusion that every church had as its essential duty under the new covenant the conduct of the mission, including support of the cross-cultural preaching such as was being conducted by Paul and his party.

Model Four: Paul's Covenant Logic

Paul related ministry to covenant in the second Corinthian letter. The entire discussion began with chapter three and concluded in chapter five. The data in the three chapters is shown below.

Chapter Three	Chapter Four	Chapter Five
Ministry is the administration of the respective covenant	Ministry means acting for the sake of others	The ministry is the ministry of reconciliation on God's behalf

Paul used two types of logic in the extended discussion of covenant ministry. First he paralleled the word covenant with the word ministry. That was typical Hebrew logic and literary style. The second bit of logic was a syllogism which related categories to each other. Syllogisms have a major premise, a minor premise and a conclusion. For example: A = B and B = C, therefore A = C. Paul's major premise began in chapter three. The minor premise was stated at the end of chapter five. The conclusion was not stated as it was so obvious. It was left for the Corinthian church to grasp.

The major premise was this: the New Covenant duty was ministry (II Cor. 3:6). Paul began with the word covenant. The servants of Christ were enabled to become servants of the new covenant. Paul meant covenant when he spoke of what was written on tablets of stone. It was the covenant, not the ministry, that was engraved on the stone tablets. He had dropped the word covenant and used in its place the word ministry. The administration of the requirements of the covenant was parallel to ministry. When Paul used the word ministry he meant the execution of the demands of the covenant. When one joined Christ, he received the remission of sins regardless of his past. The better the new covenant was administered the more people were brought to life. The preaching of the Gospel was not a work of man's righteousness, it was a work of God. It was the righteousness of God in action. Preaching was not a self-initiated behavior. It was covenantal behavior (I Cor. 9:17).

The major premise of Paul's syllogism was that the terms of the new covenant were ministry. The minor premise followed in chapter five: the ministry was the ministry of reconciliation. Ministry is service done on behalf of others, as shown by Paul in II Cor. 4 and 5. When he defined the ministry of reconciliation he put the intent of God, the sacrifice of Christ and the message of salvation all together. Without the message the act of dying for man's sins would be unknown and unaccepted. Reconciliation would not have taken place. The terms of the new covenant were to do what was necessary to be saved and then to be part of the ministry of reconciliation.

Paul continued his syllogism's minor premise by adding, "We are therefore Christ's ambassadors, as though God were making His appeal through us. We implore you on behalf of Christ..." What followed were the words God wanted all mankind to hear: "Be reconciled to God" (II Cor. 5:20).

Paul then reviewed and summarized his concept of ministry: "He who knew no sin was made to be a sin offering for us so that in Him we might become the righteousness of God" (II Cor. 5:21). Ministry and covenant were always linked in Paul's mind.

It has been the preposition of this study that the execution of the Great Commission -- the ministry of reconciliation -- is the essence of the duty of the new covenant. If the understanding of the passage in II Corinthians is correct, the proposition is fairly proved.

Model Five: New Covenant Chesed

The meaning of chesed grew through several stages. New meanings were added to former ones. The added meaning did not eliminate previous ideas, but rather built upon and assumed them to be true. In the beginning the word meant simply returning good for good received. The concept developed into the basic ethic of the Bible. The term was used more frequently than any other word to describe the character of God. Godliness was therefore the showing of good in return for the good which had been given.

Chesed was stamped upon the consciousness of every human, according to Paul. It was a moral stamp that showed the image of God in mankind. Every human knew that he owed good to someone who had shown kindness to him. Even the pagans were held to be accountable for that (Rom. 1).

The second stage in the development of the ultimate definition of <u>chesed</u> came with its use in parallel. Such development was quite natural. God made Adam and Eve and they were given a kind of informal covenant. God called and gave to Abraham the land of Canaan. He then cut a covenant with him. God saved Noah and after that cut a treaty with him. God rescued Israel from Egypt and then made a covenant with her. God first made David king and then covenanted with him. In each instance involving a covenant with God, the partner was first benefited.

Responding to the grace of God was <u>chesed</u> on man's part. However, God always specified the kind of response he wanted. The law of Moses, for example, was the kind of response God asked at that time. Failure to keep the law was failure to know God. One might not keep the commandments specifically while never intending that to be a signal to God that the relationship was over. But failure to respond at all to God's grace was depravity.

Salvation under the new covenant was achieved by God's grace in Christ. Man was expected to respond with a similar love and service to God. That was how covenant worked. When the Corinthian church collected the offering for Jerusalem, Paul complimented them saying "This service you are performing is not only supplying the needs for God's people, but is also overflowing in many expressions of thanks to God" (II Cor. 9:12). The same principle was given to Corinth regarding their support of Paul's mission. He asked, "If we have sown a spiritual seed among you, is it too much to reap a material harvest from you?" (I Cor. 9:11).

In these passages it seems clear that Paul used the concept of returning good for good received to lay a foundation for asking for money and prayer support. Because Paul had been saved he felt an obligation to God to join Him in His world vision (Rom. 1:5-14). He also felt an obligation to the rest of mankind. If one block of society received the saving Gospel they owed it to God to assist with the winning of other peoples:

> But now, since I no longer have any room for work in these regions, and since I have longed for many years to come to you, I hope to see you in passing as I go on to Spain, and to be sped on my journey by you...

When one accepted salvation there arose a moral obligation to return to Christ assistance in winning some other person.

Certain theologians insist that no response beyond a simple belief in the atonement of Christ saved a person, and they argue that any work done for God thereafter is an expression of thanks having no saving merit at all. Other theologians insist that when one accepted Christ he agreed to carry out commands of his new Lord, and that failure to do so resulted in his loss of salvation. In either case the import of mission was the same. Whether mission was the grateful response of the saved, or whether mission was obedience to a command from Christ, participation in world mission was a stimulated response. Failure to participate in mission was tantamount to moral failure and spiritual disobedience.

One ought not minimize motives for preaching, but the motive at times was less important than the fact that preaching was being done and souls were being saved by it (Phil. 1:15-18). One was certainly morally bound to serve Christ whether his salvation depended upon that service or not. But if the recipient of grace did not respond in chesed to God by being part of the ministry of reconciliation, he was immoral and judged not saved.

It was the proposition of this study that participation in the Great Commission was meeting the terms of the new covenant. Living in chesed is the mark of the saved. New Testament chesed was participation in the atoning work of Christ. Sharing that with others was the mark of the saved and the moral.

CONCLUSION

This chapter was written to make the case that execution of the mandate of Christ to disciple the nations was the essence of the duties of the new covenant. In order to do that, the entire concept of biblical covenant was reviewed. Covenants were shown to be treaties in which each partner made certain promises. The structure of typical covenants had parties, duties and promises. The New Testament scriptures abound in covenant related words and concepts.

Conducting the sacrifices was administration of a major provision of the covenant demands. Moral terms were shown to be related to the keeping of the terms of a covenant. Keeping covenant was being moral, by definition.

The apostles frequently placed their understandings of Christ and His kingdom within the frame of reference of covenants. That is, the new covenant was a new treaty with mankind with Christ as mediator, having new parties, new duties and new promises. The concept of covenant was not metaphorical or merely typological. The covenant was as real and serious as the old one has been, and obedience to it and service in it was similar in expectation even though the specific obligations changed.

The sacrifice of Christ on the cross for the sins of mankind was the central idea of the new covenant. Participation in that sacrifice was essential for salvation. Part of the actual atonement was its communication to mankind. Thus being in the body of Christ as He died for mankind's sin meant being part of His body in its resurrection also. That it turn meant preaching the Gospel so that mankind would be able to participate in the reason for the atonement -- reconciling man back to God. Man was both saved and commissioned under the provisions of the atonement. One always meant the other. For after all, what good was the death for sin if no one were reconciled by it?

Part of the covenant was the priesthood. The priesthood of the old covenant was reviewed. The entire church of Christ was shown to be the new covenant priesthood. Priests were essential mediators between God and man. Thus the church was to stand between God and all mankind with the message and fellowship of salvation. The church was the continuation of the resurrected body of Christ by which men were saved.

It was shown that Paul used a logical device to affirm the ministry of reconciliation as the duty of the new covenant. The syllogism was structured to render that conclusion.

> Major Premise: New Covenant duty was ministry.
> Minor Premise: Ministry was the ministry of reconciliation.
> Conclusion: New Covenant duty was the ministry of reconciliation.

Finally the entire moral concept of <u>chesed</u> was reviewed. <u>Chesed</u> was shown to be the major moral word of the Old Testament. It was the term used most frequently to describe Jehovah. It meant returning good to God for good He had done to us. Since the best good God had done for man was his salvation, the saved owed it to God and to the rest of lost mankind to help secure their salvation in as much as it depended upon them.

By the above procedure it was the intention of this chapter to show the high profile world mission had in the New Testament scriptures. The study was not to lay upon the people of God a burden they could not bear. Nor was it to burden the individuals in the church with a load of guilt if they had not personally gone to the foreign mission field, although a great many more ought to plan to go than do. And the churches ought to send more than they presently do.

The purpose of this article is to ask the churches to take seriously the fact that they had made covenantal promises to God that were more than just the living of a good moral life. Together the individuals of the church made up the royal priesthood. Each soul converted by a missionary who is supported by a church was led to Christ by every member of that church. In that way, at least, all can be missionaries. Being engaged in world mission is not a luxury that only the wealthy churches can afford. It is the very heart and soul of the new covenant. It is the reason the church itself exists. It is the one way a saved person can say thank you to God and make God believe he means it.

2

The Concept of Discipling in Mission

by Harry R. Baird

"Go, therefore, and disciple all the nations, baptizing them in the name of the Father, and the Son, and the Holy Spirit, teaching them to observe all the commands I gave you" (Mt. 28:19). With these words our ascending Lord left His "disciples." The imperative laid upon them a responsibility that was to result in making the peoples of this world what they were: "disciples." What a formidable task. Yet it was to be their mission, their sending.

"Make disciples" is an integral part of the divine sending. Mission is always made up of at least four components: a sender, an agent, a purpose, and an imperative. In the Great Commission Jesus is the sender, the sent are the disciples, the imperative is both "go"[1] and "make," and the purpose is to disciple all the nations.

CONTEMPORARY VIEWS AND ISSUES

As simple as this appears to be, some strong and conflicting theological positions are supported by distinct interpretations applied to Matthew's record of the Great Commission. Four current views can be stated by asking four questions: 1) When does a person become a disciple? 2) Are Christians and disciples the same? 3) How are disciples made? and 4) When is the "teaching" of the Great Commission to take place -- before or after conversion?

Some elaboration needs to be made of these four questions. First, is becoming a disciple the initial step in passing from a state of separation from Christ to the state of reconciliation with God? If so, this reconstruction considers a disciple to be one who joins in following after Jesus for any number of reasons -- curiosity, personal interest, sincere, desperate searching. Out of this clientele some make decisions and commit themselves to Jesus as Lord, are baptized and go on to perfection. According to this view, to be a disciple has a directional stance in that the disciple moves towards perfection in Christ.

Second, some authors propose that "Christians" and "disciples" are two separate concepts, and that "disciple" is a qualitative measure of being a "Christian":

> As you train young Christians to become disciples one of our primary objectives should be to help them discover their gifts (Henrichsen, 1974:132).

> The concept I am using could be summarized by saying a person becomes a disciple when he becomes stabilized in the faith, and has an outgoing commitment to the Lordship of Christ and has developed the basic disciplines of Christian living and service so that the lifelong maturing process is guaranteed, at least as much as is humanly possible (Kuhn, 1978:14).

Quite different from the above quotations is the third view that says becoming a disciple is no different from becoming a Christian. Baptism initiates one into "disciplehood." Finally, the Great Commission "teaching" is held by many to be primarily for the new person in Christ, resulting in being trained and perfected for life and service.

VARIABLES IN DEFINITIONS AND USAGE

The verb and noun forms of the word "disciple," which appear over 250 times in the New Testament, are confined to the Gospels and Acts. However, the verb form is used only four times (Mt. 13:52; 27:57; 28:19; and Acts 14:21). A review of the lexicons, dictionaries and background usage indicates that the transitive verb means "to teach," "instruct," or "make a disciple"; and in intransitive form means "to study and obey the precepts and instructions of one followed." The noun form of the word suggests "learner, pupil, scholar or follower."

In the New Testament the word is applied to specific individuals fifteen times. Small groups are also referred to as "disciples" (Jn. 13:5; 18:1,20; etc.). Specifically these groups are identified in a formal way: the disciples of John (Jn. 1:35; Mk. 2:18; Lk. 11:1: Mt. 11:2); the disciples of the Pharisees (Mk. 2:18; Mt. 22:16); and the disciples of Moses (Jn. 4:18). These followers submitted to the teaching and commands of their teacher or master. Luke speaks of great crowds as being disciples of Jesus (Lk. 6:17). The word is used variously of individuals as well as both large and small groups.

Context has a profound influence upon the meaning of words. Words mean what their author intends, relative to and as they arise out of the context in which they are spoken. To impose an etymological straight jacket on the words in the Great Commission would be erroneous. They mean what the context gives to them. We should determine the meaning of "discipling," not from isolated passages or isolated words, but from the **total** scene as presented in the Gospel and Acts.

An interesting phenomenon of word usage has recently appeared. The English translation of "disciple" has previously been a compound -- "make disciples." But no longer so. Mt. 12:52 is appropriately translated, "Every scribe who has been discipled for the Kingdom of Heaven..." The Great Commission says "Go, therefore, and disciple all nations" (Mt. 28:19). The same principle is used when the verb form is made into a substantive: "A rich man from Arimathea, named Joseph, who had become a disciple..." (Mt. 27:57). Certainly such modifications are logical and permissible.

In addition, it is not always possible to find matching word equivalents in translation. English does not provide a participial form for "faith," so "believing" fills the gap. In some cases there are gaps in the languages being translated. Such is the case with "disciple." The concepts taken from the total context of the original language can be translated with English terms for which there is no equivalent in the original.

A compilation of the various words and their usual definitions should be helpful:

USES OF THE TERM "DISCIPLE"

Disciple (noun):	a learner, an adherent or follower who follows and submits to a teacher and subscribes to his teaching.
Disciple (verb, imperative):	recruit, win, convert persons to follow and submit to a teacher or master.
Discipling (noun, participle, gerund):	the process of making disciples; the process of equipping disciples.
Discipleship (noun):	the life and living of a disciple.
Discipler (noun):	one who engages in discipling.

DISCIPLE: A WORD IN TRANSITION

The noun "disciple" last appears in the New Testament when Luke tells about Paul's return to Jerusalem from his third mission journey. Paul lodged in the house of an early "disciple, Manson of Cyprus" (Acts 21:16). Earlier in the book Luke has written that it was in Antioch that the "disciples" were first called "Christians" (Acts 11:26). Thus, the terms "disciples" and "Christians" are equated.

A dramatic use of the word "Christian" was made by Agrippa at Paul's trial (Acts 26:28). King Agrippa was a knowledgeable man "especially familiar with all customs and controversies of the Jews" (Acts 26:3). The crucifixion and the resurrection of Christ had not "escaped his notice" (Acts 26:26). "In a short time you think to make me a Christian ?" he questioned Paul (Acts 26:28). Surely, as a believer in the prophets, Agrippa was aware of the significance of the word "Christian."

Peter is the only other author who used "Christian" as a name for the followers of Christ (I Pet. 4:16). He called Christians those believers who were scattered throughout

Asia Minor. On his first missionary journey Paul evangelized in the extreme southern part of this region. On his second journey he confirmed the converts there. His stay of two and one-half years in Ephesus was highly productive, for "All the residents of Asia heard the Word of the Lord" (Acts 19:10). All of this indicates that by about 70 A.D. thousands of Christ's followers graced the provinces, cities, towns and communities of Asia Minor. When, therefore, Peter said "If any man suffers as a Christian," these thousands knew of whom he spoke. Apparently by this time "Christian" had replaced "disciple" as the popular term for referring to those of "the sect everywhere spoken against" (Acts 28:22).

The popularization of the word "Christian" did not lead other writers of the New Testament to adopt it. Paul never used "Christian" or "disciple." Instead, he spoke of the beloved of God, (Rm. 1:8); the saints (I Cor. 1:2); brethren (Col. 1:2), etc. Gentile believers in Antioch, a King of Judah and brethren all over Asia knew about "Christians" early in the Christian age. The word "disciple" had for some reason been dropped by biblical writers who used other terms for the disciples of Christ.

DISCIPLING AND THE GREAT COMMISSION

The Great Commission is expressed in a variety of ways in the New Testament[2]. Viewing each passage shows more clearly the elements contained and the way in which discipling is involved. Each of these elements can be identified in one of the records of the Commission.

THE ELEMENTS OF THE GREAT COMMISSION

1. Authorizing 2. Waiting 3. Empowering	3 elements of **preparing**
4. Sending 5. Going	2 elements of **commissioning** or **sending**
6. Proclaiming 7. Witnessing 8. Discipling	3 elements of **executing**
9. Believing 10. Repenting 11. Baptizing	3 elements of **appropriating**
12. Saving 13. Giving	2 elements of **blessing**
14. Condemning	1 element of **refusing**
15. Teaching 16. Observing 17. Feeding	3 elements of **nurturing**
18. Accompanying 19. Confirming	2 elements of **continuing**

Figure One

THE ESSENCE OF DISCIPLING

It is Matthew's rendition of the Great Commission that brings disciple-making to the center of the mission enterprise. By relying on the total New Testament context we are able to put together the components that Matthew introduces.

Discipling Begins as an Initiatory Act

When Paul and Barnabas preached the Gospel in Derbe, they "discipled many" (Acts 14:21). What did these missionaries do to make disciples? These apostles did not tarry for weeks and months discipling those already discipled. They did, however, return later to this area "strengthening the souls of the disciples, exhorting them to continue in the faith..." (Acts 14:22). They certainly did not have to make Christians out of the disciples. The context of making disciples requires them to be Christians at the same time.

The definitive act of becoming a disciple can be clearly perceived by observing the way the apostles executed the mandate. They proclaimed the Gospel, which was believed. Hearers repented and were baptized in the name of Jesus and were added to those who already had submitted to King Jesus. A disciple did not graduate into being a specialized Christian. By a precise rite of passage a person became a saint, a son, a brother, a Christian or a disciple. Luke begins early in Acts to indicate that the disciples were a specific group who had confessed Jesus as Messiah, as seen in Acts 6:1; 9:19; 11:26; 21:4 (Thayer, 1886:386).

Discipling Results in a Specific State

A disciple is a person "in state." Paul and Barnabas "made" disciples. The Lord commissioned His apostles to do something specific to non-disciples so that after it was done they were disciples. By some act, response or rite they entered **into** the state of being a disciple.

"Disciple" does have the study aspect to it, but such a meaning must not crowd out the "state" and "belonging" concepts. A disciple is an **adherent**, one who joins and becomes a part of a group by submitting to the master of that group. To "make disciples" means to make members of the body of Christ. By the time of the Great Commission "disciple" was a term that spoke specifically of those who submitted to the Lord Jesus. It was not used to refer to any would-be observer who tinkered with learning about Jesus and His teaching. Admittedly the word "disciple" was applied to uncommitted people who temporarily, flippantly or sincerely were searching for answers to life. That was a general way to identify them, and the New Testament refers to such (Lk. 6:7; Jn. 6:66). But to impose this partial concept on the entire New Testament usage of the term "disciple" is inaccurate. It is erroneous to say that Jesus sent His agents on a global mission to make incomplete followers. Jesus' concern was for people to be specifically identified with Him.

Discipling Requires an Equipping and Training Process

Discipling has a continuing aspect just as salvation has some sequential implications (Phil. 2:12). After being added, the adherent or follower does not terminate his learning, obeying and developing. Just as a baby grows up, a disciple becomes like his teacher (Lk. 6:40). All of this growth can fall handily under the rubric "discipleship," which is the life and responsibility of the disciple.

A good share of the current emphasis on discipling is on training, which is not wrong, but is unnecessarily limited. The Revised Standard Version translates Mt. 13:52 with this particular bias: "...every scribe who has been trained [discipled] for the Kingdom of Heaven." Jesus trained His apostles, Paul trained his Timothys. Timothy was told to commit the Gospel to faithful men who could teach others (II Tim. 2:2). Even though a composite view of discipling includes training the disciple, other terms can also be used to adequately describe what the disciple should do as a follower of Jesus: grow, be strengthened and be equipped. Jesus saw the necessity of supplying something more than what was implied in the word "disciple" when He added in His commission "teaching them to do what I have commanded" (Mt. 28:19). An element of teaching is involved in making disciples. Disciples must understand something before they submit to the master, but the teaching which is a prelude to becoming a disciple is not so much instruction about the Christian life as it is a heralding of the Good News so that the hearers may believe and become disciples.

Discipling Implies a Perfecting Relation

The qualitative component in discipling must be carefully distinguished from the "initiatory" and "state" elements. The previous point indicates that making a disciple is a different process from teaching him all that

Christ commanded. Becoming a Christian is not the same as
developing and growing as a Christian. Being born is not
the same as maturing. Enlisting as a soldier is not equivalent to being trained as a soldier. Often initiating terminology is used for qualitative expression, as in the queries
"Are you a born-again Christian?" or "Are you a Spirit-filled Christian?" All Christians by Biblical definition
are born-again and Spirit-filled. There are no other kinds.
But born-again and Spirit-filled are erroneously used to
indicate a supposed moral or qualitative advancement.

The Scriptures indicate that a disciple is a Christian;
a Christian is a son of God; a son of God is a saint; a
saint is a disciple; etc. Jesus could have said with equal
effect in the Commission, "Make Christians" or "Make saints"
or "Make sons of God."

As there are in fact carnal, sick, wounded, indifferent, mature and full-grown Christians, so also there are
these kinds of disciples. They, as followers, are to intensively study, honorably serve and personally grow to
manifest the characteristics of Him who called, taught,
demonstrated and consummated in His life what it means to be
faithful. But basically, to be a disciple does not imply
any more perfecting than is required of a son or a saint.

Currently the major emphasis in discipling is on
training Christians (disciples), not on **making** disciples
(converting). Disciples must be trained, but they must be
trained to reproduce others like themselves. The product of
a discipling emphasis is not a static believer, but a
living, responsible Christian who fulfills his or her
mission. Like his or her teacher, the disciple must become
a discipler. As the teacher performs, so the learner must
imitate. Initiation, equipping, perfecting and reproducing
are the major elements in a composite view of discipling.

MODELS FOR DISCIPLING

The two prominent models of discipling in the New Testament are those of Christ and Paul. Immediately contrasts
between them become evident and should be noted. Jesus was
highly selective and provincial; not everyone could be an
apostle. Only Jews were candidates. He specially endowed
and authorized the apostolate to be the depository of His
revelation for the world. Paul, receiving this revelation,
bridged selectivity and universality. Jesus was the secret
prepared to be disclosed at a particular time in history.

Paul was to herald the secret exposed to him for all times and to all men.

Jesus was confined to Palestine; Paul's responsibility encompassed the world. The primary object of Jesus' attention was the house of Israel. Paul, of the house of Israel, went to the Gentile world. Jesus trained in the midst of His own people; Paul discipled in many different cultures. They were on different sides of Pentecost, the moment of the empowerment by the Holy Spirit. They were at the opposite end of the establishment of the Church.

The two models are that -- models, not exact patterns. Neither is absolute for all situations but must be adapted according to the need. The first disciples after Pentecost scattered under persecution into all the country, proclaiming the Word of God. They did not have a closely regulated and concentrated period of instruction, like the Twelve, to equip them before they were scattered. Their basic equipment was an active faith, gifts and power of the Holy Spirit, and a passion for souls. With such little training were they really disciples? According to some modern-day definitions they were not.

Jesus' Model of Discipling

Matthew divides his data about Jesus into five parts corresponding to the five books of the Pentateuch. Chronological sequence and geography are not chief concerns of Matthew. The author directs all his material toward one focal point -- the Great Commission. Of all the New Testament writers, only Matthew gives the Commission in terms of disciple-making. Two of his five divisions deal specifically with that subject: discipleship (3:1-7:29) and apostleship (8:1-11:1). The other main themes are Revelation (11:2-13:53), the Church (13:54-19:1), and Judgment (19:1-26:2); all of which become vital parts of the second description of His model given below.

1. Relational or Personal. Jesus prepared an apostolate through intense personal relationships. Much has been made of the time that Jesus spent with the Twelve. However, the evidence points to the probability that Jesus spent most of the first year of His ministry -- and possibly more -- looking over the field, choosing His apostles, and being involved in a ministry with John the Baptist. The most that Jesus spent with His apostles in intense personal time was 20-24 months. John's Gospel records barely 30 days of the ministry of Jesus. In addition, many interruptions took place, and the trio of Peter, James and John were often alone with Jesus. None of these limitations detracts from the personal time He spent with His disciples, but accentuates how deep and intense their relation with Him must have been.

Significant weight is often placed on the one-on-one basis of the Jesus model. But the smallest breakdown of numbers among the Twelve was three. If and when individual instruction was given, others were present (Jn. 21:15-19).

2. Instructional or Observational. Immediately after Jesus is introduced by John the Baptist, Matthew cites Him giving detailed instruction (Mt. 5-7). Matthew continues with the extensive teaching of Jesus in the parables of the Kingdom (Mt. 13), in private lessons on ecclesiology (13:54-19:1), and in Christology (16:13-20). Matthew is also very precise in recording those occasions when Jesus confronted the contrary Jewish system and those who misunderstood and resisted His purpose. In no other Gospel is the direct conflict between Jesus and His opponents so vivid. These disciples, steeped in such a system as they were, had to change their worldview, their approach to the Kingdom of God. One way to change that view was by observing their Master in direct and open clash with the issues.

3. Laboratorial or Experiential. Jesus not only taught and demonstrated, He required "hands on" experiences. The apostles needed a taste of what they were going to get into after the Ascension. So Jesus gathered them together and sent them out on a short-term mission (Mt. 10:1-25). This experience spilled over into what was to become their ministry after the Resurrection and the Commission. The Twelve were on their own. They were free to blunder and make mistakes, which they undoubtedly did as some of them had done on other occasions when Jesus was not present to oversee them (Mt. 17:19-21). Later He corrected them.

Jesus provided the model for His apostles, leading them into exercising in His presence what they would come to do in His absence. He pronounced woe on Jewish cities that did not believe (Mt. 11:20-24). The desire for a sign on the part of the Scribes and Pharisees led Him to introduce the unimaginable idea that Nineveh and the Queen of the South would judge the Jews for not accepting Christ (Mt. 12:38-45). He went to the district of Tyre and Sidon where a Canaanite woman became the center of attention. The crumb she asked for was the banquet provided through the Great Commission (Mt. 15:21-28). His incident of the two sons (Mt. 21:28-32) and the parable of the landowner (Mt. 21:33-46) resulted in the Jewish establishment perceiving that Jesus proposed God's rejection of them in favor of someone else.

Above everything else Jesus set His own career, as spoken by the prophet Isaiah, as the model for the Great Commission to bring hope to all the peoples of the world (Mt. 12:15-21). In this prophetic declaration the core of the Commission unfolds.

In summation, all the relational and doctrinal teaching of the Master was brought to fruition by laboratory experiences, where the apostles experimented, tested, applied, and were corrected concerning what they had been taught. He not only verbally taught them; He showed them and let them copy His example and implement His instruction.

Paul's Method of Discipling

The Pauline model of discipling was ordered and directed by the Lord Himself (Acts 9:15-16; 26:16-20). How Paul's activities unfolded under a variety of circumstances give us a model that can be utilized in particular situations.

It is remarkable that one man accomplished so much. In a few short years Paul evangelized four provinces: Galatia, Asia, Macedonia, and Achaia. He also raised his eyes to look upon horizons far beyond these. Paul sought four goals: to win souls (make disciples), to plant churches (incorporate disciples), to perfect and equip the brethren (qualify disciples), and to expand the outer borders of Christian witness (multiply disciples). Wherever he went and to whomever he spoke or wrote, he pressed hard for these end products. These goals showed his conceptualization of the Great Commission. He never isolated these goals from each other. They are inseparable in the purpose of God and were so in the life of the apostle. This understanding of Paul's purpose and method can relieve the weakness in many efforts in the expansion of Christianity.

One way to describe Paul's ministry is in terms of motion. He was restlessly, almost compulsively, going to every city of note from Antioch to Spain that he might preach the Gospel and make disciples. In most cases he stayed in each place long enough to establish a church or be run out of town. Many times it was both.

Mobile or Missionary Model. The linear movement. This model has the spearpoint-thrust dimension. It expresses the "go," the "sending," and the "all peoples" statements of the Great Commission. It describes Paul's initial penetration of the Gentile world (Acts 13:4-14:8). There is no indication that he, Barnabas and Mark encountered a single Christian, but many were receptive to eternal life. The excursion was successful aside from the fact that their helper left them before they arrived on the intended field and that Paul was stoned and left for dead. The first major stepping-stone outside the Jewish world was laid.

His second penetration into the non-Christian world began at Antioch (Acts 13:22-23). Macedonia and Achaia were destined now to receive the witness about Jesus. The Holy Spirit directed Paul to by-pass Asia as a discipling target and to respond to the Macedonian call, which led him to Philippi. After some victories at Philippi, he descended the Achaian peninsula proclaiming the Gospel as far as Corinth, where he stayed for eighteen months. On returning to Antioch he stopped at Ephesus, the gem of Asia. He committed himself to return, if God willed, and thence journeyed by himself to Antioch.

His promise to return to Ephesus initiated his third linear thrust into the pagan world (Acts 18:23-21:17). This was his longest missionary journey in terms of time. It was also perhaps his most successful. By it he filled a gap in the mighty swath of Christianization that swept from Cilicia west and north around the Aegean Sea and south to Greece. Previously he had by-passed Asia. From the Ephesian center he pushed out into the surrounding areas until "all who lived in Asia heard the Word, both Jews and Greeks" (Acts 19:10), thus completing a gigantic arch in which a vital Christian witness was established.

Churches by the dozens were planted; disciples by the thousands were made. Contacts through persons and letters would be continued, but new fields would be entered. Accompanied by Luke and Aristarchus, the faithful disciple went into yet another field to be harvested by means of an appeal to Caesar. Paul must complete the vision and the commission to disciple the Gentile world (Acts 26:15-20). Luke indicates that in Rome the discipler, while under confinement of Roman guard, was "**preaching** the Kingdom and **teaching** concerning the Lord Jesus Christ" (Acts 26:31), a perfect example of the Great Commission model of making disciples. How unfortunate it is that accurate and detailed data is not available about his trip to Spain, if he indeed did go there (Rm. 15:28). Such data would indicate what the harvest was in that land so far from Jerusalem.

The Cyclical Movement. Paul never failed to return to the places where he had made disciples. Backtracking by the same route from the last stop on his first campaign, he stopped at each city "strengthening the souls of the disciples, encouraging them to continue in the faith." He "appointed elders for them in every church; having prayed with fasting, they commended them to the Lord" (Acts 14:22-23). Specific responsible persons were designated to "look to" the task of taking care of the disciples.

The first leg of his second mission thrust was given to the same type of ministry: "strengthening the disciples." He said to Barnabas, who was later replaced by Silas, "let us go back and visit all the towns where we preached the word of the Lord, so we can see how the brethren are doing" (Acts 15:36). And so they went through Syria and Cilicia "strengthening the churches" (Acts 15:41). Continuing through these areas, they came to Derbe, Lystra and Iconium. As they visited one town after another, they passed on the decisions of the Jerusalem conference and "the churches grew strong in the faith, as well as growing in numbers" (Acts 16:4-5).

The pattern recorded by Luke showed that on his second journey Paul did not spend time making disciples until after he arrived in Macedonia. All, or most, of his work was nurturing until he got beyond the perimeter of the area he had previously evangelized.

From Macedonia to Corinth he made disciples. In Corinth, after Timothy and Silas arrived from Berea, he "devoted full time" to persuading and teaching Jews and Greeks (Acts 18:5). For eighteen months he continued his soul-winning advances with detailed efforts at perfecting those who became Christians.

He did not alter his methodology in his third penetration into pagan territory. Leaving Ephesus, he "exhorted" the disciples (Acts 20:1), crossed the sea west to Greece, and spent three more months "teaching" those he had won to Christ during his eighteen months' stay. After ninety days of "strengthening" the disciples, he gathered some of his trained workers, traveled north by land through Macedonia, took ship and eventually arrived at Miletus, where he notified the elders at Ephesus to meet him on the seashore. He counseled them, prayed with them, and departed never expecting to see them again (Acts 20:17-38).

In this manner, Paul structured his actions to fulfill the purpose of his life as derived from the commission given to him. His was the mobile or missionary model.

Stationary or Church Model. What did Paul do when he stayed in a particular place for a long time? Only his stay at Ephesus can be considered here.

Church-Center Discipling. Arriving at Ephesus, where he had left Priscilla and Aquila, he entered the synagogue and for three months spoke the word of God. The turn of events brought about a hardening against the Gospel. A valid assumption is that the status quo of the synagogue refused to accept what the Gospel demanded about the Gentiles; so Paul took the disciples and went to the hall of Tyrannus and there he stayed for two full years (Acts 19:9-10). Here the church was housed and the great mission of the Church was executed from this group until "all the residents of Asia, both Jew and Greek heard the Word."

From the fragmentary information available about how Paul related to the church, we have reason to assume that he must have deeply involved the congregation in that discipling enterprise. The Ephesian letter, written some years later, is highly missiological, which implies that the church was indeed a discipling organism in the composite sense.

Formally Instructional. It seems most probable that Tyrannus was a philosopher and did not use his quarters from eleven A.M. to four P.M. At these hours Paul undoubtedly expounded the scriptures and initiated his evangelistic activities to penetrate all Asia. The atmosphere of the hall of Tyrannus was surely somewhat academic and in harmony with the educational customs of the day. Can it not be surmised that this same atmosphere pervaded the way Paul presented the Gospel? Is it unreasonable to think that Paul arranged those studies according to the Jewish pattern for training initiates and members of the priesthood? Can we say that in our day some counterparts of Paul's discipling method are found in a formal Christian academic environment? The core subject matter is surely the same.

Team-Assisted. Most of the time Paul was accompanied by a group, called by some an "apostolic band." When he and Silas revisited Lystra on the second journey, the brethren spoke well of Timothy, who had developed into a valuable worker while Paul was on his third-year furlough. So Paul accepted him as an associate.

With Paul at Ephesus were Erastus, Timothy, Trophimus, Tychicus, Priscilla, Aquila and possibly more. What did these team members do? Surely they went to Paul's teaching sessions at the hall of Tyrannus. They were trained to do the work of an evangelist, to help deliver messages, resolve problems, smooth disturbed waters, give encouragement, set the church in order and strengthen the brethren[3].

This task force was not allowed to remain idle. Paul trained and commissioned them for service. He must have demanded high qualities and rigorous discipline (Acts 15:38-40). Returning from his third campaign he gathered a number of workers along the way to take with him to Jerusalem. Perhaps the senior missionary wanted his young apprentices to become culturally oriented and to get acquainted with what was going on in Jerusalem and the Jewish nation. Erastus and Timothy were with him on this trip from Ephesus to Greece, where he stayed ninety days. On his way north through Macedonia to return to Jerusalem, he picked up Sopater at Berea, Aristarchus and Secundas at Thessalonica, Luke at Macedonia, Gaius of Derbe, Tychicus and Trophimus of Ephesus and maybe others. It is remarkable that in so many cases the disciples are listed in pairs, and that they were out in various cities and churches performing their responsibilities.

House-to-House. Besides the "school room," Paul activated public and house-to-house proclamation (Acts 20:20). This work was initiatory discipling, for he preached to bring them to "repentance toward God and faith in our Lord Jesus Christ" (Acts 20:21). He was not satisfied with inviting people to come to his lessons; he went out to them. This procedure may also indicate that his activities at the hall were more formal and perhaps for more selective persons -- more for training disciples than for making disciples.

Correspondence. Paul left a document within the reach of every church he planted. He instructed that some of his correspondence be shared by churches (Col. 4:16). His letters became as important to building up the Body of Christ as reading the Torah was to edifying the Jew.

A brief review of the above characteristics of Paul's model of discipling indicates the thoroughness with which he entered an area. In simple direct terms he chose a territory, literally surrounded and saturated it with proclamation, baptized repentant believers, formed Christian communities, strengthened and built up the brethren with exhortation and instruction, trained select persons formally and informally and by demonstration, deployed workers to places of need, wrote letters to solve problems and promote the faith, lifted his eyes to untouched fields, and then pointed his life toward them to repeat the same cycle.

CONCLUSION

Discipling is a mission imperative. It is a core commandment in the Divine sending. The holistic approach to discipling is both practical and essential simply because the desperate needs of a complex world are so diverse. A multitude of people groups, in an almost unbelievable number of circumstances, must be discipled.

The modeling done by Jesus and Paul is a demonstrative answer to the who, what and how questions about discipling. Because all the ingredients are available, only the level of vision and willingness place limitations upon the execution of this holy task.

NOTES

[1] The participle "going" absorbs the imperative force of "make."

[2] Mt. 28:18-20; Mk. 16:15-18; Lk. 24:44-49; Jn. 20:21; 21:15-17; and Acts 1:4-8.

[3] Col. 4:10-12; II Tim. 4:9-20; Titus 3:12-13, etc.

BIBLIOGRAPHY

Henrichsen, Walter A.
   1974   <u>Disciples are Made Not Born</u>. Wheaton: Victor Books.

Kuhn, Gary W.
   1978   <u>The Dynamics of Discipleship Training</u>. Grand Rapids: Zondervan Books.

Thayer, Joseph Henry
   1889   <u>A Greek-English Lexicon of the New Testament</u>. New York: American Book Co. (corrected edition).

3

God and the Gods: Expect Footprints

by Frederick W. Norris

God's ultimate revelation of Himself and thus of the Good News to humankind is Jesus Christ. That claim forms the center of the Christian faith. It or statements similar to it express the realities which would be preached and taught by Christians. Indeed, the truth it refers to warrants the work of the Church. When its ultimacy is sacrificed, Christian mission becomes limp, often purposeless. Telling the story of Jesus in order that those listening may become a part of His body is an essential aspect of the missionaries task.

Therefore, if we were to talk about the primary concerns of mission apologetics, we would deal first with Jesus Christ as He is depicted in the New Testament and prophesied about in the Old Testament. All kinds of questions come to mind in relationship to that constellation of issues. Who is this Jesus? Are the reports about Him trustworthy? Is there ever enough evidence to support the proclamation of one person as divine, human and Lord of the universe? Properly, many books and articles have been devoted to such inquiries.

What is envisioned here, however, is only a small part of that venture. In some ways it is removed from the foundational issues which would form the structure of any fundamental theology program. It operates from within a community of faith; it assumes that Jesus is Lord and that scripture is normative for Christian faith and practice; it presupposes that Christian mission is legitimate. This approach is not taken because no explanations of such basic commitments are called for, that is, because all one can do is tell the story again. Neither does it assume that living the Christian life is any less important than telling the story of Jesus. Yet this approach does see the importance of preaching as retelling. What the present chapter focuses upon is the knowledge which all missionaries have that their relations to other cultures and religions often determine the success or failure of Christian mission. If then, one takes Christian scripture as normative for faith and practice, how it treats other cultures and religions is crucial. For missionaries who are striving to be biblical, the way in which the Bible deals with other views of ultimate values will determine how they face the different faiths embodied in the lives of the people where they serve.

There has been no lack of concern with other religions among Christians. The history of Christian missionary efforts has indicated how widely varied the approaches have been (Neill, 1964 and Rosenkranz, 1977). Some have insisted that all the indigenous religion and as much of the native culture as possible must be avoided. They say, "Only preach the Word." At the other end of the continuum, some have suggested that each religion has its own validity and all are striving toward a common goal. Thus if there is a mission of the Church it is to help the poor and needy, not to preach yet another gospel. In a recent article Arthur Glasser has described six ways of facing other religions which he sees as having dominated Christian missiology. According to his description the first three have viewed Christianity as "superior to other religions," while the last three have seen it as "on a par with other religions." The approaches he notes are:

> 1. **Radical Displacement.** Christianity with all its Western cultural baggage is transplanted whole and the ethnic religion is brushed aside as valueless.
>
> 2. **Discontinuity.** The uniqueness and superiority of Christianity are assumed; though Christianity is regarded as having no real point of contact with the other religion, it nonetheless seeks to adapt itself to the cultural forms of the people.
>
> 3. **Recognition of Uniqueness.** Each religion is recognized as a unique unity to be respected;

comparisons are possible, when honestly made at roughly equivalent levels of belief and practice, but Christianity is regarded as obviously superior.

4. **Legitimate borrowing.** Since it is granted that there are many points of contact between all religions due to the commonality of their human dimensions, Christianity borrows freely from them in order to be truly indigenous.

5. **The Gospel as Fulfillment.** Christianity is presented as either the literal fulfillment of other religions (as the New Testament fulfilled the Old Testament), or as the capstone of the highest aspirations one finds expressed or intimated in the scriptures of other religions.

6. **Relativistic Syncretism.** Every religion -- Christianity included -- is regarded as representing the spiritual quest of humankind seeking God. One finds the truth latent in all and takes the best from each. Through religious encounter and dialogue, understanding of one's own faith is enlarged and enriched by the other religion. Incompleteness diminishes and there is ongoing movement toward the ultimate truth, which may be brought even nearer by encounter with yet other religions (Glasser, 1983:205).

Glasser himself finds shortcomings with these categories. He is particularly concerned with anyone who might find all of these approaches to be valid because in his view such a person would be "overlooking the nuances of the Bible and have only a limited knowledge of the non-Christian religions" (1983:205). What is intended in this chapter is a look at the Bible to see how it deals with other cultures and the religions within them in order that those biblical "nuances" may become clearer.

CULTURE AS A MEANS OF COMMUNICATION

In the last half of the 19th. century there was serious talk among some scholars about the possibility that the Holy Spirit had created the language of the New Testament as a special vehicle for recording Christian revelation (Milligan, 1922:58-62).[1] Most of those who had been involved in the highest levels of scholarly investigation had begun their study of Greek in classical literature. It was thus obvious to them that the Greek of the New Testament was not that of ancient Greece. Although some literature from the first century of our era was available, it also had a different vocabulary and at times a different syntax from the writings within the canon. Similarities between the language of the Septuagint and New Testament Greek were found, but those did not explain the latter.

At about the same time various mission efforts in non-European cultures, particularly in the cultures of the East, were revived and increased. In nearly every case these early European or North American missionaries were quick to move their work into the languages and cultures where they lived. Often these missionaries began conversation with native speakers, produced grammatical and lexical studies and undertook the translation of the Bible into the languages of their regions (Latourette, 1944). The overriding concern was to bring the Word of God to other peoples. But the presupposition for such work, whether considered and stated or merely assumed, was that the Christian scriptures could be made clear in other languages. Most of these missionaries were struck by the differences between their own culture and that of the land in which they worked. They often opposed various food taboos, marriage practices, dress codes, etc. Thus, they cannot be accused of an unthinking syncretism. Yet they did, almost without exception, create biblical translations which went directly against some views of the character of New Testament Greek. If in this instance those views had been correct, it would have been preferable, perhaps necessary, for God to create some new language in each of the cultures, one quite different from the usual speech of each region. Only then could the content of His revelation to humanity be made clear to another language grouping.

The view that the Holy Spirit had created New Testament Greek, however, proved to be wrong. Archaeological expeditions and chance finds both in the field and in libraries began to uncover pieces, particularly the papyrai, which were composed in a Greek like that of the New Testament. Many of these writings, largely comprised of personal letters and daily business correspondence or records, were filled with both the vocabulary and syntax which marks the Greek of the New Testament. Instead of the language of the earliest Christian witnesses having been created by God especially for the purpose of revelation, it turned out to be the <u>lingua franca</u> used in most of the Mediterranean world. The early work of Deissmann (1910) and the masterful studies of Moulton and Milligan (1930), made it abundantly clear that God did not need to find special speech in order to make His will known. He was perfectly capable of communicating through the means which were available in everyday conversation. That truth obviously did not demand that all words or phrases kept exactly the same denotations or connotations which they had previously been given. New relationships were necessary.

It is also the case that certain concepts and attitudes which are found within the culture and language were not taken over in the New Testament. Much can be learned by watching what was chosen and what was left behind. The old cliche, "Bible names for Bible things," has merit. Not all forms of "love" were selected as descriptive of God's love affair with humankind. And even the use of the word <u>agape</u> apparently received deeper content within its context.

When second century Christian writers began to describe God in terms of aloofness, <u>apathes</u>, they made good connections with philosophical and religious concerns within Mediterranean Hellenistic culture. But they and the later Fathers who followed them injected into their teaching about God a conception of aloofness which is not in any way a part of the biblical witness.[2] The word <u>apathes</u> does not occur in the Septuagint or the New Testament; the reality it describes is not there. God could use daily Hellenistic, Koine speech as the vehicle of revelation; no new language was necessary. But not all of the culture or the entire language was claimed as descriptive of His revelation. It was not necessary for God to start from scratch and create a language to encompass His truth. But some adjustments and deletions of the language available for the purpose did occur.

Theologically, we should have expected as much. The virgin birth of Jesus Christ indicates that something new is occurring, something which is not like every other birth. Yet the manhood of Jesus, as portrayed in scripture, is not different from the humanity of any other inhabitant of earth. He has unusual powers, yet He also was on occasion without knowledge, overcome with emotion and subject to great pain. As the book of Hebrews claims, He was tempted in all points as we are, yet He did not sin. He took on our humanity but in the process He changed it back to what it had been. He became man, but He did not become sinful. The incarnation of Jesus Christ, the coming of the Son of God as a full-blooded human, should have indicated that humans and their cultures can be employed as the means for communicating God's revelation of Himself. The papyrai, which usually record daily speech employed in the Mediterranean basin during the Hellenistic era, afford another analogue of the incarnation. For the purpose of expressing revelation, Koine Greek underwent some changes; in certain instances it was given new meanings. Specific aspects were rejected. But it remained the human speech of everyday discourse.

Perhaps those 19th. century missionaries, and missionaries from most every era, have seen something which was clearer to them because of their constant closeness to the necessity of the incarnation. In any event their successes in winning those of other cultures and languages to Christ has been rooted in an analogue of the incarnation itself. When the Lord of the universe became man and dwelt among us, humanity was changed. But it was the humanity which God had created so long ago, not a chimera, not a humanity which only seemed to be there. It was a broken humanity which could still serve the purpose. Every human culture and language goes through some change when the Gospel takes residence within it. But every missionary must remember that the new culture and the new language is capable of receiving and making clear that Gospel. The chimera, the appearance of the ease in which one saw the truth in the home culture and language as opposed to the difficulty of expressing it in the new culture and language, is only that: a fantasy. As contemporary linguists and missiologists agree, every language and thus every culture can become the means of communication for the Gospel.

OTHER RELIGIONS AS ANALOGUE, AS SUBSTANCE OF REVELATION

When we examine scripture carefully, however, it goes farther than indicating that culture and language have been the means of communicating the Gospel. It indicates that the values of various cultures, of different systems of truth -- even those ultimately opposed to Christian revelation -- have provided analogues for and even substantial aspects of Christian truth.

This does not mean that the writers of scripture affirmed everything which they observed in the surrounding cultures and all which they saw in other religions. The Old Testament describes a severe struggle against Canaanite, Egyptian, Babylonian, Assyrian and other cultures and religions. The Pentateuchal laws and ceremonies often were meant to separate Israelites from their neighbor's customs and beliefs. In the books which tell of the conquest, the judges and the monarchy, the attempt to remain pure is a constant theme. That same concern emerges in the prophets. Within the New Testament the epistles in particular describe Christian battles against both a legalistic Judaism and an idolatrous paganism. Limits are set; boundaries are drawn. There is no sense of anything and everything being a true revelation of God.

Yet that strong witness does not take away the power of other insights, the force of the truth that both other cultures and religions can be analogous to and indeed already contain some of the substance of biblical revelation.[3] The first indication of this is to be found in the Old Testament. The names for God which appear within the patriarchal narratives of Genesis are on more than one occasion taken from or shared with various groups within the ancient Near East. The "god of the fathers" appears to have been an unnamed figure related to nomadic tribes and their sense of family tradition while the god "El" appears to have been a Canaanite deity associated with various shrines. Both the comparative evidence of extra-biblical texts and two of the ancient traditions within the Pentateuch suggest that this was the case. Particularly in Ex. 3 and Ex. 6 the revelation of God's personal name, Yahweh, to Moses is viewed as something extraordinary. Before then God was not known by that name. As Ex. 6:3 makes clear, God told Moses that he had appeared to Abraham, Isaac and Jacob as El Shaddai, but He had not made His name Yahweh known to them.

A third tradition, however, employs the name Yahweh as early as the creation account in Gen. 2 and has Eve call God by that name. Here Abraham, Isaac and Jacob know God by His name Yahweh as do the Philistines Abimelech, Ahuzzath and Phicol (Gen. 14:22; 26:25-28; 28:13). This tradition evidently sees God's telling of the name Yahweh to Moses as something different but not a new revelation. Taking all three Old Testament traditions together as an expression of truth indicates that Israel was able to assimilate different names of other gods, such as the "god of the fathers," as at least partially revelatory of Yahweh Himself (Alt, 1967:1-100). Earlier experiences of deity, both those associated with a nomadic life and those associated with a more settled existence, were seen as capable of inclusion in the general history of God's self-revelation.

The figure of Melchizedek proves to be a particularly interesting indication of how Israel dealt with other religious traditions. This king of Salem, a Canaanite, worships the god "El Elyon" and accepts one-tenth of Abraham's spoils after the latter's victories. According to the narrative Abraham accepts Melchizedek as a priest and sees his worship as compatible with praise to Yahweh (Gen. 14:17-24). The psalmist says that Melchizedek formed a special order of priests, one which was not dependent upon the line from Levi (Ps. 110). Later Melchizedek is selected by the Christian communities as an analogue for true Christian priesthood (Heb. 5-7). All this occurs even though Melchizedek appears in the Genesis narrative without previous introduction and no connection with the line back to Adam and Eve. His worship is affirmed by Abraham, but scripture does not say that he learned it from Jewish circles. Exactly what the meaning of Melchizedek is has been much disputed.[4] But perhaps he represents one of two options: either a Canaanite priest/king who worships God truly, or a figure from the history of Israel because of the centrality of that city in Jewish tradition. In either case, he is evidence that for Israelites Yahweh was active elsewhere than in the earliest familial lines of the Jewish heritage. He made Himself known under various names and among different peoples, even among Canaanites whom Israel so often opposed as deadly enemies.

Old Testament wisdom literature is not reticent to use the wisdom from other cultures and literature. It borrows directly from at least Egyptian wisdom and most probably from other sources as well. Proverbs 22-24, particularly 22:17 - 23:11, relies upon an Egyptian document called the "Teaching of Amen-em-ope." The similarities of the two documents demands that there is some direct relationship between them. The "Teaching of Amen-em-ope" is dated prior to the book of Proverbs. What appears to be the best suggestion is that those collecting the various proverbs of our Old Testament book had found use for this ancient Egyptian wisdom. They either translated parts of it themselves or more probably employed a translation of it which was accessible to them. The point of this incident is to see that inspired Old Testament writers and compilers incorporated Egyptian wisdom into their own statements of God's truths. They evidently did not find that step to be a dangerous syncretism which destroyed the integrity of Yahweh's revelation, but a recognition of His activity in other cultures.[5]

Within the New Testament we find a similar pattern. In the epistles to the Romans, Paul indicates that all humanity has had witness to God, a viewpoint which echoes a number of the Psalms. But many, particularly the pagans, have abandoned what could be known of God and have given themselves over to the desires of the flesh. At no point does Paul compromise the ultimacy of God's revelation in Jesus Christ; neither does he anywhere insist that there is salvation outside of Christ. He argues that both Jew and Gentile have fallen short and stand in need of Jesus as Savior. Yet he does speak of conscience, perhaps of natural law, which everyone possesses including the pagans. Gentiles could follow it and then be either condemned or excused by living up to its precepts. Since the Jews were unable to live according to the Old Covenant, it is probable that pagans would experience similar difficulties. Even if Paul in this important aside does not state unequivocally that some will be excused on the day of judgement if they live according to their conscience or an inward law of nature, he does notice that what a pagan believes about right and wrong may well be correct. If in those final days, Gentiles have lived according to their consciences, there may well be a strong witness to their partial good intentions and good deeds, all of which occurred outside the circle of Jewish law or specific Christian revelation.[6]

Perhaps the important inferences for contemporary Christian mission which can be drawn from Paul's points are three. First, no culture to which a missionary goes is without a witness to Almighty God. We do not go to make God known for the first time; we go to make Him known in His full revelation in Jesus Christ. Pagan conscience, or perhaps a natural law, already has indicated some truth about God. Second, the mission of the Church is not compromised by knowing that God has witnesses in any land upon the earth. Paul clearly insists on the finality of revelation in Jesus Christ. That is incontestable. He spoke of the possibility that a good conscience might give witness at the judgment day, but he spent his life preaching Christ to those same pagans. He evidently found no inconsistency in being an active Christian evangelist and in raising the possibility of living according to conscience, perhaps according to natural law, even though in practice he found that possibility overwhelmingly denied. Third, it should not be strange to find people in any land who seem to live in ways very similar to those described in scripture as Christian ideals. It would be totally false to assume that any culture is without its redeeming features, that any group of people is without its outstanding faithful and moral leaders. Paul in Ephesus found friends among the Asiarchs (Acts 19:31), even though those people were pagan priests who led a political league of cities in Western Asia Minor. Paul fought a legalistic Judaism and an irrelevant paganism, but he found those whom he admired both within Judaism and paganism.

The digest example of Paul's preaching found in Acts 17 perhaps goes even deeper. He praised the Greek leaders assembled at the Areopagus for their religious sensitivity. They had many statues -- things made by human hands which could not in the end represent deity. But they were concerned, even interested enough to have a statue to the unknown God. Paul could not brook their idolatry (Acts 14:15-17; 17:16), but he did not -- as Irish missionaries in Europe centuries after him -- overturn their idols immediately in order to discuss their idolatry. He looked beyond their statues and saw an honest attempt to reach up toward God.

Perhaps deeper still, he was willing to quote their poets as understanding some truth about the creating and sustaining God whom he wished to proclaim. We must never forget that the phrases "in Him we live and move and have our being" and "for we are indeed His offspring" first appeared among Greek poets. In fact that wisdom seemed to be so strong within various Hellenistic theologies that it is difficult to place the quotations with any one author. Many shared those views. Paul still preached the resurrection of Jesus, something which was repulsive to certain of his hearers. He did not adjust the message to their cultural background; he was not involved in syncretistic dilution of the Gospel. Yet he did insist by quoting their poets that not all their traditions were false. He claimed what they already knew as a part of the truth about God's nature.

Someone might insist that this approach to the statues and the poets is just good rhetoric, a proper employment of things within the experience of the hearers so that the crucial point could then be made. Perhaps this is true. Yet such an insight should not be coupled with the suggestion that Paul really did not value the Athenian religious sensitivity and wedded to the implication that he did not think their poets spoke the truth. Such views would involve Paul in a duplicity which does not fit what we know of him or the Gospel which he proclaimed. It also would not be consistent with the Old Testament patterns discussed above. We should humbly admit that other value systems are not all wrong. If we look deeply enough we will find in each culture, in each religion God's partial witness to Himself.

It is tragic that Biblical positions such as these employed here have not always been understood. Not recognizing the use within the Bible of various names for God, some of which came from religions other than that of mainline Judaism, has caused much damage to Christian mission which might have been avoided. Some efforts in China were destroyed by deep distrust of employing any well established names for ultimate deity which already existed in that language and culture. Translations were withdrawn and whole groups of missionaries sent home or restricted because some thought that a new Chinese phrase for God would have to be created which did not carry the older cultural and religious connotations. At times when those most interested in faithful Christian mission decry the "destruction" of the Bible caused by modern historical-critical scholarship, it would be good to remember that if Christian missionaries had known how Genesis deals with the "gods of the fathers" and the various names for deity, they might have been willing to employ well established names for God in China and elsewhere.[7] Sadly, in many mission fields the preaching of Jesus Christ as the ultimate revelation of God has been hampered by strong resistance to the use of any truths imbedded in the indigenous cultures and religions, even though Paul's preaching and writing indicate that he found such truths outside of Judaism and Christianity.

Perhaps one further step is worthy of discussion. If the Bible can employ other religious traditions as both analogues to and partial substance of God's revelation, we should not be surprised when other religions cast new and interesting light on the meaning of the Bible. Having lived in another culture myself -- even though it was a European one -- but more pertinently having listened to missionaries report their work for a number of years, I am struck by how often the analogues and the substance found in other cultures tend to make even scripture itself more striking not only for those in the other culture but for us. Some of the studies in this volume show both how God has not left Himself without witness and how much of the very structure of the Gospel found elsewhere can bring fresh insight and excitement to our reading of scripture. In teaching within a seminary context, and listening within a congregation, I find that scripture is often clarified in strange ways by the search to bring the Gospel into a different culture.

CONCLUSION

The ultimacy of God's revelation in Jesus Christ is not to be compromised by the Christian. It is the center of Christian faith and mission. But God is not without witness in other lands. When we go to those cultures we must look both for the truth which He has already revealed there and for the people who most nearly live the life which He requires. As part of Christian mission we do not bring all new truth to a false society. We bear witness to the final revelation of God in Christ in the midst of many genuine seekers after and speakers of truth.

Precisely because we do not hold within our limited understanding all the truth, nor do we represent all the heights of civilization, we approach other peoples with humility -- not weakening the claim of Christ -- but recognizing the witness of God. In the Spirit we search with them for the fulness of truth. We cannot be haughty nor colonial, condescending nor proud. Together we will learn to be disciples of Christ.

To return then to Glasser's description of six approaches, we find that none of them is truly expressive of biblical nuances and that particularly the differentiation between the first group of three and the second group of three is invalid. If one takes scripture with great seriousness as the paradigm for mission, then it leads the way toward "legitimate borrowing" and viewing the "Gospel as fulfillment." Borrowing is legitimate, not because of a shared humanity -- although in the deepest sense we are all persons, all human beings. The Christian borrows because God has made Himself known in various ways and only finally in Jesus Christ. Scripture does not see the approaches of borrowing and fulfilling as ones in which the revelation of God to Israel and in Jesus Christ is "on a par with other religions." What it does insist upon is the ultimacy of God's self-disclosure in Jesus Christ and the fact that in each place, in each culture, in every religion we should expect some footprints of God Himself.

That does not mean that we will be beyond the problems of subjectivism or syncretism -- issues which can indeed weaken the finality of God's revelation. But it does point up both our dilemma and our dynamic. If we take scripture as normative for both faith and **practice** then we, as much as scriptural figures, writers and compilers, must dare to look for God's footprints outside scripture. To be biblical people we have no other choice.

NOTES

*This article is dedicated to the memory of Toyozo Wada Nakari (1898-1984). As a convert from Shinto and Zen Buddhist commitments and a specialist in Old Testament studies, he left his imprint on my concerns for Christian mission. He is a colleague sorely missed.

[1] Milligan (1922) discusses the issue and notes that Rothe, a dogmatician in Germany during the 1860's, had taken the position that Koine Greek was a language especially created by God.

[2] The entry under apathes in Arndt and Gingrich (1979) shows that it was not used either in the New Testament or Septuagint translation of the Old Testament. However, the entry under that word in Lampe (1961) indicates how frequently it was used by early Christian writers as descriptive of God's nature.

[3] It should not be assumed that the biblical texts discussed in the rest of this chapter represent all those which give evidence of religious borrowing or the Christian fulfillment of certain themes in other religions. Those selected here are typical, but they do not exhaust the number available.

[4] Von Rad (1971) and Brueggemann (1982) deal with the difficult figure of Melchizedek. Morris's attempt (1976) to connect Melchizedek with Shem and thus the line of Judah distorts the text in Hebrews, draws on later Jewish tradition and fails to recognize the meaning of the names for God in the passage.

[5] Scott (1965:20-21, 135-136) explicates this view. McKane (1970:369-406) presents a similar explanation although he emphasizes the Israelite editor's freedom in using the material. According to McKane the editor "alters its order and imagery and inserts instructions of his own and from other sources" (1970:371). Tate (1971:71) thinks there might have been a common source behind the Egyptian and Israelite works, one he considers "probably" to have been Canaanite. In that case the borrowing by the Israelite editor would have been from a Canaanite tradition, thus keeping the borrowing point much the same.

[6] Kasemann (1980:61-68) emphasizes that Paul's major point is the lost condition of both Jews and Gentiles. But he asserts that Paul's statements in Romans keep him from

sharing Luke's apologetic concerns in Acts 17. It is my opinion that precisely the views of Rom. 2:14-16 suggest the influence in Acts 17. Cranfield (1975:155-163) thinks the reference to Gentiles is to Gentile Christians. But the comparison between Jews and Gentiles in Rom. 1-2 would not include all humanity if ethne means only Gentile Christians. Then the claim in Rom. 3 that all have fallen short would not have been previously supported as the rhetorical development of the letter assumes.

[7]Malan (1856) insisted that both mission practice and translations of the Old and New Testaments demanded that words for God already established in the culture and its religions should be employed. He noted that the attempt to transliterate the Latin deus into other languages had failed miserably. But he did not know or had not accepted some of the Old Testament scholarship which would indicate that the Old Testament itself borrowed some names of God from the surrounding religions.

BIBLIOGRAPHY

Alt, Albrecht
    1967 "The God of the Fathers," in Essays on Old Testament History. New York: Doubleday & Co., Inc. (trans. by R. A. Wilson).

Arndt, W. F. and F. W. Gingrich
    1979 A Greek-English Lexicon of the New Testament and Other Early Christian Literature. Chicago: Univ. of Chicago Press.

Brueggemann, Walter
    1982 Genesis: A Bible Commentary for Teaching and Preaching. Atlanta: John Knox Press.

Cranfield, C. E. B.
    1975 The Epistle to the Romans, Vol. I Edinburgh: T. & T. Clark.

Deissmann, Adolf
    1910 Light from the Ancient East. London: Hodder & Stoughton. (trans. by L. Strachan).

Glasser, Arthur F.
    1983 "A Paradigm Shift? Evangelicals and Interreligious Dialogue," in Contemporary Theologies of Mission. Grand Rapids: Baker Book House.

Kasemann, Ernst
   1980   Commentary on Romans. Grand Rapids: William B. Eerdmans Pub. Co. (trans. by G. Bromiley).

Lampe, G. W. H.
   1961   A Patristic Greek Lexicon. Oxford: Clarendon.

Latourette, Kenneth Scott
   1944   The Great Century in North Africa and Asia. New York: Harper and Brothers.

Malan, S. C.
   1856   Who is God in China, Shin or Shang-Te? London: Samuel Bagster & Sons.

McKane, William
   1970   Proverbs. Philadelphia: Westminster Press.

Milligan, George
   1922   Here and There Among the Papyrai. New York: Doran Company.

Morris, Henry
   1976   The Genesis Record. Grand Rapids: Baker.

Moulton, James and George Milligan
   1930   The Vocabulary of the Greek New Testament Illustrated from the Papyrai and other Non-Literary Sources. London: Hodder & Stoughton.

Neill, Stephen
   1964   A History of Christian Missions. Baltimore: Penguin Books.

Rosenkranz, Gerhard
   1977   Die Christliche Mission. Muenchen: Chr. Kaiser Verlag.

Scott, R. B. Y.
   1965   Proverbs - Ecclesiastes. Garden City: Doubleday.

Tate, Marvin
   1971   "Proverbs," in The Broadman Bible Commentary, Vol. 5. Nashville: Broadman Press.

Von Rad, Gerhard
   1971   Genesis: A Commentary. Philadelphia: Westminster Press. (trans. by J. Marks).

4

Missions in Revelation: Research in Progress

by James C. Smith

The Bible is a missionary book. As children most of us learned that the golden text of the Bible is John 3:16. Later we added verse 17 as an inseparable part of that text. This is the constant theme of Archibald McLean's <u>Where the Book Speaks</u> (1907). More recently, John Stott has been more specific by affirming that the eternal God of the Old Testament is a missionary God, that the living Christ of the gospels is a missionary Christ, that the Holy Spirit of the book of Acts is a missionary Spirit, and that the young church of the epistles is a missionary church (1977:31-91). Many theologies of mission stop here as Stott did in his "Biblical Basis of Missions."[1] Knowing Stott, having heard his expositions and having read them, I am sure he would have included the Apocalypse had the schedule allowed for a fifth exposition. I am therefore bold to add the closing sequel: "The coming kingdom of the Revelation is a missionary kingdom."

The last book of the Bible is a neglected one. It is easy to understand why. It is full of strange numbers, colors, images, sounds, places, visions, conflicts, judgments, signs, wonders and scenes. And most of those writing about it contribute to the confusion by bringing their own presuppositions, contexts and prejudices rather than allowing the book to speak for itself. A major principle in studying the Bible is to understand the context or setting in which a particular book is written. But even that is dependent on the words it uses and especially how it describes itself. Most readers of Revelation, especially those in missionary contexts, will not have the benefit of the study resources available whose heritage is primarily from Western Christendom. On the other hand, unless those under such influences recognize them and seek to transcend them, they only contribute to the complexity or confusion.[2]

Like the rest of the Bible, the book of Revelation is a missionary book (DuPreez, 1970:152). This article will attempt to show that it is missionary in its self-descriptions, it is missionary in its style and structure and it is missionary in its themes and vocabulary. It unfolds the purpose of God from Creation to the consummation, in heaven as well as on earth. It is cosmic in its coverage. It is a missionary book.

IT IS MISSIONARY IN ITS SELF-DESCRIPTIONS

The book describes itself in at least six ways in its entirety and in at least five ways in its various divisions.

Revelation and Apocalypse

"The Revelation of Jesus Christ" appears in the first verse and gives the book its name, Revelation and Apocalypse, a transliteration of the Greek apokalupsis. Of the eighteen times this word is used in the New Testament, it appears but once in this writing in its noun or verb form (Winter, 1978:70). Of the remaining uses, five refer to the Gospel, five refer to the gift of wisdom or insight, five refer to the coming of Christ and one refers to the glory and wrath associated with such coming. Writers therefore have a tendency to fill its meaning from the apocalyptic writings of the Old Testament (largely the book of Daniel) and its contemporary forms rather than from the content and structure of the book itself. The word apokalupsis means "an uncovering," and the later actions of "opening the scroll" and "breaking the seal" should speak to this uncovering more than any other. "To show," deiknuo, is the writer's explanation of the word (Rev. 1:1) and he employs it another seven times -- more than any other New Testament writer -- which when combined with the Gospel of John account for nearly half its usages. The phrase also introduces the major visions of Revelation (4:1; 17:1; 21:9-10; 22:1,6,8). "What must soon take place," "For the time is at hand," and "Who is and who was and who is to come" combine the sense of immediacy and end-time characteristic of apocalyptic writings and eschatology (the study of last things).

The Word of God and the Testimony of Jesus

This combination appears five times in the book -- though "words" is plural in one case and the phrases are reversed in another. Both phrases are strong Johannine words, logos and marturia. The words are equally strong when referring to Christ.

Prophesy

This word means "to speak forth" and appears nineteen times in the New Testament -- seven of them in Revelation. The definite article "**the** prophesy" or the strong pronoun "**this** prophesy" appear four times which should enforce that **this book** should provide its primary meaning. While the primary meaning of prophesy is "telling forth," the related meaning of "forthtelling" is evident in the visions and their sequences. The phrase "in the Spirit" enforces this dimension. The testimony of Jesus as the Spirit of prophesy (Rev. 19:10) keeps the book in clear Christological context.

A Written Book

Another dominant Johannine word, grapho, appears in Revelation twenty-nine times -- and only in its verb form. The article "a" or "this" is the word with which the writing opens and closes. Revelation is **a** book (3 usages), **the** book (9 usages) and **this** book (5 usages) as pointed out by Winter (1978:107). And while most versions and translations distinguish between "book" and "scroll" in chapter 5, the Authorized Version does not and may be more close to the mind of the writer. It should be noted that the word for "the little book" in chapter 10 appears only here in the New Testament. Other words or phrases are used to describe the various parts of the drama. These usually introduce or close a section or are peculiar to a section or interlude.

What the Spirit Says and In the Spirit

"What the Spirit says" is limited to the churches in chapters 2 and 3. "In the Spirit" introduces the four main visions of the book. The phrases cannot be separated as they describe the instrumentality of God.

Others

The "mystery of God" in 10:7 appears to be equivalent to prophesy and is consistent with its broader New Testament usage in relation to gospel, revelation and purpose of God.

Each time God's judgments or acts reach a climax they are summarized in different ways. "The ark of the covenant was seen within its temple" closes chapter 11. "Now the salvation and the power and the kingdom of our God and the authority of His Christ have come" climaxes the victory in heaven (12:10).

It is interesting that in a book which is distinguished by its parallels and counterparts, there appear to be none for revelation, prophesy, writing, book, mystery and gospel. This is distinctive and in harmony with a missionary faith and its missionary book. The missionary message is a revealing. It is a revelation of a person, Jesus Christ, and concerns what is, and what was, and what is to take place hereafter. So, it is also history, testimony, prophecy and prophecy-mystery. It is written and can be shared. It is of the Spirit and can be appropriated.

IT IS MISSIONARY IN ITS THEMES

The Nature of God

The God of the Apocalypse is a God who gives revelation of Himself. As a God of the Spirit of the prophets, He is a God who testifies or witnesses. He is the God of history and the King of the ages. He is the God of eternity, the "I am that I am" God who lives forever and ever. He is the God of creation and the God of the covenant. He is the God and Father of Jesus Christ. He is the sovereign, regal, reigning and ruling God. He is the one seated on the throne. He is the holy and true one. He is the Lord God almighty. He is the God who judges and avenges. So, He is not only holy and true, but just and true. He is the God of heaven, the God who shelters with His presence and the God who makes all things new. He is worthy so He is the worshipped one. He dwells with men and they are His people. The God of the Apocalypse is a missionary God.

The Jesus Christ of the Apocalypse is the promised, anointed, saving one, the faithful and true witness. He has a sharp two-edged sword and is Himself the Word of God, the Amen. He is the firstborn of the dead, the living one. Like His Father, He is the "I am" -- the self-existing one. As the first and the last, He is the coming one. He is the male child but also the Son of Man and the Son of God. As the ruler of the kings on earth He is the lord of the earth. He is also the Lord of the church. As one who sits upon the clouds, the bright and morning star, He is the Lord of glory. In short, He is the Lord of lords and King of kings. He is the Spirit, yet He sends out the seven spirits of God. He is the holy one. Supremely in this book He is the Lamb, combining in Himself lordly rule through self-giving sacrifice. Because He was slain and ransomed men for God from every tribe and tongue and people and nation, and made them a kingdom of priests for God, the Jesus of the Apocalypse is a missionary Christ.

The Spirit of the Apocalypse is a missionary Spirit. He is the complete, perfect Spirit, who with the Father and the Son, are the Godhead of the Bible -- and of this book. He is the enabling Spirit. It is "in the Spirit" on Patmos, at the throne, in the wilderness and in Jerusalem that John sees and writes. He is the speaking, communicating, applying Spirit, so He is also the Spirit of prophecy. He is the Spirit sent out into all the earth. He is the inviting, wooing Spirit who says "Come!" The Spirit of the Apocalypse is a missionary Spirit.[3] That the descriptions of the Father, of the Son and of the Holy Spirit are similar is a characteristic of Johannine literature and of the message of this book.

The Idea of Covenant

Those who see covenant as the key to understanding the Bible as a whole (Smith, 1981) or as the major theme of the mission enterprise (DeRidder, 1975; DuPreez, 1970) point out the covenant form of the letters to the seven churches, the commission of 22:17-19 and the explicit reference in 11:19: "Then God's temple in heaven was opened, and the ark of His covenant was seen within His temple; and there were flashes of lightning, loud voices, peals of thunder, an earthquake, and heavy hail." As DuPreez summarizes, "God causes His kingdom to come by means of His universal covenant sovereignty," and "God, by virtue of His right to reign as universal lord of the covenant in Christ, gathers from all nations a universal covenant people, i.e. a people drawn from Jews and Gentiles alike" (1970:152-167).

The Concept of the Kingdom

Just as some see the major theme in missions as the covenant, others see it as the kingdom of God (Ladd, 1981:51-69; Stewart, 1956:7-74). While the kingdom theme is introduced in chapter 1 and is localized in the seven churches, it is central in the triumph of 11:15 and 12:10. It is unmistakably clear that the book of Revelation is the answer to the model prayer of Jesus: "Thy kingdom come."

James C. Smith							75

Form of the Commission

Our forefathers delighted in affirming that the Bible contains facts to be believed, commands to be obeyed, warnings to be heeded and promises to be enjoyed. DeRidder summarizes these as Preamble, Demand and Promise (1975:178-179). He then compares the commissions in Mt. 28, Mk. 16, Lk. 24, Jn. 20 and Acts 1. Unfortunately, he fails to see that Rev. 22:17-20 is its sequel:

> The Spirit and the Bride say "Come." And let him who hears say "Come." And let him who is thirsty come, let him who desires take of the water of life without price. I warn every one who hears the words of the prophecy of this book: if any one adds to them, God will add to him the plagues described in this book, and if any one takes away from the words of the book of this prophecy, God will take away his share in the tree of life and in the holy city, which are described in this book. He who testifies to these things says, "Surely I am coming soon." Amen. Come, Lord Jesus.

The Sweep of Mankind

The universality of the Apocalypse is clear from four reappearing words or phrases. The **whole world** appears sixteen times in the New Testament and is usually translated "the inhabited world." That is its consistent meaning in the Apocalypse. The most frequent word translated world in the Bible is kosmos from which we get cosmic or cosmological. It can mean the created, geographical world as well as the corrupt, passing world. It is used in the sense of created world in Revelation (11:15; 13:8; 17:8).

Those who dwell upon the earth usually refers to those unresponsive to God's love and judgments and is sometimes translated as "earthlings." Those who perceive the Apocalypse as 'other-worldly' should be reminded that "the earth" appears in Revelation more than any other book of the New Testament. The major section of the book, sometimes described as "Christ and the world," covers 60% of the writing.

The phrase **mankind** or **men** appears in eight references. But the fourfold phrase, **tribes, tongues, peoples and nations** dominates present missiological thought. This phrase occurs seven different times in the book, never in the same order and with the words "kingdom and multitude" substituted for tribes twice. The context for two are redemption and deliverance. The setting for two others are judgment and of the remaining three, opportunity. Mission strategists see people groups as the principal way of penetrating the vast billions on earth. Missiologist Donald McGavran see this phrase as illustrating his homogeneous unit principle: "Men like to become Christians without crossing racial, linguistic or class barriers" (1970:198).

The Dynamics of Prayer

A recurring theme in the Apocalypse is worship and praise. Doxologies abound. "Power and wealth and wisdom and might and honor and glory and blessing" (5:12) are complete in number and are exhaustive in praise. Some see a liturgical analysis as the key to understanding this book. Other have written books on the praise passages alone (Coleman, 1980). Those who see the glory of God as the object of creation and the key to scripture find much to support their view in the book of Revelation.

The prayers of the saints are an important part of the throne scene of Revelation 5 and 8. Prayer participates, not only in the worship in heaven, but also in the unfolding, shaping and climax of history. Prayer participates in the vengeance, vindication and victory of our Eternal, Almighty God. This is prayer which enables all of God's people to hasten the climax of history. D. T. Niles notes, "The world rocks to its foundations and God's people are at prayer. It is their one form of direct participation in the rule of God" (1961:64). One of the most important things any Christian can do for world evangelism is to pray.

IT IS MISSIONARY IN ITS STYLE AND STRUCTURE

Symbols

The book of Revelation is a book of symbols. Symbols have the unusual capacity to communicate meaning in ways which can be described and sensed, but not necessarily explained. Since they can combine color, sound and form, imagination can be involved as well. In Revelation there are creatures: lions, oxen, eagles, dragons, beasts and horses mixed with multiple eyes, wings and horns. There are stones by the dozens. There are numbers by the score. Color is added to color. There is a rainbow, white garments, golden crowns, glass-like crystal, scarlet beasts and a woman in purple. There are the elements: earth, water, fire and wind. Sound echoes upon sound: voices, thunders, trumpets, harps, shouts, cries, wails, and earthquakes. Pictures crowd upon pictures: robes washed in blood, fire from heaven, lightning in the sky, falling stars and hurling millstones, an angel in mid-heaven and a beast from the abyss. Many of these are from the Old Testament. Niles notes that within the four-hundred and four verses of the book, there are five-hundred and eighteen quotations from the Old Testament apart from countless suggestions of it (1961:32). These symbols and images are not always limited to the same or single meaning. Many persons and images have their parallels or counterparts. But exuberance of symbolism offers no license for arbitrary allegorizing or speculative interpretation (Niles, 1961:32).

Time and Space

There is a different perception of time. While there is mention of past, present and future, they interact and intermix. There is a way in which certainty communicates imminency. Another characteristic of this kind of writing is how the meaning of the past and present is unveiled and understood in the light of the final end, even participating in it. There is also a different perception of space. The book takes on cosmic dimension: in heaven, on earth and under the earth and all therein. Here, too, there is interaction and intermixture. But one has the feeling when this occurs that it is in the writer's clear design.

Internal Structure and Literary Devices

More and more students of the Apocalypse are agreeing that the structure and literary composition are an inseparable part of its meaning. Literary devices are at home in poetry, drama and apocalyptic writings. Image clusters reinforce each other. Preannouncements and cross references have an integrating effect. Repetition, especially in cyclic form and interlocking or interlacing is obvious. Hendricksen uses the phrase "progressive parallelism" to describe it (1961:48). Fiorenza adds that of "conic/concentric spiral" (1979:26). I see the book as a cyclic-conical form of repetition within an indivisible whole with a continual forward movement toward fulfillment. Fortunately, most peoples of the world can sense the book readily, identify with it quickly from their oral or written lore, and learn from it appreciatively.

THE SUB-THEME OF POWER IN REVELATION

Most students of the book outline it under a given theme or primary emphasis, such as visions, sevens, chronology, christology, judgment and victory, chapters, and combinations. It is clear that the revelation of Jesus Christ is the subject, if not the theme, of the book. Given that as theme, I submit that a parallel or sub-theme is power.

Let us review the book in sequence from a power-theme point of view for one application of its missionary message.[4] The book opens with a self-description as revelation and prophecy, with a blessing for one who reads aloud, who hears and who keeps what is written. This is followed with a greeting from the Godhead and closes with a doxology of "Glory and dominion/power forever and ever, amen." Then follows the first vision of one like a son of man, "whose face was like the sun shining in full strength" (1:16).

Summary of Chapter One. God has inherent power. He is the Alpha and Omega: He is the Lord God, who is and was and is to come. He is the Almighty. The one like a son of man is authoritative by description, though only His face is described by a 'power-word.'

Letters to the seven churches follow. Each is introduced with some description of the one like a son of man. Each is commended, warned or corrected, and has a promise to the one who conquers. Thyatira is distinguished with the promise, "He who conquers and who keeps my works until the end, I will give him power over the nations, and he shall rule them with a rod of iron, as when earthen pots are broken in pieces, even as I myself have received power from my Father" (2:26-27). This one who knows everything about the churches says of the one in Philadelphia, "I know that you have but little power, and yet you have kept my word and not denied my name" (3:8).

Summary of Chapters Two and Three. Those who conquer have delegated power, just as the Son of God has power received from His Father. The church in Philadelphia has a little authority. The word itself carries the meaning of delegated power.

The second scene shifts to a throne in heaven and praise to God for His eternality and for His creative worth: "Worthy art Thou, our Lord and God, to receive glory and honor and power, for Thou didst create all things, and by Thy will they existed and were created" (4:11). The throne scene continues into chapter 5 where the one on the throne holds a sealed scroll. John weeps because there is no one in heaven or on earth or under the earth able to open the scroll or to look into it. He is told by one of the elders, "Weep not; lo, the Lion of the tribe of Judah, the root of David, has conquered, so that He can open the scroll and its seven seals" (5:5). This Lion of the tribe of Judah, this Root of David is a Lamb. And as He takes the scroll, the four living creatures, the twenty-four elders and thousands of angels say with a loud voice, "Worthy is the Lamb who was slain, to receive power and wealth and wisdom and might and honor and glory and blessing" (5:12). These are then joined by "every creature in heaven and on earth and under the earth and in the sea, and all therein, saying, 'To Him who sits upon the throne and to the Lamb be blessing and honor and glory and might forever and ever'" (5:13).

Summary of Chapters Four and Five. The slain Lamb is worthy to receive both power and might forever along with wealth, wisdom, honor, glory and blessing.

Chapter six continues in heaven as the Lamb opens six of the seals. The living creatures bid, "Come," and introduce the four horses and horsemen of the Apocalypse. The first was a white horse whose rider had a bow and received a crown and "he went out conquering and to conquer" (6:2). The second horse was red. "Its rider was permitted to take peace from the earth, so that men should slay one another; and he was given a great sword" (6:4). The third was black. Its rider had a balance in his hand and he was told, "A quart of wheat for a denarius, and three quarts of barley for a denarius; but do not harm oil and wine" (6:6). The fourth was a pale horse whose rider's name was Death, and Hades followed him. "And they were given power over a fourth of the earth, to kill with sword and with famine and with pestilence and by wild beasts of the earth" (6:8). When the fifth seal was opened, John saw under the altar of the souls of those who had been slain for the word of God and for the witness they had borne. They cried out with a loud voice, "O Sovereign Lord, holy and true, how long before Thou wilt judge and avenge our blood on those who dwell upon the earth?" (6:10). Each is given a white robe and they are told to rest a little longer, until the number of their fellow servants and their brethren should be complete, who were to be killed as they themselves had been.

The sixth seal shows the creation in convulsion and everyone from highest to lowest seeks to hide "from the face of Him who is seated on the throne, and from the wrath of the Lamb; for the great day of their wrath has come, and who can stand before it?" (6:16-17).

Chapter 7 is usually seen as an interlude between the sixth and seventh seals. The chapter opens with the four angels standing at the four corners of the earth restraining the four winds of the earth that none might blow on earth or sea or against any tree. These four angels "had been given power to harm the earth and sea" (7:2). Another angel from the rising of the sun and with the seal of the living God told them "not to harm the earth or the sea or the trees till we have sealed the servants of our God upon their foreheads." There follows the sealing of the hundred and forty-four thousand out of every tribe of the sons of Israel. They are joined by a great innumerable multitude from every nation, tribes, peoples and tongues standing before the throne and before the Lamb. And they are joined with the angels, the elders and the living creatures who fall on their faces before the throne and worship God. Blessing and glory and wisdom and thanksgiving and honor and power and might be to our God forever. They are then described in words of delivering, fulfilling, keeping, completing power.

Summary of Chapters Six and Seven. The horses and riders have permitted, limited power. And while not stated in words of our study, the Sovereign Lord and the Lamb are perceived by the martyrs and by everyone of earth as having judging, avenging, wrath-power.

Chapter 8 continues in heaven. The opening of the seventh seal was followed by about half an hour of silence. And then seven trumpets were given to the seven angels before God. Another angel stands at the altar with a golden censer. In it was incense mingled with all the prayers of the saints on the golden altar before the throne. These rose from the hand of the angel before God. Then the angel takes the censer, fills it with fire from the altar and throws it on the earth. There follows the cataclysms of peals of thunder, loud noises and flashes of lightning and an earthquake. At the sound of the first trumpet, a third of the earth, trees and all green grass was burnt up. The blowing of the second trumpet resulted in a third of the sea becoming blood with a third of the living creatures dying and a third of the ships destroyed. The third trumpet resulted in a blazing star from heaven falling on a third of the rivers and on the fountain of waters making the water bitter-to-death. The fourth angel's trumpet resulted in a third of the light from sun, moon and stars darkening a third of both day and night. Chapter 9 describes the fifth and sixth angels and their trumpets. The fifth angel was given the key to the shaft of the bottomless pit. Furnace-like smoke darkened the sun and air. From the smoke came the locusts of the earth, "And they were given power like the power of scorpions of the earth" (9:3). So torturous was their sting that men will long to die but not be able to. These horse-like locusts are a composite of horses, humans, lions and winged creatures. "Their power of hurting men for five months lies in their tails." Their king is the angel of the bottomless pit, whose Hebrew name means Destroyer. When the sixth angel blew his trumpet, a voice from the altar before God said, "Release the four angels who are bound at the great river Euphrates." These had been held ready for the hour, the day, the month and the year to kill a third of mankind. The troops of cavalry numbered ten-thousand times ten-thousand. These horses with lion's heads have power in their mouths and in their tails. And a third of mankind was killed. Even then the rest of mankind did not repent of the works of their hands of worshipping demons and idols or of their murders or their sorceries, immoralities or thefts (9:20-21).

Summary of Chapters Eight and Nine. The angels receive and blow trumpets. The consequences are limited to a third. They are restrained and partial. The fifth angel receives the key and opens the shaft of the bottomless pit, releasing the locusts of the Destroyer. Their power is given from beyond, is permitted and directed and limited. The troops of cavalry are likewise limited in killing a third of mankind.

Chapter 10 is introduced with a mighty angel coming down from heaven with a little scroll in his hand. This angel says there is to be no more delay, "But that in the day of the trumpet call to be sounded by the seventh angel, the mystery of God, as He announced to His servants and prophets, should be fulfilled" (10:7). Then John is told to take and eat the little scroll which would be bitter to the stomach but sweet as honey to the mouth. And he was told, "You must again prophesy about many peoples and nations and tongues and kings" (10:11).

Summary of Chapter Ten. While only the angel is described as mighty, the mystery of God to be fulfilled and the prophesy about many peoples and nations and tongues and kings communicates the source and means of power.

Chapter 11 has two parts. Verses 1-14 are an interlude featuring the two witnesses and intervenes between the sixth and seventh trumpets. Verses 15-19 are the seventh trumpet and announce "The kingdom of the world has become the kingdom of our Lord and His Christ and He shall reign forever and ever." John is given a measuring rod to measure the temple, the altar and those who worship there. The witnesses are to be granted "Power to prophesy for 1260 days, clothed in sackcloth." They are not to be harmed lest their foes are doomed to be killed. They have power to contain the rain, to turn water to blood, and to smite the earth with every plague as often as they wish. After their testimony is finished the beast that comes from the bottomless pit will make war on them, conquer and kill them. Men from peoples, tribes, tongues and nations will look at their dead bodies and refuse to let them be buried. And earthlings will rejoice because these two prophets had been a torment. But after the period had passed, breath from God entered them, and in the sight of their foes, they went up to heaven in a cloud. A great earthquake killed seven-thousand and the rest who were terrified gave glory to the God of heaven.

Summary of Chapter Eleven. The witnesses have delegated power over the elements and plagues. God has resurrecting, ascending power. The Lord God and His Christ have reigning power, rewarding power and destroying power. The chapter closes with the opening of God's temple in heaven and the appearance of the ark of the covenant within the temple.

Chapter 12 introduces the signs, wonders and portents. Tenney sees chapters 12-14 as an interlude of "the personages and the angels" that intervene between the trumpets and the bowls. He sees it as featuring seven persons: the woman, the dragon, the man child, Michael, the beast from the sea, the beast from the earth and the Lamb (1957:32-41). Ellul calls this chapter -- along with chapter 11 -- "the keystone" (1977:65-99). He sees the two witnesses of chapter 11 as "an exact synthesis of the work of Jesus" (1977: 80). He insists that it is the grand design of the book that "he is situated precisely in the exact center of the Apocalypse at the juncture between the first part, which is historical (church and history), and the second part, which is transhistorical, to eventually metahistorical (judgment and new creation)" (1977:80). So, he sees chapter 12 as the Incarnation taking place in heaven. His argument is persuasive, especially when he identifies the Incarnation as the new covenant.[5] He states:

> The New Covenant cannot be better described
> than as the heart itself of God; and a covenant
> which cannot be put in question, since now a
> true identification of God with man is realized.
> It is an eternal covenant, since this ark is no
> longer on earth like that of Moses and David;
> but it is the covenant made by the unity in the
> person of Jesus of the totality of man with the
> totality of God (Ellul, 1977:82).

The male child which the woman bore and which the dragon sought to devour is "one who is to rule all the nations with a rod of iron" (12:5). There follows a war in heaven where Michael and his angels and the dragon, who is thrown down in defeat, is then identified as that "ancient serpent who is called the Devil and Satan, the deceiver of the whole world. What 11:15 is to earth 12:10 is to heaven:

> Now the salvation and the power of the kingdom
> of our God and the authority of His Christ have
> come, for the accuser of our brethren has been
> thrown down, who accuses them day and night be-
> fore our God. And they have conquered him by
> the blood of the Lamb and by the word of their
> testimony, for they loved not their lives even
> unto death (Rev. 12:10-11).

The scene now shifts to earth where the pursuit of the woman by the dragon continues. When the woman is delivered, the dragon turns his wrath to "the rest of her offspring, on those who keep the commandments of God and bear testimony to Jesus." Chapter 13 describes the beast from the sea and the beast from the earth. To the former, the dragon "gave his power and his throne and great authority." The beast was allowed to exercise authority for forty-two months. It was allowed to utter blasphemies against God and it was allowed to make war on the saints and to conquer them. And its authority extended over every tribe and people and tongue and nation. The beast from earth looks like a lamb but speaks like a dragon. It exercises all the authority of the first beast. It is allowed to work signs, to give life and speech and to cause non-worshippers to be killed. It causes all to be marked with the number 666.

Chapter 14 provides a heavenly counterpart with the one-hundred forty-four thousand who had been redeemed from the earth as the first fruits for God and the Lamb. Another angel flying in mid-heaven has the eternal Gospel to proclaim to those who dwell on earth, to every nation and tribe and tongue and people. A second announces the fall of Babylon the great, applies it specifically to anyone who worships the beast and its image. The second of seven beatitudes follow. "Blessed are the dead who die in the Lord henceforth." "Blessed indeed,' says the Spirit, 'that they may rest from their labors, for their deeds follow them!" This chapter closes with one like a son of man joined by angels -- the one having power over fire -- in reaping the ripe harvest of the earth. Niles notes that at the end of every age, harvest must come; that at the close of every crisis, the consequences must be reaped -- it will be a harvest of repentance, a harvest of retribution, a harvest of remorse, and finally, a harvest unto rest (1961:81-82).

Summary of Chapters Twelve through Fourteen. The male child has ruling power. The woman sheltered has escaping power. God who has inherent power, and His Christ, who has authoritative power, manifest their conquering power through the power of the Lamb's blood, the Word's testimony and their selfless deaths. The dragon has assumed power which it gave to the beast which has allowed power, limited power. God, the Lamb, one like a son of man and His angels have retributive, harvesting power.

Chapters 15 and 16 cover the last seven plagues and the seven bowls. The scene is heaven and the occasion is praise to God by those who had conquered the beast and its image and the number of its name. The song they sing is the song of Moses, the servant of God, and the song of the Lamb: "Great and wonderful are Thy deeds, O Lord God the Almighty! Just and true are Thy ways, O King of the ages! Who shall not fear and glorify Thy name, O Lord? For Thou alone art holy. All nations shall come and worship Thee, for Thy judgments have been revealed" (15:3-4).

The temple out of which the seven angels took their bowls -- and which no one could enter until the seven plagues were ended -- is filled with smoke "From the glory of God and from His power." The first bowl of foul and evil sores was poured on the earth. The second bowl was into the sea in which everything living died. The third bowl was in the rivers and fountains of water which became blood. The fourth bowl was directed to the sun which was allowed to scorch men with fire. "They cursed the name of God who had power over these plagues, and they did not repent and give Him glory." The fifth bowl was poured on the throne of the beast. And the result was darkness. These men likewise cursed the God of heaven for their pain and sores and did not repent of their deeds. The sixth angel poured his bowl on the river Euphrates whose water was dried up. This released foul spirits from the mouth of the dragon and leads to the battle of Armageddon. The last bowl was poured into the air, followed by a fourth description of cataclysms centering in the great earthquake which split the city into three parts and hailstones rained on men from heaven.

Summary of Chapters Fifteen and Sixteen. The Almighty God is praised for His just, true and holy judgments which are inseparable from His glory and power. The judging power on the earth is finished.

Chapters 17 through 20 trace this judgment upon the great harlot, the great city Babylon, the beast and false prophet (the second beast), the dragon or serpent who is the Devil and Satan, and upon Death and Hades. The woman drunk with the blood of saints and the blood of the martyrs of Jesus is "Babylon the great, mother of harlots and of earth's abominations." The beast on which she rides has some of the characteristics of the sovereign God. It is also linked with the seven hills and seven kings who are to receive royal power and kingly authority for one hour. One in purpose, they give their power and authority to the beast and make war on the Lamb who conquers them. The king and the beast turn and destroy the very woman who had dominion over them. They are the very instruments of God in doing this: "For God has put it into their hearts to carry out His purpose by being of one mind and giving over their royal power to the beast, until the word of God shall be fulfilled." Chapter 18 describes the authoritative angel from heaven brightening earth with his splendor and detailing in poetic form the fall of Babylon. The mighty city, Babylon, has been judged by the mighty Lord God. Chapter 19 opens with a fourfold doxology of the mighty voice of a great multitude in heaven crying "Hallelujah! Salvation and glory belong to our God, for His judgments are true and just; He has judged the great harlot who corrupted the earth with her fornication, and He has avenged on her the blood of the servants." They are joined by the twenty-four elders and the four living creatures in a similar song of praise. Then the voice of the multitude, like the sound of many waters and of mighty thunder peals: "Hallelujah! For the Lord God Almighty reigns. Let us rejoice and exult and give Him the glory for the marriage of the Lamb has come, and His bride has made herself ready" (19:6-7).

For a second time we see a white horse. The rider is judged Faithful and True and his name is The Word of God. He smites the nations with a sharp sword from his mouth and rules them with a rod of iron. He treads the wine press of the fury of the wrath of God the Almighty. His other name is King of kings and Lord of lords. The beasts and the kings with their armies make war against the horseman and his army. The beast and the false prophet are captured and thrown alive into the lake of fire. The rest are slain by the sword from the rider's mouth.

Chapter 20 describes the binding of the Devil for a thousand years and his final destination in the lake of fire. Then those beheaded for their testimony for Jesus and for the Word of God and who had not worshiped the beast nor received its mark came to life and reigned with Christ for a thousand years. The second death has no power over these. But as priests of God and Christ, they reigned with them a thousand years. Satan is then loosed from his prison, gathers the nations of the earth for battle and surrounds the camps of the saints in the beloved city. But fire from heaven then consumes them and the Devil joins the beast and the false prophet in everlasting torment. The only remaining enemies are Death and Hades. All were judged by what they had done. Then Death and Hades were thrown into the lake of fire followed by those whose names are not found written in the book of life. So there is consummated in eternity what was achieved on earth when Jesus was raised: the last enemy to be destroyed is death (I Cor. 5:26).

Summary of Chapters Seventeen through Twenty. The ten kings have limited power and transfer that delegated authority to the beast. But the Lordly, Kingly Lamb conquers them. The purpose of God is greater than the royal power of the beasts. Mighty Babylon yields to the mighty Lord God. Mighty voices in heaven acknowledge the Almighty God who reigns. The Faithful and True, the Word of God, the King of kings and Lord of lords rules the nations. And death is powerless. An angel seizes, binds and seals the Devil for a thousand years. Satan is loosed and cast into the lake of fire. Every description shows his ultimate powerlessness. He whose freedom and might seemed limitless is now powerless. It is the same with Death and Hades. "Where death is thy sting? Where grave thy victory?"

Chapter 21 opens with a new heaven and a new earth and the five other "new things" which contribute to its wholeness: new peoples, new Jerusalem, new temple, new light and new paradise. The God who makes all things new is with his new people in the new Jerusalem. Those who conquer have this heritage, but the others -- the cowardly, the faithless, the polluted, the murderers, fornicators, sorcerers, idolators and all liars -- are in the fiery lake of second death. One of the angels who administered the last plagues now shows John Babylon's counterpart, the holy city Jerusalem coming down out of heaven from God. Its twelve gates carry the name of the twelve tribes and its twelve foundations the names of the twelve apostles. It is templeless and lightless. The Lord God Almighty and the Lamb bring the temple and its light. The kings of the earth and nations bring their glory to it. Its holiness will exclude those who practice abomination and falsehood and receive only those who are written in the Lamb's book of life. A river of life flows through the city. And on either side of the river, the tree of life with its monthly fruit and leaves for the healing of the nations. The servants of God worship Him and see His face and with Him they reign forever.

Summary of Chapter Twenty. For God to dwell inseparably with His people is the meaning of a new heaven and a new earth. This is the consummation of the former things. Together with the Lord God Almighty and the Lamb they will reign forever and ever.

Chapter 22:6-21 is the epilogue. It parallels chapter one with the same symmetry with which the counterparts are matched throughout the main body of the book. The only power word in the section is the seventh beatitude: "Blessed are those who wash their robes, that they may have the right to the tree of life and that they may enter the city by the gates." But the Lord, the God of the spirits of the prophets, the God who sends His angel to show His servants what must soon take place, the God who is coming soon, the God who is worshipped, the recompensing, repaying God, the 'I am the Alpha and the Omega, the first and the last, the beginning and the end' God corresponds to the God of the entire book and especially to the God and Father to whom is glory and dominion forever and ever. He is the God of the prophecy of this book. If anyone adds to them, God will add to him the plagues described in this book. And if anyone takes from the word of the book, God will take from him his share in the tree of life and in the holy city described in this book. He is the God of the unchanging revelation which He has given.

Jesus likewise sends His angel with His testimony for the churches. He is the Lord of the church, the root and offspring of David, the bright and morning star. He is the king of Israel and Lord of creation. He is the coming Lord and He is the Lord of grace.

Summary of Chapter Twenty-Two. The God of the spirit of the prophets, the God of the angels, the God of the servants, the God of the prophecy, the coming God is the God of all. He is the Lord God Almighty. And Jesus is the Lord of all whose grace is with all the saints.

ANALYSIS OF POWER

1. God the Almighty has inherent power. His power and glory fill the temple. He has praise power, plague power, sovereign power and retributive-judging power. He has abiding, keeping power.

2. Jesus has bestowed or delegated power. It is shared power with the Father. He also has authoritative, conquering power, ruling power.

3. The overcomers or conquerors have delegated power, conquering power, deathless power, sonship power, reigning power, and access power.

4. The punishing agents have power. Horse and riders are permitted power. Angels and messengers have delegated power, restraining or controlled power, releasing power, fire-power, and pronouncement power. Locusts have permitted power and limited, controlled power. Horses/troops of cavalry have destructive power. The two witnesses have delegated power.

5. The foes or the enemies have power. The dragon has assumed power which it gave to the beast. The beast has allowed power, but very vast: over every tribe and tongue and people and nation. Another beast (false prophet) has delegated power, allowed, limited power. The ten kings have allowed, limited and transferable power. The woman -- the great city, Babylon -- has limited power. Satan has controlled power.

This is the paradox of Revelation -- and ultimate reality as well -- that in the Incarnation initially and in the Crucifixion finally, the all powerful God of all humbled Himself, took the form of a servant, and tasted death for everyone (Phil. 2:5-11). That is apparent weakness at its weakest. But because of His obedience to death -- His total selflessness -- God raised Him from the dead and exalted Him to His own right hand as His eternal Son and sovereign Lord. That the slain Lamb could also be the conquering Lord of lords and King of kings could only happen in the fulfilled purpose of God.

The all powerful God and reigning Lord restrained Themselves in repeated severe mercies until repentant mankind is dissuaded from his ways or won to the God who seeks him through the very act of judgment. Such restrained power speaks to the missionary enterprise in profound ways.

1. Missionaries go out at the command and care of a missionary God. They also go out of a self-giving love for that God and for those peoples in whom they seek to dwell. Those missionaries are sent out by self-giving people.

2. Sending peoples usually send from strength: commitment strength, economic strength, national or political strength. Receiving peoples usually receive in weakness: weak economically, weak technologically, weak politically. (We sometimes make the mistake of perceiving them to be weak culturally, a blatant and uninformed error).

3. But perceptive missionaries recognize that the real power struggle is not against flesh and blood, but against the principalities and powers, against the world rulers of the present darkness, against the spiritual hosts of wickedness in the heavenly places (Eph. 6:2).

4. Such a struggle introduces us to what is known in missionary anthropology as "the power encounter." Missiologist Alan Tippett has written extensively on this subject. While his findings are beyond the immediate limits of this study, they are invaluable to its application.[6]

> Now to Him who is able to strengthen you according to my gospel and the preaching of Jesus Christ, according to the revelation of the mystery which was kept secret for long ages but now is disclosed, and through the prophetic writings is made known to all nations, according to the command of the eternal God to bring about obedience of faith -- to the only wise God be glory for evermore through Jesus Christ! Amen. (Rom. 16:25-27).

NOTES

[1] I scanned several existing sources to assist me in locating books or articles on the subject of missions and the Apocalypse. Dickerson (1982) had nothing. However, there were a limited number under the theme, Commissions, but they centered exclusively in the Gospels and Acts. Anderson's bibliography on the theology of mission was similar (1966). A scanning of the Apocalypse in New Testament Abstracts from 1967 yielded but one entry with an explicit missionary perspective. Most focused on particular words or isolated phrases and were dominated by either the liturgical or the doctrinal -- usually from denominational and traditional mindsets. The book reviews were a helpful exception.

[2] It is not inappropriate to speak of "The Western Captivity of the Apocalypse." Even the few missionary writers seem enslaved by western mindsets and parochial patterns. The two most refreshing exceptions are Ellul (1977) and Niles (1961). While both have rather conventional backgrounds and academic experiences, they are able to transcend most of them in stimulating ways.

[3] The counterparts of these are the three unclean spirits like frogs (16:13), the spirits of devils (16:14), and foul spirits (18:2). The others most obvious are the two women, the two cities and the two responses of praise and woe.

[4] My review of the power theme is derived almost exclusively from 1) a review of the power-words in the Apocalypse: kratos, exousia, dunamis, iskun, megas; 2) the word most often translated "conquering" or "victory," and 3) the family of words related to "reigning" and "ruling." Strauss (1973) is distinctive in combining the Christological with the power theme in his outline "The Lord of ..." His book is distinguished in other values as well.

[5] My appreciation of Ellul's analysis, his Christology and some of his other theology does not extend to his rather radical existentialism or his ambivalent universalism.

[6] In a statement of genuine humility Tippett referred to "the whole area of power and functional substitutes in each of which area I think I have written more than anybody else and here I have had virtually no models" (1974:15). The reader is directed initially to Tippett's lectures presented at Lincoln Christian College and Seminary which were later published in book form (Tippett, 1969).

BIBLIOGRAPHY

Anderson, Gerald H.
   1966   Bibliography of the Theology of Missions in the Twentieth Century. New York: Missionary Research Library.

Coleman, Robert
   1980   Songs of Heaven. Old Tappen: Rebel Pub. Co.

DeRidder, Richard R.
   1975   Discipling the Nations. Grand Rapids: Baker.

Dickerson, G. Fay (ed.)
   1982   Missions: A Bibliography Selected from Atla Religion Data Base. Chicago: American Theological Library.

DuPreez, James
   1970   "Mission Perspective in the Book of Revelation." The Evangelical Quarterly. 42:3:152-167.

Ellul, Jacques
   1977   Apocalypse: The Book of Revelation. New York: The Seabury Press.

Fiorenza, Elisabeth Schussler
   1981   Invitation to the Book of Revelation. Garden City: Image Books.

Hendriksen, William
   1961   More than Conquerers: An Interpretation of the Book of Revelation. Grand Rapids: Baker.

Ladd, George Eldon
   1981   "The Gospel of the Kingdom," in Perspectives on the World Christian Movement, ed. by S. Hawthorne and R. Winter. Pasadena: Wm. Carey Lib. 51-69.

McGavran, Donald A.
   1970   Understanding Church Growth. Grand Rapids: Wm. B. Eerdmans Pub. Co.

McLean, Archibald
   1907   Where the Book Speaks. New York: Fleming H. Revell Co.

Niles, D. T.
   1961   As Seeing the Invisible: A Study of the Book of Revelation. New York: Harper and Brothers.

Smith, Mont W.
   1981   What the Bible Says about Covenant. Joplin: College Press Pub. Co.

Stewart, James S.
   1956   Thine is the Kingdom. Edinburgh: St. Andrew Press.

Stott, John R. W.
   1977   "The Biblical Basis of Declaring God's Glory," in Declare His Glory, ed. by David M. Howard. Downers Grove: InterVarsity Press. 31-91.

Strauss, James
   1973   The Seer, the Savior, and the Saved. Joplin: College Press Pub. Co. (revised edition).

Tenney, Merrill C.
   1957   Interpreting Revelation. Grand Rapids: Wm. B. Eerdmans Pub. Co.

Tippett, Alan R.
   1969   Verdict Theology in Missionary Theory. Lincoln: Lincoln Christian College Press.

   1974   "The Anthropological and Ethnohistorical Pilgrimmage of a Missiologist." Unpublished paper.

Winter, Ralph and George Wigram
   1978   Word Study Concordance. Pasadena: William Carey Lib.

Part Two

HISTORY OF MISSIONS

"In many and various ways God spoke of old."

Heb. 1:1

5

Alexander Campbell's Conception of Mission

by William J. Richardson

From the very beginning of his career as an editor Alexander Campbell expressed concern for the conversion of the world and for appropriate means to achieve that goal. He regarded evangelism as a necessity; the love of God bestowed upon mankind in the person of His Son must be known in order to bear its fruit in human life.

> God's love of the world, His benevolence toward His ignorant, erring, and rebellious offspring, must be apprehended, known, and relied on, before any change in our views of His character, or of our conduct can be effected. And as the testimony given of the person, character, mission and work of Jesus Christ His Son, is that which developes [sic] this kindness, grace, favor, benignity, or philanthropy of God our Father, that testimony must be known, or relied on, before it can operate on our hearts ... our understandings, wills, passions, appetites, and conduct (Campbell, 1828a:6:466).

Believers, he once declared, should seek to fulfill this aim not only because of the mandate to do so but because the philanthropy of God moves them to desire "the reformation and salvation of men" (1831a:235).

Campbell also shared the conviction of his father, Thomas, that the reformation and unity of the church are necessary means of fitting the church to carry out this task, a conviction sometimes obscured by the controversies in which he was involved, particularly in the early years of his editorship of the **Christian Baptist**.

Despite this commitment to the evangelization of the world Campbell was known among his contemporaries as one of the foremost of the "anti-missionary Baptists" His was probably the most effective voice raised against the missionary programs of the major denominations of his day, attacking their institutions, their methods and goals. In later years, however, Campbell appears to have espoused some of the types of institutions and conceptions he earlier condemned. Where in the 1820s he disavowed the use of the term **missionary** and denounced extra-congregational societies, in the 1830s and 1840s he laid out a principle of extra-congregational cooperation, became president of a missionary society, and employed the word **mission** to describe the task of converting the world to Christ. Any attempt, therefore, to deal with Campbell's conception of Christian missions must set for itself two goals: first, understanding of his so-called "anti-missionism;" and secondly, elaborating his concept of the nature and task of the Christian missionary enterprise.

CAMPBELL'S EARLY OPPOSITION TO "MISSIONARY SCHEMES"

Campbell's opposition to the missionary programs of his day did not arise from a denial of the use of means in conversion, such as the preaching of the Gospel. In this respect he saw himself as differing from most revivalists of his day who, although they used the revival technique, conceived of the possibility of regeneration occurring "without any knowledge of the Gospel" (1824a:50). If this position were applied with rigor it would obviate the need for evangelism. Moreover, he vehemently rejected the "two seed in the spirit" theology of the anti-missionist Daniel Parker because its rigid predestinarianism assigned no role to human decision in response to the Gospel (1829a:637). Campbell's "anti-missionism" stemmed rather from his opposition to the use of what he considered inappropriate means. It was his conviction that the church, the congregation of God, is now the only authorized means of making the divine philanthropy known to the world.

> The church of Jesus Christ is, in **propria forma**, the only institution of God left on earth to illuminate and reform the world (1824f:16).

This conviction formed the basis of most of the points he raised in opposition to the "missionary schemes" of his day in an article "Remarks on Missionaries" (Campbell, 1824f:13-17).

Because of his high view of the nature and role of the church it was inconceivable that its glory could be "transferred to a human corporation [such as Bible Societies]... The church is robbed of its character by every institution, merely human, that would ape its excellence and substitute itself in its place" (1824g:1:33). This indictment fell not only upon missionary and Bible societies, but upon all the various societies coming into being in the first third of the nineteenth century.

Campbell's opposition also focused upon what he perceived to be methods inconsistent with the stated objectives of the various societies. Especially repugnant were some of their schemes for raising money and such practices as naming to boards of directors of societies persons who were either skeptics or otherwise uncommitted to the professed ideals of those societies. On one occasion he expressed displeasure over the appointment of General LaFayette to the directorship of the American Bible Society (1824j:123). Moreover, those schemes were too expensive. Basing his calculations on the annual report of the United Foreign Missionary Society mission to North American Indians he concluded that it had cost $762.76 for each of its four converts in twelve years of operation (1824e:81-83).

Furthermore, he saw these missionary societies as instruments for the advancement of the cause of certain sects and particularly of their clergy (1824d:64-66). In addition, Campbell held the conviction, shared by Jeffersonians, Unitarians, free thinkers, as well as many Baptists and Methodists, that the promoters of the societies had as their controlling aim the establishment of a national creed. In 1825 he reprinted a "circular" published by the friends of The National Tract Society whose contents supported his claim that these missionary, Bible, Sunday School and tract societies were "great religious engines, fitted and designed for the predominance of the leading secretaries who set them a-going, ultimately tending to a **national creed** and a religious establishment (1825:55-60).

Two other factors weighed even more heavily in Campbell's thought in his earlier years. One was the conviction that the reform of the church, including its unity, was necessarily antecedent and prerequisite to serious attempts to evangelize the nations. The church could only be effective as it became a model of the religion of Christ and exhibited the unity that comes through mutual relation to Christ.

> We are convinced that the character of the 'Christian Communities' is the greatest offense or stumbling block in the way of the conversion of the world ... therefore the only hopeful course to convert the world is to reform the professors of Christianity (1824i:41-42).

He urged believers to "return to the religion of our common Lord, as delivered unto us by His holy apostles. Model your churches after the primitive model," because churches will then be edified and multiplied "with accessions until all flesh shall see the salvation of our God" (1824i:41-42). Again:

> An attempt to convert pagans and Mohametans [sic] to believe that Jesus is the Son of God, and the **sent** of the Father, until Christians are united, **is** also an attempt to frustrate the prayer of the Messiah, to subvert His throne and government (1824b:135).

The other factor -- crucial to understanding Campbell's earlier opposition and an important key to understanding the later modification of his views -- is the fact that Campbell at this time equated the terms **missionary** and **apostle**. In the light of this understanding he rejected the term **missionary** as no longer appropriate and likewise regarded as mistaken any schemes predicated upon use of this term. In Campbell's view there were but two grand missions instituted by God. One was the mission of Moses and Joshua. Moses was the great apostle of God to the Israelites; thus, God's missionary. The second mission, to which all others were subservient, was the Father's sending of His own Son to the world as His great apostle or missionary, and the Son's sending His missionaries to perfect this grand mission. The missionaries of Christ were the twelve and the seventy sent out during His ministry and those who received the commission in person after the Resurrection and who were later empowered by the Spirit on Pentecost to carry it out. All the above had special qualifications:

> Thus all the missionaries, sent from heaven,
> were authorized and empowered to confirm their
> doctrine with signs and wonders ... to satisfy
> the most inquisitive of the origin of their
> doctrine (Campbell, 1824f:14).

Because he thus equated **missionary** and **apostle** he contended that once the Gospel had been preached to all the world "the missionary work was done" (1824f:14). Unless one supposed oneself to possess the powers enjoyed by these missionaries, one should not liken his commission to theirs.

Campbell still contemplated the spread of the Gospel through the world but conceptions of the task and the means employed to fulfill it must be other than those implied by the use of the term **missionary**, a usage which he believed to be the capital mistake of modern missionary schemes. It was the enlargement of his understanding of the scope of the New Testament use of **apostle** that was to become a significant factor in the later modification of his views concerning the Christian mission and the means of fulfilling it.

CAMPBELL'S MODIFICATION OF VIEWS ON MISSIONS

No specific date can be given as the time that Campbell began to advocate a more vigorous program of evangelism and to articulate the case for organized cooperation in missionary endeavor, but the views he expressed in the late 1840's were quite different from those to be found in the early volumes of the **Christian Baptist**. Yet the change was not made abruptly. Moreover, while he no longer asserted that world evangelism must await the reformation and unity of Christians, he continued to hold to the plea for union in truth. For example, in 1827 while praising the Mahoning Association for its appointment of Walter Scott as evangelist or "messenger of the churches," he noted that such activities must be carried on concomitantly with efforts toward Christian unity.

> It is hoped that all Christians will turn their
> attention more to good works and to the conver-
> sion of those around them, and to the union of
> all disciples on primitive grounds, in order
> that the whole world may be brought under the
> dominion of the Root and Offspring of David[1]
> (1827a:382).

An important development in Campbell's thought came in his emphasis upon cooperation in later issues of the Christian Baptist. In 1828, he affirmed the propriety of churches in association "co-operating in any public measure" in which they may agree, citing the example of the Mahoning Association's appointment of Scott as "their messenger to proclaim the word" (1827b:419). He did insist, however, that such associations could not claim juridicial or legislative power over congregations.

In 1831, Campbell began a series, "The Co-operation of Churches," expressing the conviction that on New Testament grounds such cooperation is necessary, even though the manner of it is left to the discretion of participating churches (1831c:437). The Lord, he declared, had "committed the salvation of men" to both the agency of the Spirit and the agency of man. "He has now left it to the church to convert the world." While the means empowered through the ages have been subject to corruption and perversion, nevertheless the "Gospel has reached us ... we are now rejoicing in the hope of the glory of God ... the abuse of any means is no argument against the use of them" (1831c:437). Moreover, he declared, the fear of failure to use means properly had resulted in leaving "wholly undone the most important duties" (1831a:236).

Interesting also is the fact that in this same period Campbell acknowledged that support of societies could be regarded as a matter of individual conscience. "Many of our brethren contribute to Missionary and Bible Societies and Sunday Schools, with all their imperfections. Let every man, we say, be fully persuaded in his own mind, and act consistently" (1832b:616).

In 1841 Campbell began a lengthy series of articles on the subject of "the Christian organization," aimed at setting forth a "scriptural system of co-operation" to fill the need for "concentrated effort in building the common cause" (1844:44). The spread of the Gospel was chiefly, though not solely his concern. His observation of the churches had led him to conclude:

> There is, however, little or no co-operation; no general organization; no mutual understanding; no coming together in one place in case of emergency, and for the dissemination and support of the Gospel and mutual encouragement of one another in the work of the Lord (1841:543).

He affirmed that "both by precept and example" the New Testament teaches "the necessity of united and concentrated action in the advancement of the kingdom" (1842:62-63). He did not, however, find a set form that such an organization should take, although he rejected the Congregationalist, Presbyterian, Methodist and Episcopal forms as suitable models. Nor did he see the question as having to do with the fundamental order of the church; he emphasized that he had not changed his views on the nature of the church from his **Christian Baptist** days or from his more recently published "Extra on Order."

In this series Campbell distinguished between "private duties," which were the concern of particular congregations, and "public duties of all the churches in their associate character, as one body." He considered organization for carrying out public duties necessary, while insisting that such an organization must not interfere with the performance of private duties of "each particular community" (1843:84).

This series on organization is worthy of more extended study because of the way it reflects the development of his thinking. It is significant also for the response it elicited, as it caused some consternation among persons otherwise sympathetic toward Campbell's views. It also led to a spirited but friendly exchange between the editor and an Episcopalian, who agreed with Campbell's premise concerning organization but insisted that only the evolved order of the post-apostolic age represents God's intention for the church.

Campbell continued to argue the need for some type of organization for cooperation. In 1849 when a general convention at Cincinnati -- set up first as a delegate body -- established the American Christian Missionary Society, Campbell accepted the presidency of the organization and actively defended it and its program. Of the accomplishment of that convention he wrote:

> it is the glory ... of the first convention ever assembled of our brethren, that then and there they unanimously resolved, in the name of the Lord, to institute, to organize, and put into operation, a society for spreading salvation and civilization over all Lands, so far as the Lord will give them means and the opportunity (1850b:76).

FACTORS IN CAMPBELL'S CHANGE OF VIEWS

There has been much debate over whether Campbell's later attitude on missionary organization differed from that of his **Christian Baptist** days. The reformer himself insisted there had been no fundamental change; it was abuses of the principle rather than the principle itself that he had earlier opposed (1832b:614-615). Later, in a reply to Jacob Creath, Jr. he justified the 1849 convention, declaring that a convention is "either scriptural or unscriptural, good or bad," depending on its objective (1850a:637-8). Similar explanations of Campbell's views were given by his contemporaries, D. Burnet, W. Pendleton and R. Richardson.[2]

More recent authors are convinced a change of views had indeed occurred and adduce factors -- political and social as well as theological -- to account for it. We can only summarize their arguments recognizing that such a treatment cannot adequately represent their thinking. Not all the arguments are of equal merit or validity but must be cited as significant efforts to deal with an important problem of historical interpretation. Frederick West attributes Campbell's change of mind to a philosophy of history emphasizing the millennium, accompanied by belief in the role and destiny of the United States, a vision which required "greater social planning" including new forms of organization for the Disciples (West, 1948:164-211). Lunger sees Campbell's change of mind as due to his acceptance of denominational status for the movement (Lunger, 1954). In addition to the above, Lambert cites a move by Campbell toward more conservative social and economic principles, following Clay's American System model, which had their counterpoint in "more of a mood to consider the social limits of individual action." He alludes also to such factors as Scott's work as an evangelist for the Mahoning Association; the union with the Christian Connection which forced him to rethink his position on independency; the fact that Campbell could not oppose distribution of the Scriptures, even if done by a Bible Society; and the influence of Campbell's friend D. S. Burnet who was also a staunch supporter of the society principle (Lambert, 1980:308-315). Hughes attributes the change to a shift of emphasis from "radical restoration" to the "theme of unity;" hence for Campbell the silence of scripture need no longer prohibit the use of expedients in carrying out the command to preach the word. This shift of emphasis, says Hughes, included a commitment to civil religion, a type which differed from that of the founding fathers in being grounded in revelation rather than in the presuppositions of Deism (Hughes, 1976:44:87-103).

However difficult it might be to identify all the factors involved, it is necessary to recognize that Campbell had undergone a change of views. This does not mean that he had departed from his basic commitment to New Testament Christianity or to the plea for union in truth; however, he no longer asserted that world evangelism must await the achievement of this aim. He never wavered in concern for the conversion of the world, but modified his views in such a way as to affect not only his attitude toward the missionary society but also his concept of the way of carrying out the task and his understanding of the status of the personnel involved in carrying it out.

A factor in this change, which has either been overlooked or given insufficient attention, is Campbell's enlarged understanding of the scope of apostleship. In 1823 he had opposed the use of the term **missionary** because it was the equivalent of the term **apostle**; hence to invoke the use of the term **missionary** was to claim apostolic status and function, a claim he would not allow. He had likewise restricted the term **ambassador** as synonymous with **apostle** and **missionary** and hence had refused to apply that term to any class of ministers today (1824h:20-21).

At that time Campbell had conceived of only two orders of apostleship in the New Testament -- that of Christ and of those He personally sent out as "His missionaries to perfect the grand mission." He had ridiculed the notion that a parallel could be drawn between the commissioning of a missionary today and the commissioning of Paul and Barnabas as seen in Acts 13 (1824f:15-17).

However, as early as 1827 Campbell began to make reference to "messengers of the churches," a designation he gave to Walter Scott's status upon the latter's appointment as evangelist of the Mahoning Association (1827a:382). He found sanction for such usage in II Corinthians 8:19-23, where this term is applied to persons chosen by the churches to travel with Paul in collecting benevolent funds (1831a: 238). The term "messengers of the churches," is a rendering of apostoloi ekklesiōn (II Cor. 8:23). In an article written in 1832 Campbell identified apostoloi ekklesiōn, "apostles of the congregations," as a third order of apostles; "persons chosen and sent by the congregations on special errands." He conceived of the status of "messengers of the churches" in like manner (1832a:196). "Messenger of the church" could refer to any person, male or female, sent on any errand by a particular congregation (1827b:419).

Also, the term might designate persons appointed by churches meeting in association to carry out tasks reflecting the interests they shared in common, such as the conversion of the world. "The primitive churches in certain districts did co-operate in choosing certain persons for the work of the Lord, and these persons when chosen were called 'messengers of the Churches'" (1831a:238).

The role of such messengers varied according to need and circumstance. A particular church might appoint one to "carry twenty dollars for the congregation in New York to that in Columbus" (1827b:419), or to represent it in a "co-operation meeting" such as the one in "the Western District of Virginia and the neighboring counties of Ohio" which Campbell served as president (1836:184-185). An association of churches might appoint messengers "on all errands connected with the peace and prosperity of all the churches, and with the conversion of the world" (1835b:522).

> The first churches did exercise the right of selecting from among themselves brethren for the accomplishment of special purposes ... I dont [sic] mean political purposes; not literary ones, as such, nor commercial ones -- I mean ecclesiastical purposes -- matters which regard the conversion of the world and the welfare of the churches (1831b:240).

Hence, it was a step quite in keeping with his developing understanding of the concept of "messengers [apostles] of the churches" that Campbell came finally to regard this term as synonymous with the term **evangelists** and **missionaries** when applied to those whose errand was that of preaching the Gospel (1849:269). They represented a different order from the original apostles commissioned by the risen Lord. Therefore, they could be called missionaries without any derogation of the office of the "Apostles of Christ" upon whose unique witness rested the faith of the church throughout the ages.

Thus, at the same time that Campbell was developing a case for the cooperation of churches he was coming to an understanding of a function of ministry appropriate to the concept of cooperative action undertaken by churches to evangelize the world. However much the other factors cited above may have entered into the modification of his views, it cannot be said that Campbell proceeded without due consideration for the authority which he sought to bring to bear upon all issues confronting the body of Christ.

ROLE OF THE CHURCH IN MISSION

Campbell never wavered from his conviction that the church is God's chosen instrument for the conversion of the world. In 1857 he wrote:

> Has not the Lord commanded the Gospel to be preached to all the world ... till He personally appear on the field Himself and call the world to judgment? This is the identical mission of the church; this is her duty, her privilege, her honor, as it is now and will ever be her chief glory and her highest happiness (1861:544).

There could be no succession to the apostolic office; as the "Lord's prime missionaries" they could not "transfer their office to others" (1861:563). But the function of proclaiming the apostles' message had devolved upon the church. The church cannot replicate "what Christ, the Holy Spirit, and the Apostles have done;" her task is rather to "guard the precious deposite [sic], to preserve the oracles, to hold them forth, to sound forth and proclaim the word" (1832c:248).

STRATEGIES FOR MISSION

Although his conception of the church's role in mission remained unchanged, Campbell's view of its implementation underwent revision. His earlier strategy emphasized the church's exhibiting the Gospel to the world -- as the necessary concomitant to communicating the Gospel by preaching.

> An organized society of this kind, modeled after the plan taught in the New Testament, is the consummation of the manifold wisdom of God to exhibit to the world the civilizing, the moralizing, the saving light, which renovates the human heart... The Christian religion is a social religion, and cannot be exhibited to the world, only when it appears in this social character (1824f:16-17).

Hence as a "project for spreading the Gospel" Campbell proposed that a congregation take up residence in a heathen land, its members wearing the same type of clothing and supporting themselves in the same manner as the natives, holding forth "in word and deed the saving truth," thus "allowing their own works and example to speak for their religion." He was persuaded that "in process of time, a more solid foundation for the conversion of the natives would be laid, and more success resulting, than from all the missionaries employed for twenty-five years" (1824f:16-17). This project was never put into operation; by the time the Disciples got around to engaging in missions overseas other strategies had been adopted.

In some ways the strategy described above resembles the recently proposed concept of mission known as "Christian presence;" it differs, however, in that it conceives of conversions to Christian faith and of participation of converts in the church as its main goals.

Campbell's later strategy focused upon the cooperation of churches in sending missionaries to evangelize other areas, because the world is the field of the whole church. The whole church ought to cooperate in the important cause of sending the Gospel to all nations as far as in its power. For this cause congregations should join in prayers and in choosing and sending out "proclaimers," and in contributing to their support (1832c:244-249).

Thus the strategy of the American Christian Missionary Society in the 1850s, of sending out missionaries, differed from that which he outlined in the 1820s. To Campbell's mind this difference did not constitute a reassessment of the role of the church in God's purpose. The proposals themselves are not contradictory. The earlier strategy could still have been pursued in combination with or conducted parallel to the program later adopted. The differences between the two programs are significant, however, for the way they reflect the development of Campbell's thought in the years intervening.

GOAL OF THE MISSION

For Campbell the goal of mission in its broadest terms is the salvation of mankind, defined in terms of the reformation or renovation of human life and its beatification, the model being in the image of Christ (1828a:466-467). But "renovation" does not describe merely the final state of things; the social state of man now could be changed, the world "Christianized" (1824f:16). Campbell believed a time would come when society would be "fully civilized" (1861:69). Such a state would come only when each individual member of society is civilized, "when all the powers of his animal, intellectual, moral, and religious nature are fully developed in subordination to his ultimate and eternal destiny" (1861:55). Thus he linked world evangelism with his hope for the millennium, a time when **"Jesus Christ will -- govern the world by religion only, and that by the operation of a single principle,"** the "principle of love" (1861:371-374).

In Campbell's view the Gospel envisions the transformation of relations among persons in society -- as a consequence of the renovation of the persons who comprise society. He rejected the proposal, put forth by Robert Owen in their 1829 debate, of renovating human nature by environmental conditioning. Owen saw man as a determined being, "formed according to the nature, kind and qualities of the circumstances in which he is permitted to live;" hence the only way to change people was by changing the circumstances (1906:26). Campbell admitted that environment plays a role in developing personality. But to proceed from this view alone, he declared, is to attempt to found a social system upon one-half man, the animate, overlooking his moral nature.

> Society is not a number of persons covering a certain piece of ground like the trees in our forests. They must congregate upon some stipulations, express or implied. These stipulations are to be performed and consequently, responsibility and accountability forces itself upon Mr. Owen in defiance of the powers of his imagination (1906:393).

It is to man's moral nature that the principle of love embodied in the Gospel makes its appeal. Thus, Campbell saw the contrast between the Christian system and that proposed by Owen:

> What is the pith of his philosophy? Why, it is this. **Transplant a crab tree and it becomes an apple tree.** But the great reformer's philosophy was **engraft a new scion.** Such is the exact difference between the scheme of Mr. Owen and the founder of Christianity (1906:367).

Campbell did not disparage activities aimed at improving social and political systems but he held the conviction that the ultimate amelioration of the human condition must come through the Gospel.

THE MISSIONARY TASK

The missionary task could be simply defined, even though it might involve a variety of functions. It is to evangelize -- to bring persons into Christian status, or relation to Christ, and to edify or nurture persons in that relationship. Here again the church plays a vital role. The church is the agent of converting persons to Christ; once converted they must be gathered into congregations, under the guidance and teaching of elders, where they may be nurtured in the faith and the attendant responsibilities of discipleship (1851:508-509).

The distinction between evangelism and edification also called for a corresponding distinction between preaching and teaching. Preaching is announcement, the proclamation of the facts of the Gospel, with a view to winning persons to allegiance to Christ. Teaching is setting forth the meaning of the facts of the Gospel (doctrine) for the purpose of helping converts to grow in the faith. "To make known the fact is to preach, and to explain the meaning of that fact is to teach" (1824a:76). Throughout his career Campbell was insistent on maintaining this distinction; the functions of preaching and teaching must not be confounded. The fact that an evangelist might "have both these works committed to his hands ... does not make them one and the same, any more than preaching and baptizing are one and the same act because performed by one and the same person" (1861:536-537).

MINISTRIES FOR MISSION

In his view of ministry Campbell sought to hold in perspective his insistence on the role of each member of the congregation in evangelism and his belief in the propriety of a church, or churches in cooperation, sending out evangelists. He accepted the implications of the priesthood of believers; every disciple is "one of the Lord's freedmen and priests" with "full power and privilege to attend upon every part of the Christian institution" (1831a:237). In **The Christian System**, published in 1835, he declared: "A Christian is by profession a preacher of truth and righteousness, both by precept and example" (1835a:64). Even earlier he had declared that every Christian is a missionary (1829b:640). In one of his missionary addresses he was led to remark: "A silent Christian is an anomaly in creation" (1861:532).

At the same time he recognized the necessity of there being in the church persons to whom these functions were specifically assigned, a "standing and immutable ministry... of Bishops, Deacons, and Evangelists" (1835a:60). These had diversified functions, which he outlined as follows:

> **Bishops,** whose office is to preside over, to instruct, and to edify the community ... and to watch for their souls ... compose the first class ... **Deacons,** or servants, ... constitute the second ... **Evangelists,** however, though a class of public functionaries created by the church, do not serve it directly; but are sent out into the world, and constitute the third class of functionaries ... **Evangelists,** as the term indicates, are persons devoted to the preaching of the word, to the making of converts, and the planting of churches (1835a:60-62).

As we noted earlier, when applied to those persons given the function of preaching, converting, planting of churches, Campbell regarded messengers of the church, evangelists, and missionaries as filling the same office.

MISSIONARY METHODS AND PROCEDURES

Campbell saw the actual functioning of a mission as a fourfold purpose: 1) selecting and appointing evangelists, including giving them prayer and financial support; missionaries "ought to be freed from all necessity of providing for themselves and families" (1861:548); 2) preaching the Gospel and making converts; 3) gathering the converts into congregations; and 4) leaving them in the care of elders (bishops) and deacons for their edification. As a process so described he believed that "the missionary spirit and the missionary work are essentially the same." At the same time there would be diversity in "the condition of the missionaries and the condition of the field" (1861:535-536).

> In this, as in every other work, there is a time and a place, there are conditions and circumstances, which call for special attention, special development and special application (1861:535-536).

As an example of this diversity he cited the differences in the discourses "in the four Gospels or in the Acts." Although "the same in sense and purport" these discourses were diversified in style and manner, in general and special details." He attributed this phenomenon to differences in the missionary context where these discourses were given (1861:535-536).

In an 1835 treatise Campbell laid out what he described as "ORDER -- as respects the Labors of an Evangelist." It contains several principles or procedures to be followed in a missionary situation (1835c:523-525). As the following will show, he limited his discussion in this treatise to the factors leading up to the making of converts, presumably because he had elsewhere dealt with procedures for setting congregations in order.

1. The field of endeavor should be chosen with great care. As with the case of a farmer choosing a farm, one must "consider the soil" and whether his capacities are sufficient to meet the challenge of that field. Elsewhere Campbell recommended: "If we [the American Missionary Society] cannot evangelize the whole world, let us send out our missionary evangelists to such fields as promise the most fruit"[3] (1861:542)

2. The field should be cultivated in order to evoke a friendly hearing of the Gospel. The evangelist "takes the people as he finds them. He is courteous ... humble, affable, communicative." He avoids involvement in politics or in family or neighborhood disputes. He is guided by the maxim of speaking the truth in love. "He removed the darkness, not by inveighing against it, but by presenting the light, and seeks to reform the world more by persuasion than by denunciation" (1835c:523-525).

3. As a corollary to beginning with people where they are the message must be adapted to the status of the hearers. "The evangelist preaches not to every man as if all the world were Jews, Samaritans, or Infidels." The goal is the same in all cases -- to make disciples; but the situation of each hearer determines the kind of overture to be made (1835c:523-525).

4. Persons must not be pressed into obedience until first they have come to the conviction that Jesus is the Christ. The appeal to obedience is grounded in motives contained in the Gospel. "It is not the fire of hell, but **the love of God**, on which he delights to dwell."

5. Apostolic precedent must guide the evangelist in his preaching. The message centers in Christ and not in a theological system.

> He preaches Christ and not the Spirit, nor any theory of spiritual operations. He ... seeks to make converts to Jesus Christ, and not to a theory of redemption. It is the person and the office of Emmanuel, and not the speculative philosophy of the schools, to which he invites the attention of his audience (1835c:523-525).

Moreover, in answer to the question, "What shall I do?" the evangelist should answer "in the very words of the Apostles." So as far as the Gospel, faith and obedience are concerned the missionary must, as it were, "begin at Jerusalem, where the Lord commanded His Apostles to begin."

This concern for the apostolic <u>ordo salutis</u> -- the order in which faith, repentance, baptism, remission of sins, the Holy Spirit appear in the "evangelical economy" -- remained with Campbell throughout his career. He did not charge the major religious bodies with omitting any of these items but rather of presenting them in an order different from that which flows naturally from the Gospel as a proclamation about Jesus of Nazareth, the arrangement reflected in Acts. To change that order in effect changes the Gospel.

> A very different tune is played upon the same notes when the arrangement of them is changed, and so different Gospels are preached upon the different ordering of these items (1828b:486-488).

SUMMARY

Alexander Campbell was not a missiologist in the twentieth-century meaning of the term, nor was he informed by some of the insights open to missiologists today from such dsiciplines as anthropology or sociology (at least under those names). He cannot of course speak specifically to the issues we face today. Nevertheless his approach might well contribute to our dialogue, if not to our understanding, at least in the following particulars.

1. Priority in missionary procedure is determined by the distinction between addressing to persons the claims of Jesus for their allegiance (proclamation) and instructing them in the meaning and implications of the Lordship of

Jesus for their life (teaching). Both functions belong to the missionary task, but one, the proclamation, precedes and lays the ground for the other.

2. While Campbell viewed sending the word of life to "nations in darkness" as the "work of greater importance" he did not discount the mandate to care for the temporal needs of people (1861:522).

3. His project for converting the world set forth in the second issue of the **Christian Baptist** called for setting the church in the midst of the pagan community, thus avoiding the "mission station" approach, although later on one occasion he made reference to 'missionary' stations to describe the society's work.

4. The missionary should be aware of "contextual" factors in the field of his endeavor. He "takes the people as he finds them," adjusting accordingly his mode of dealing with them and his manner of communicating the Gospel.

5. The church played a vital role in his thinking -- as the institution divinely appointed for mission and as the fellowship into which converts are drawn in fulfillment of their discipleship. As the instrument of mission the church must exhibit Christ and the reconciliation brought about by the Gospel; therefore the appeal for restoration and unity are inseparable from mission. The mission cannot wait; but efforts to carry it on must be accompanied by efforts to make the church "the glorious church" of Christ's intention.

NOTES

[1] Only a few years later he put evangelism, unity and restoration in juxtaposition as follows: 1st. Nothing is essential to the conversion of the world but the union and cooperation of Christians. 2d. Nothing is essential to the union of Christians but the Apostles' teaching or testimony (1835a:87).

[2] D. S. Burnet, "The Christian Baptist and Missionary Bible Societies," Preface to Eighth Edition, **Christian Baptist**; W. K. Pendleton, Ed., **Millennial Harbinger**, (1866), 497-498; R. Richardson, **Memoirs of Alexander Campbell**, Cincinnati, (1897), II:130.

[3] However, Campbell supported the continuance of the Jerusalem mission of Barclay despite limited results (1861:527).

BIBLIOGRAPHY

Campbell, Alexander

1824a "A Familiar Dialogue between the Editor and a Clergyman." Christian Baptist. 1:76-77 (1889 edit).

1824b "A Restoration of the Ancient Order of Things - No. II" Christian Baptist. 2:135 (1889 edit).

1824c "Address - No. IV" Christian Baptist. 1:48-50 (1889 edit).

1824d "Another Scheme to Defraud the Public." Christian Baptist. 1:64-66 (1955 edit).

1824e "Missionary Report." Christian Baptist. 1:81-83 (1955 edit).

1824f "Remarks on Missionaries." Christian Baptist. 1:13-17 (1889 edit).

1824g "Reply to Mr. Robert Cautious." Christian Baptist. 1:33-34 (1889 edit).

1824h "The Clergy - No. I" Christian Baptist. 1:18-21 (1889 edit).

1824i "The Conversion of the World." Christian Baptist. 1:40-42 (1889 edit).

1824j "Worthy of Imitation." Christian Baptist. 2:123 (1889 edit).

1825 "Priestly Ambition." Christian Baptist. 3:55-60 (1955 edit).

1827a "Miscellaneous Letters - No. I" Christian Baptist. 5:381-383 (1889 edit).

1827b "Reply to Mr. W." Christian Baptist. 5:418-420 (1889 edit).

1828a "Ancient Gospel - No. VIII" Christian Baptist. 6:466-467 (1889 edit).

1828b "Ancient Gospel - No. IX" Christian Baptist. 6:486-488 (1889 edit).

1829a   "New Periodicals." Christian Baptist. 7:636-637
        (1889 edit).

1829b   "Sermons to Young Preachers - No. IV" Christian
        Baptist. 7:639-640 (1889 edit).

1831a   "The Co-operation of the Churches - No. I"
        Millennial Harbinger. 235-238.

1831b   "The Co-operation of the Churches - No. II"
        Millennial Harbinger. 240-242.

1831c   "The Co-operation of the Churches - No. IV"
        Millennial Harbinger. 435-438.

1832a   "Apostles." Millennial Harbinger. 196-199.

1832b   "Reply to Epaphras." Millennial Harbinger.
        614-617.

1832c   "The Co-operation of the Churches - No. VI"
        Millennial Harbinger. 244-250.

1835a   The Christian System. St. Louis: Christian
        Pub. Co.

1835b   "Order - As respects Messengers." Millennial
        Harbinger. 519-523.

1835c   "Order - As respects the Labors of an Evangelist."
        Millennial Harbinger. 523-525.

1836   "Co-operation Meeting." Millennial Harbinger.
        184-185.

1841   "The Nature of the Christian Organization - No. I"
        Millennial Harbinger. 532-537.

1842   "The Nature of the Christian Organization -
        No. II" Millennial Harbinger. 59-64.

1843   "Church Organization." Millennial Harbinger.
        82-86.

1844   "Organization." Millennial Harbinger. 42-45.

1849   "Church Organization - No. III" Millennial
        Harbinger. 269-271.

1850a "Conventions - No. V" *Millennial Harbinger*.
       637-641.

1850b "The Christian Missionary Society - No. I"
       Millennial Harbinger. 73-76.

1851 "Support of the Christian Ministry - No. I"
       Millennial Harbinger. 508-511.

1861 *Popular Lectures and Addresses*. St. Louis:
       Christian Publishing Co.

1889 *Christian Baptist*. St. Louis: Christian Pub. Co.
       (13th. edit).

1955 *Christian Baptist*. Nashville: Gospel Advocate Co.
       (7 vols).

Campbell, Alexander and Robert Owen
   1906 *The Evidences of Christianity: A Debate*.
         St. Louis: Christian Pub. Co.

Hughes, Richard T.
   1976 "From Primitive Church to Civil Religion: The
         Millennial Odyssey of Alexander Campbell."
         Journal of the American Academy of Religion.
         44:1:87-103.

Lambert, Byron C.
   1980 *Rise of the Anti-Mission Baptists: Sources and
         Leaders, 1800-1840*. New York: Ayer Co.

Lunger, Harold L.
   1954 *The Political Ethics of Alexander Campbell*.
         St Louis: Bethany Press.

West, Frederick Robert
   1948 *Alexander Campbell and Natural Religion*.
         New Haven: Yale University Press.

6

Revival and the Restoration Movement

by Max Ward Randall

Within the Restoration movement the term "revival" may connote a phenomenon often found in frontier religious life, but which its leaders have rejected. For some, revival consists of little more than an ecstatic joy that leaves the believer as unsettled as he was before. To many evangelicals, including Restorationists, to have a revival means only to generate an accelerated concern for religion, called a "revival meeting." Accession of many additions would affirm that a "revival" had taken place.

When believers pray for revival they usually desire "a purifying and vitalizing of the existing Church" (McGavran, 1970:163). With many historians, revival is the means by which God renews His Church to carry out the divine task of evangelizing the world.

REVIVAL IN SCRIPTURE

God gives revival. David prayed: "Wilt Thou not revive us again: that Thy people may rejoice in Thee?" (Ps. 85:6). Isaiah exclaimed, "For thus says the high and lofty One that inhabits eternity, whose name is Holy; I dwell in the high and holy place, and also with Him who is of a contrite and humble spirit, to revive the spirit of the humble, and to revive the heart of the contrite" (Is. 57:15).

Revival is the work of God. "O Lord, I have heard Thy speech, and was afraid: O Lord, revive Thy work in the midst of the years, in the midst of the years make it known;

in wrath remember mercy" (Hab. 3:2). This principle was often illustrated in both Israel and Judah as they cried in prayer and repentance, and God revived them.

The book of Acts describes an awakening of the people of God. Through the Gospel, according to Peter, "times of refreshing shall come from the presence of the Lord" (Acts 3:19). The development within Acts begins with the spiritual awakening on Pentecost. On that day the promise of the Holy Spirit was fulfilled. Jesus' disciples became daring Gospel advocates. It was God who revived them.

J. EDWIN ORR'S DEFINITION OF REVIVAL

J. Edwin Orr knows more about revivals than any other historian. He says:

> An Evangelical Awakening is a movement of the Holy Spirit in the Church of Christ bringing about a revival of New Testament Christianity. Such an awakening may, of course, change in a significant way an individual only, or it may affect a larger group of people; or it may move a congregation, or the churches of a city or a district, or the whole body of believers throughout a country or continent, or indeed the larger body of believers throughout the world. Such an awakening may run its course briefly, or it may last a whole lifetime (Orr, 1965:265).

He goes on to add that though they come about in various ways there are common aspects to all revivals. These aspects include: 1) the importance of prayer; 2) a hunger for the Word of God; 3) the desire for holy living; and 4) preaching with power.

REVIVAL IS THE RESULT OF PRAYER

When revival occurs it comes to those who pray earnestly and who long for it. Such prayers in the history of the Awakenings are numerous. The last years of the 18th. century were a time of discouragement. Bishops Madison and Provoost shared the fears of Chief Justice Marshall that the Church could not be revived. In New England twenty ministers, out of despair, issued a call for a 'Concert of Prayer' (Orr, 1965:21). Those men, desperate because of the prevailing impiety and the corruption of public morals, were joined in earnest prayers until the tide turned.

Prayer at Hampden-Sydney College.

Following the Revolution the more prestigious colleges were fountains of immorality and unbelief. When the situation changed, it took place gradually. A few students of Hampden-Sydney college in Virginia came together to pray. Unbelievers broke up the meeting until the college president opened his study for the intercessors. Half the students became Christians in a short time (Orr, 1965:21).

Prayer at Williams College.

Five students from Williams College, during the summer of 1806, meeting regularly in a grove to pray, were driven from the trees to find protection from a thunderstorm. In the shelter of a haystack they prayed for power to reach the millions unsaved around the world. The storm subsided and the sun broke through. God's presence illuminated their hearts, and Samuel J. Mills expressed what became their rallying cry: "We can do it if we will." The American missionary enterprise began with that haystack compact.

Prayer was a key in the beginnings of the Restoration movement.

Restoration churches are aware of Walter Scott who was chosen as evangelist for the Mahoning Baptist Association at a meeting in New Lisbon, Ohio in 1827. There were fifteen men, eleven affiliated with the Campbell movement, three associated with Barton Stone and the Christian Churches, and Scott from the Haldane persuasion called the Church of Christ.

In the Mahoning Baptist Association in 1827 there were seventeen churches. Thirteen of thirty-four individuals baptized that year had been excommunicated. In the previous year only eighteen had been baptized (Baxter, 1874:89).

The men at New Lisbon were deeply committed. They met on the Lord's Day at sunrise in the Baptist meeting house for prayer and praise and continued till eight o'clock. For hours their petitions were lifted to the Father. To these men emphasis upon restoring the Church was not enough; they knew they needed to pray.

The reformation gathered momentum from the beginning of Scott's evangelistic labors. By the end of 1828 one-thousand had been added to the churches of the Mahoning Baptist Association. Membership had doubled.

Many were convinced that the means of proclaiming the Gospel had been rediscovered. The one-thousand added over just twelve months was proof of divine power. They observed victories over denominationalism and unity among sectarian bodies (Richardson, 1868:2:181-183). Through laborers within the Mahoning Association in 1829, another thousand were baptized (Campbell, 1830:415).

By 1832, 25 thousand were part of the new reformation (Scott, 1832:72). In 1833 Campbell noted that during the previous seven years there had been tremendous growth. In that year alone ten-thousand were added, with some 100,000 a part of the movement (Garrison and DeGroot, 1948:324). In 1836 Cox published the following statistics: "Christians, one-thousand churches, three-hundred ministers, thirty-thousand members. Reformers or Campbellites have been computed at one-hundred fifty thousand" (Cox, 1836:472). These statistics bear testimony to the growth of the churches. The prayer factor is obvious, and the Restoration Movement was affected by the prayer-motivated climate that was an important factor in the awakenings of the 1790-1830 years.

The Place of Prayer in the Revivals of 1857 to 1860

The place of prayer was also apparent in the revivals of 1857 through 1860 that became worldwide in their outreach (Orr, 1964:6). In 1857 a revival began in Ontario which soon reached the States. On December 1 a convention met at Pittsburgh under the Presbyterians. The agenda had to do with revival. "Two hundred ministers and many laymen attended, and much time was spent in prayer" (Orr, 1964:10). In September a noonday prayer meeting was announced at the Dutch Reformed Church in downtown New York City. "Within six months, ten-thousand were gathered daily for prayer" (1964:11). This awakening swept New England, through the valley of the Ohio and as far as Texas.

In 1858 prayer meetings were flourishing in Louisville, Kentucky. The March 27th. **Daily Courier** recounted that meeting houses were overflowing. Within weeks four simultaneous gatherings were being held. Similar events took place in Lexington, Covington, Frankfort and other cities (Orr, 1965:120-121). Daily meetings in Cincinnati grew. In Cleveland the attendance approximated two-thousand. Prayer meetings were started in Indianapolis. In Detroit meetings were held in Baptist and Congregational churches. In St. Louis union meetings were attended by all classes. Towns in Illinois, Wisconsin and Minnesota were also affected.

Prayer is a Characteristic of Revival in Other Countries

In November 1859 the **Millennial Harbinger** spoke of the revival in Ireland.

> It must not be thought of as confined to one town, nor to one country. Communications from some thirty places are now before us, and its range is widening (Campbell, 1859c:626-627).

A month earlier the **Harbinger** had related the news of the revival in Scotland. After the Union Prayer meeting,

> the whole congregation rose and joined in the Doxology, 'Praise God from Whom all Blessings Flow.' To the honor of Scotland the news of the American Revival was received with implicit confidence and unfeigned joy by the ministers and members of the Scottish churches and a union prayer meeting was established in Aberdeen (Campbell, 1859d:571).

HUNGER FOR THE WORD OF GOD A PREREQUISITE FOR REVIVAL

Desire to feed upon the Word is an essential part of revival. Without it, revival cannot take place (McGavran, 1970:166). Disciplined study of the Word was a concern of Alexander Campbell. While aware of the expansion of the Methodists, Baptists, Presbyterians and others in 1858 and 1859, he was ambivalent towards that growth because those churches gave little attention to the study of Scripture.

While denominational churches were growing because of revival, Campbell insisted that Restoration churches were growing because "of the cause we plead." Wrote Campbell:

> The cause we plead has not been more successfully pled for many years, so far as we are posted, than during the present year. Some five-hundred additions by immersion are reported during the last month (1858b:594).

Another Restoration leader was quoted, "We desire only to urge the claims of the Gospel, as, at least, the only revealed instrumentality through which the Spirit of God accomplishes the conversion of the sinner (Campbell, 1859a: 230-231).

Restoration leaders could not, however, avoid relating the growth of the churches to the revivals affecting denominations all over American and Europe (Randall, 1983:354).

PURITY AND HOLY LIVING ALWAYS THE CONSEQUENCE OF REVIVAL

McGavran has observed:

> Though it is often accompanied by powerful emotions -- trembling, weeping, agonizing prayer, and feelings of great joy and peace -- revival is no mere emotional binge. It is a restoration of New Testament Christianity. Humility, "brokenness," and yielding of self to God our righteous heavenly Father result in confession of sin and restitution of those sinned against (1970:167).

This realization was also Barton Stone's conviction, following the Cane Ridge revival experience.

> But that cannot be Satan's work, which brings men to humble confession and forsaking of sin, to solemn prayer, fervent prayer and thanksgiving, and to sincere and affectionate exhortation to sinners to repent and go to Jesus the Savior (Rogers, 1847:35).

As a result of the 1858 revival in Louisville, Kentucky, "such had been the improvement in the city's morals and such were the reports from the rest of Kentucky and the other states, that it was thought by the press that the millennium had arrived at last" (Orr, 1965:120-121).

When Godfearing men and women cry for, and God gives revival, Christian behavior becomes practical for every aspect of life. One filled with the Spirit will confess and reject sins previously deeply hidden. Wicked practices are broken. The Holy Spirit establishes new standards of love, mercy and justice. Those revived become the champions of social reform.

REVIVAL MOTIVATES GODLY MEN AND WOMEN TO RESTORE NEW TESTAMENT CHRISTANITY

Men whose preaching touched the founders of the Restoration movement reveal that revival provides motivation to restore the Church. Revival moves devout men to study the Word with the object of restoring the biblical pattern.

John Glas

John Glas, 1695-1773, a Scotch Presbyterian, determined to make the Scriptures his rule of faith and conduct. He was possessed "by the doctrine of the glorious Gospel." His emphasis "that the Kingdom is essentially spiritual, and is independent of state control, as well as support of the secular arm" brought opposition from his denomination, and he was excommunicated (Hornsby, 1936:10). Alexander Campbell was "well acquainted with all that controversy, since Glas was excommunicated by the high church of Scotland, for preaching that Christ's Kingdom is not of this world" (Campbell, 1826:229).

The followers of Campbell, Scott, Stone and others who came after John Glas, longed for the restoration of New Testament Christianity. With their belief that the Church is a society ordained by God, the autonomy of the local church, their keeping of the Lord's Supper each first day of the week, their emphasis upon a plurality of elders for each congregation and their practice of mutual exhortation, they have revealed the influence of the Glasites.

The Haldane Brothers

Robert Richardson refers to the reformatory movement then progressing in Scotland from which Campbell received his first impulse as a religious reformer. His reference was to Robert and James Haldane. Robert was born in 1764 and James was born in 1768. Both men, at approximately the same time, gave their lives in religious service. At the beginning of their ministry they were members of the Church of Scotland. It was their desire to motivate to greater strength all who were disciples of Christ. Significant was the prominence they gave to "the authenticity and inspiration of the Holy Scriptures" (Murch, 1962:17). They took the Bible alone as their rule of faith and practice.

The rejection of the extra congregational church was one of the decisions made by the Haldanes. They embraced a congregational form of government with a plurality of elders. "It was adopted as a principle that ecclesiastical usages should be conformed to the practice of the apostolic churches" from then onwards (Richardson, 1868:1:129). In early 1808 James Haldane decided no longer to baptize children. In April he was immersed, and Robert followed his example. Both brothers became advocates of immersion for believers only. They had taken another move towards the restoration of the New Testament Church.

Bishop James Madison

On May 26, 1786, Madison preached before the convention of the Episcopal Church of Virginia. He gave emphasis to Christian unity and the nature of creeds in perpetuating division. He was focusing upon one of the foundation stones necessary for the restoration of biblical Christianity.

> Those things alone should be held as essentials, which our Lord and master hath fully and clearly expressed, and which therefore cannot require the supposed improvements and additions of men. They [the human articles of belief] are to be avoided because the Scriptures, being the sole ground of faith, afford the only test by which purity of doctrine is to be ascertained. He who would search for the truth must search for it in the Scriptures alone.
>
> Would to God, those dissentions, which too much abound among Christians, could at this moment be banished from amongst us (Madison, 1786).

In 1829, 43 years after Madison's sermon, Alexander Campbell first saw a copy and was amazed at its content.

> I have not met in any one extract so many of the sentiments advanced in this work; nor have I seen so exceptional an exposition of my "particular views" from any pen: nor did I know, til yesterday, that any man in the United States had spoken so much good sense on these subjects (Campbell, 1829:578).

Madison, a product of the awakenings, was an advocate of biblical restoration years before Campbell came upon the scene, and is an excellent example of the dynamic at work through the Awakenings which motivates godly men to restore the Church revealed in the Scriptures.

Rice Haggard

Rice Haggard was born in Virginia in 1789. He joined the Methodist Church and became a preacher, being ordained by Bishop Francis Asbury (Barrett, 1908:269). Later, when he became convinced that the doctrine was not in full accordance with Bible teachings, he returned to Virginia and asked for his release from the Methodist Church.

When, in 1793, James O'Kelley seceded from the Methodist Church, Haggard and O'Kelley stood together. They assumed the name of Republican Methodists, but on August 4, 1794 Haggard stood before the Republican Methodist conference and urged the acceptance of the name "Christian" (MacClenny, 1950:116).

Haggard was at the Springfield Presbytery at Cane Ridge, Kentucky in June, 1804. Barton W. Stone recalled that at that meeting Haggard proposed the adoption of the name "Christian" (Rogers, 1847:50). Haggard had written a pamphlet entitled "An Address to the Different Religious Societies on the Sacred Import of the Christian Name." It was printed in Lexington, Kentucky in 1804 and five years later was reprinted in the **Herald of Gospel Liberty** published by Elias Smith of the Christian churches of New England.

It is obvious that the three segments of the Christian Church had some acquaintance with each other's work and a sense of being part of one enterprise (Randall, 1983:80-81). Each knew Rice Haggard and were influenced by him.

Haggard advocated the restoration of the church. McNemar, one of the co-signers of the **Last Will and Testament of the Springfield Presbytery** was acquainted with Haggard. Following his signing, McNemar wrote:

> And as the groundwork of this vast kingdom, they proposed to seize upon the sacred name "Christian," and so draw into union all who wished to be called by that worthy name. The plan of this great kingdom was drawn up by Rice Haggard, and published in the year of 1804: which proposed, as the leading foundation principles, simply to worship one God -- acknowledging one Savior, Jesus Christ -- have one profession of faith, and let that be the Bible -- one form of government, and this to be the New Testament -- the members of one church (McNemar, 1808:97).

The concern of Haggard was to reunite the Church. In his pamphlet he offered nine proposals. The first four, as listed by NcNemar were: 1) we are to worship one God; 2) acknowledge one Savior, Jesus Christ; 3) have one confession of faith, and let that be the Bible; and 4) let us have one form of discipline and government, and let this be the New Testament.

Likely Haggard was acquainted with prominent men like
James McGready, Henry Patillo, John Wesley and George Whitefield, all of whom saw the evils of division fostered by
denominational names.[1] There is no doubt about the effect
Samuel Davies had upon Haggard. Davies was a scholar who
contributed to the establishing of the Presbyterian church
in Virginia after 1748. In 1759 he was appointed president
of the College of New Jersey (Princeton) where he served
until his death. Three volumes of sermons came from the pen
of Davies. In the first was his address on "The Sacred
Import of the Christian Name." It had a likeness to Rice
Haggard's pamphlet, and there were parallelisms between Haggard's tract and Davies' sermon.

In Davies' sermon is a footnote referring to "Dr. Grosvenor's excellent essay on the Christian name" published in
London in 1728. Grosvenor's pamphlet was entitled "An Essay
on the Christian Name, Its Origin, Import, Obligation, and
Preference to All Party Denominations." The biblical text
was the same as used by Davies in his sermon and Haggard in
his tract, Acts 11:26. Davies had Grosvenor's sermon before
him as Haggard had Davies' before him. Parallelisms between
Grosvenor in the 1720's are to be found in Davies in the
1750's and in Haggard in 1804.

However, emphasis upon the name Christian no more began
with Grosvenor than it did with Davies or Haggard. Grosvenor referred to Dr. Fuller of London and his paper "Best
Name on Earth." He also quotes from Tertullian who pleads
for the Christian name, from Luther who objected to one
calling himself by Luther's name, and from Calvin who
insisted that only the Lord and Master should be named with
no man's name in opposition to Him.

Thomas Campbell

That revival motivates men to restore New Testament
Christianity can be proven through the ministry of Thomas
Campbell. He was a product of the second Great Awakening.[2]
Thomas Campbell was a champion of Christian Unity and the
restoration of the Church. His **Declaration and Address** has
been described as "one of the greatest contributions that
American Christianity has made. It has been called the
religious Declaration of Independence -- declaring the
Church free from bondage to human creeds, human names, and
human lordship" (Smith, 1930:52). The **Declaration** was published in 1809, twenty-three years after James Madison's
sermon to the convention of the Episcopal Church in Virginia

in 1786. Madison's and Campbell's studies were much alike, and comparisons are recommended to all concerned about the restoration of the New Testament Church.

Glas, the Haldanes, Madison, Haggard and Thomas Campbell are six leaders of the eighteenth and nineteenth centuries who became advocates, through the Great Awakenings, of a return to New Testament Christianity. Others such as Wesley, Whitefield, Edwards, Grosvenor, Davies, O'Kelley, Hodge and McGready, from a diversity of theological backgrounds were searching for ways to return to the New Testament pattern. Most pre-dated the Restoration movement. All enunciated principles essential for the restoration of New Testament Christianity. These principles gave emphasis to the authority of the Scriptures; the responsibility of the Christian before God and the right of private judgment; the evil of sectarianism; and that the way of unity in the body of Christ is through conformity to the Scriptures. Some were closer to the pattern than others, but out of the Awakenings, all came to advocate a return to the pattern revealed through the Scriptures, and they all impinged upon the formation of the Restoration movement.

Even so, many touched by the Awakenings were unwilling to become obedient to the Word. They embraced an emotional kind of religion, that when the excitement died, left them in a worse state than before. However, this does not deny that Revival motivates godly men and women to restore New Testament Christianity. Restoration of the Church is necessary, but unless prayed for, longed for and deliberately sought and to some degree obtained, in the classic sense it does not really occur.

REVIVAL MOTIVATES MEN AND WOMEN TO PREACH WITH POWER

This power will manifest itself in the conversion of souls. Other evidences will be apparent -- an emphasis on prayer, a study of the Word, a concern for the poor, a demonstration of Christian liberality, a sense of responsibility for mission and a commitment to godly living -- but a determination to reach the lost is the foremost proof of the reality of revival. Without it, revival is to be questioned.

The growth of the Church is a consequence of power generated through Revival. The growth of the Restoration movement churches provides an example. D. S. Burnet reported in Missouri in 1858:

> Seventy five accepted the terms of the Gospel.
> On Thursday last, a scene occurred, the like of
> which was never before witnessed here -- the
> baptizing of some fifty or more persons at the
> same time. On Monday morning a large number
> were baptized, in the presence of one of the
> largest assemblages that ever convened here on
> a like occasion   (Campbell, 1858a:418-419).

Continuing growth of Restoration churches was reported by Campbell through 1858 and 1859. From Missouri at Berry 159 additions (1858c:656); from Kentucky 150 additions in a period of six weeks at Carlisle and Sharpsburg; about 150 additions in Belle Aire, Barnesville and Beelers Station (1858c:658); from Salado 200 additions (1858d:718); and from Owen Country, Indiana, 400 additions (1859b:118).

Late in 1859 W. K. Pendleton wrote a significant article in the **Millennial Harbinger** in which he revealed the explosive growth of churches of the Restoration for that year.

> The year has been one of great activity among
> the disciples. Never has the Gospel been pro-
> claimed with more earnestness or its power
> more joyfully manifested in the conversion of
> souls. From every part of the wide union the
> story of its triumphs is sent up to us, and we
> feel fully warranted in saying, that during the
> last twelve months not less than thirty or forty
> thousand converts have been enlisted under the
> banner of the cross. Hundreds of churches have
> been planted   (Pendleton, 1859:706-707).

Significantly, through 1858 and 1859, all the churches combined in the United States, as a result of the revival, grew by more than one-million members (Sweet, 1973:311).

J. Edwin Orr emphasizes that:

> The main effect of an Evangelical Awakening is
> always the repetition of the phenomena of the
> Acts of the Apostles, which gives one a simple
> account of an Evangelical Awakening, one that
> revives believers, then converts sinners to God.
> In this way, an Evangelical Awakening may be said
> to effect the revitalizing of the lives of nomi-
> nal Christians, and of bringing outsiders into

vital touch with the divine dynamic causing such
Awakening -- the Spirit of God (Orr, 1965:265).

THE IMAPCT OF REVIVAL IN INDIA

Early in 1903, the Presbyterian Church at Mawphang in northeast India began to pray for an outpouring of the Holy Spirit upon the churches of Khasia as well as the rest of the world. These meetings became fervent in 1904, and in 1905 at a meeting of the Mawphang church, a revival began which manifested itself in prayer, weeping and praise. The usual pattern for meetings was broken when the chairman called on two men to pray. Others also prayed. The following Sunday the spirit of intercession took control, and it became impossible to close the service. There was much simultaneous prayer, praise and weeping. The awakening soon spread to other parts of India.

The Khasi Hills tribes practiced human sacrifice until after the beginning of the twentieth century. The awakening affecting the Christian community brought a conviction of sin which soon turned to rejoicing and praise. Missionaries disapproved as it began but changed their minds as they witnessed the transformation of nominal Christians and the conversion of hundreds to the Lord.

By 1906 news of revival had spread throughout Assam. At Nowgong in 1907 all the churches gathered to pray for the salvation of the lost. The awakening had spread to north of the Brahmaputra River by 1907. From there it moved to the Naga Hills of Nagaland. Numbers were won in the Imphur field of Nagaland in 1907. Many were added as evangelism among the Nagas accelerated.

Interest among the Mizo tribe from the Lushai Hills was kindled through news of the Khasi Hills awakening among the Baptists. Membership increased, only to be followed by persecution and a return to heathenism. The Church was set back, with some of the leadership despairing of it ever recovering. But in 1913 the revival again ignited the Mizos of the Lushai Hills. By 1919 it had spread to three areas, among the Tripura and to Manipur state. Four thousand were converted. Head hunting tribesmen became believers.

> One effect of these revivals, within a generation, was to make head hunters into a predominantly Christian people, inhabiting India's most Christian and most evangelical area, in zeal far

surpassing the early evangelized fields, as well as the places which claimed a thousand years or more of a traditional Christianity (Orr, 1973: 137).

There is more to this story as it is touched by the American Restoration movement. Professor Randall met Mr. T. Lunkim, Christian leader of the Kuki people, while studying at Fuller Theological Seminary. Lunkim, an illiterate tribesman until 21 years of age, was converted by the American Baptists. Handicapped in his witness, he largely educated himself and ultimately found his way to Serampore College where, in four years he earned three college degrees, graduating with honors. Following college, the India Bible Society employed him to translate the entire Bible into his own Kuki tribal tongue, which he did in four years, from Greek and Hebrew.

By the 1970's it was Lunkim's dream to win the Meitei to Christ. The Meitei, also of Manipur state, approximate about one-million people and are largely animistic with a thin veneer of Hinduism covering their belief in spirits. Because of his determination to win the Meitei, Lunkim found his way to Fuller's School of World Mission in 1975 to best learn how to win these people.

But Lunkim had not reckoned with decisions already made by the Baptist and Presbyterian denominations. Though they had been working with the Meitei since 1960, they had not planted a single church. When Lunkim expressed his determination to work among that tribe, the above denominations refused to cooperate with him. At that moment Lunkim determined that he would evangelize the Meitei whether the denominations supported him or not.

Lunkim sought the aid of Professor Randall, who, with others, determined to help him get back to northeast India. They found support for him to begin evangelizing the Meitei.

In 1976 the decision was made in India that the new work would be called the Christian Church, giving emphasis to biblical restoration. The Kuki Christian Church became the first tribal church in the fellowship. There are now Kuki, Meitei, Zomi and Thangkhai Christian Churches among others, particularly in northeast India but also in Burma.

In 1977 a daily fifteen minute radio broadcast in the Kuki language was initiated. Beginning in 1982 a similar program has been beamed daily to the Meitei. These broadcasts are an aid in restoring the Church and they are a factor in converting animistic tribesmen. Thousands have been won. In 1982 there were some 260 churches with a membership of 330,000 associated with the work.

This evangelistic activity has been indigenous from its beginnings. There could be no witness if it were to depend on western missionaries, for the government will not permit them to serve in the area. Evangelism must be done by national leaders. If the Great Commission is to be fulfilled, it will be done by national evangelists laboring among their own people, culture and language.

Antecedents of this Restoration movement are to be found in the late 19th. and early 20th. century awakenings in northeast India. The Christian Church in Manipur would be first to credit the Presbyterian and Baptist Churches out of which many Restoration churches have come. The movement would not have happened without them. The growth of these denominations was motivated by revival.

Unity, prayed for by our Lord, is so presented that churches are uniting into one fellowship. Excitement has been stimulated, generating zeal for preaching the Gospel. Thousands of animists and Hindus are leaving their old religion in northeast India and turning to the Lord.

The worldwide awakening of the early twentieth century

> was the most extensive Evangelical Awakening of all time, reviving Anglican, Baptists, Congregational, Disciple, Lutheran, Methodist, Presbyterian, Reformed and other evangelical bodies throughout Europe and North America, Australasia and South Africa, and their daughter churches and missionary causes throughout Asia, Africa and Latin America, winning more than five million folk to an evangelical faith in the two years of greatest impact in each country (Orr, 1975b:112).

THE IMPACT OF REVIVAL ON RESTORATION CHURCHES IN AFRICA

Restoration movement churches have also benefited from the awakenings which influenced South Africa, Zimbabwe, Zambia, Malawi, Zaire and other countries in Africa. Christian church missionaries were influenced by the denominations in Africa in the early 1920's and 1950's. They were impressed with the educational programs that several denominational churches had in southern Africa for half a century. The Methodists, Anglicans, Dutch Reformed and Baptists in South Africa, had expanded their school systems due to the awakenings of the late 19th. and early 20th. centuries. In other parts of the continent missionaries were similarly influenced. No schools were in Malawi as late as 1875. Within thirty years, changes had come. The Church of Scotland, the United Free Church of Scotland, the Zambezi Industrial Mission and the Paris Evangelical Mission, by 1905 had a total of 311 schools with as many as 22,208 pupils.

At the beginning of the 20th. century missionaries had difficulty persuading African parents to permit their children to attend school. By 1924 early resistance had changed. By 1936 demand for schools was greater than the missionaries could supply (Randall, 1970:71).

Missionaries of American Christian Churches were aware of this growing hunger for education. They also observed that usually where there were schools there were corresponding churches. It was easy to conclude that if they would reach the tribes, they would best do it through schools which would assist in planting churches. Within fifteen years of their arrival in Zimbabwe they had 40 schools with thousands of pupils, and where there was a school there was a church.

A similar pattern was implemented by Christian Church missionaries in Zambia. Schools were built and churches were begun. Zambia was entered by these missionaries in 1961 while still Northern Rhodesia. In 1964 it gained its independence, and at once changes came. The government was prepared to take over all primary schools. The Zambia Christian Mission turned over its schools to the Department of Education in 1968, but with one request: that the missionaries be allowed to remain in Zambia to focus attention on the planting of churches. They were given that privilege. The result has been dozens of churches and thousands of converts.

The Zambian Minister of Education said in 1967:

> It is on the foundations so carefully laid by these early pioneers [the early missionaries] of half a century ago that the educational system of today has been built (Zambia Press Release No. 1387, 1967).

The pioneers he referred to had come to Zambia as a result of what Orr called "the most extensive Evangelical Awakening of all time" (1975b:112). The New Zealand Churches of Christ were affected by that revival and it was they who gave assistance to the American Christian Churches when the latter entered Rhodesia in 1956.

Though the American missionary enterprise did not get under way until half a century after the awakenings of the early 1900's, it designed its program after the pattern established by the denominations affected by the revival, including the New Zealand Church of Christ Mission.

CONCLUSION

Revival is a factor in the growth of the kingdom, whether among churches in America or on the foreign fields. Foundations of the work in India and Africa are to be found in many denominational agencies whose history goes back to the late 19th. and early 20th. centuries. Christian church missionaries owe a debt to the pioneers for the patterns they established and the foundations they laid.

Hopefully, it may be observed that an effort to return to the doctrine of the apostolic church and a greater emphasis upon Christian unity has been more strongly advocated by the missionaries supported by Restoration churches than those of the denominations. At best, however, they have enjoyed only partial success, because they are often as sectarian as those of the denominations they are trying to correct. Though they stand in need of God's grace as do their denominational neighbors, the marvel is that God has poured out His grace and mercy, especially in times of revival and awakening, and He will again.

Because churches of the Restoration movement have been affected directly or indirectly by successive awakenings as have other churches, they are constrained to pray for further revival, that the Lord's Church might be renewed so that millions still lost might be saved.

NOTES

[1] See Randall 1983:80-93.

[2] See Orr, 1965:55; 1975a:140; Latourette, 1971:4:198 and McAllister, 1954:60-64.

BIBLIOGRAPHY

Barrett, J. Pressley
   1908   The Centennial of Religious Journalism.
           Dayton: Christian Publishing Association.

Baxter, William
   1874   Life of Elder Walter Scott. Cincinnati:
           Bosworth, Chase and Hall.

Campbell, Alexander
   1826   "Reply to R.B.S." Christian Baptist. 3:229.

   1829   "James Madison, D.D." Christian Baptist.
           7:578-580.

   1830   "Mahoning Association." Millennial Harbinger.
           414-415.

   1858a "Progress of Reform." Millennial Harbinger.
           418-419.

   1858b "Progress of Reform." Millennial Harbinger. 594.

   1858c "Progress of Reform." Millennial Harbinger.
           656-658.

   1858d "Progress of Reform." Millennial Harbinger. 718.

   1859a "Converting Influence." Millennnial Harbinger.
           229-231.

   1859b "Progress of Reform." Millennial Harbinger.
           117-119.

   1859c "Revival in Ireland." Millennial Harbinger.
           626-631.

   1859d "The Religious Revival in Great Britain."
           Millennial Harbinger. 568-575.

Cox, F. A.
   1836   The Baptists in America. New York.

Garrison, Winfred E. and Alfred T. DeGroot
   1948   The Disciples of Christ: A History. St. Louis:
           Christian Board of Publication.

Hornsby, John T.
   1936   John Glas: A Study in the Origins, Development, and Influence of the Glasite Movement. Unpublished Ph.D. dissertation, The University of Edinburgh.

Latourette, Kenneth Scott
   1971   A History of the Expansion of Christianity. Vol. 4. Grand Rapids: Zondervan Pub. Co.

MacClenny, W. E.
   1950   The Life of James O'Kelley and the Early History of the Christian Church in the South. Indianapolis: Religious Book Service.

Madison, James
   1786   A Sermon Preached before the Convention of the Protestant Episcopal Church in the State of Virginia. Richmond: Thomas Nicholson.

McAllister, Lester G.
   1954   Thomas Campbell, Man of the Book. St. Louis: Bethany Press.

McGavran, Donald A.
   1970   Understanding Church Growth. Grand Rapids: Eerdmans.

McNemar, Richard
   1808   The Kentucky Revival. Cincinnati: Art Guild Reprints.

Murch, James D.
   1962   Christians Only. Cincinnati: Standard Pub. Co.

Orr, J. Edwin
   1964   The Second Evangelical Awakening. Fort Washington: Christian Literature Crusade.

   1965   The Light of the Nations. Grand Rapids: Eerdmans.

   1973   The Flaming Tongue. Chicago: Moody Press.

   1975a   The Eager Feet: Evangelical Awakenings 1770-1830. Chicago: Moody Press.

   1975b   "Definition and Discussion." Unpublished paper.

Pendelton, W. K.
   1859   "Our Progress and Prospects." *Millennial Harbinger*. 706-714.

Randall, Max Ward
   1970   *Profile for Victory in Zambia*. South Pasadena: William Carey Library.

   1983   *The Great Awakenings and the Restoration Movement*. Joplin: College Press.

Richardson, Robert
   1868   *Memoirs of Alexander Campbell*. 2 Vols. Philadelphia: J. B. Lippincott and Co.

Rogers, William
   1847   *The Cane Ridge Meeting House*. Cincinnati: Standard Pub. Co.

Scott, Walter
   1832   "Religious Denominations." *The Evangelist*. 72.

Smith, Benjamin Lyon
   1930   *Alexander Campbell*. St. Louis: Bethany Press.

Smith, Elias
   1840   *The Life, Conversion, Preaching, Travels and Sufferings of Elias Smith*. Boston: privately printed.

Sweet, William Warren
   1973   *The Story of Religion in America*. Grand Rapids: Baker Book House.

Zambia Press Release
   1967   "Zambia Press Release No. 1387/67."

7

Unity and Mission in the Restoration Movement

by C. Robert Wetzel

From the initial proclamation of the imminent appearance of the Kingdom of God, the unity of the citizens of the Kingdom has always been seen as integral to the successful fulfillment of the mission of the church. Jesus had to deal with contention and rivalry among His closest followers. He dealt with it by commanding absolute love for God accompanied by the same kind of love for one's neighbor. Obviously, a house divided against itself would not stand.

Division is rooted in human frailty. Hence rather than pride of place Jesus interpreted greatness in terms of humility: "He who is greatest among you shall be your servant; whoever exalts himself will be humbled, and whoever humbles himself will be exalted" (Mt. 23:11-12).

Jesus' prayer in Jn. 17 links inextricably the unity of His followers with the successful fulfillment of their mission: "May they be brought to complete unity to let the world know that You sent Me..." (Jn. 17:23). The very oneness of God implies unity and orderliness. Heaven is not ruled by an Olympian Council with its contentious deities divided by rival passions. Rather, "the heavens declare the glory of God; the skies proclaim the work of His hands" (Ps. 19:1). Both physical and moral law find their unity in the purposive creative force of a single Lawgiver. Jesus as the only begotten of the Father is one with the Father, and thus He prays for the believers "that all of them may be one, Father, just as You are in Me and I am in You" (Jn. 17:21).

Why should this prayer for unity play such a significant role in the climactic days of Jesus' ministry? He simply understood human weakness. Satan would always assault the Kingdom at its weakest point, and human pride is too often a vulnerable gate. The transformation called for in the life of the believer can be a slow and difficult process. Hence Jesus anticipated the strain on the young church to preserve its unity even as it enjoyed initial success. The happy picture of Acts 2:42-47 was soon to be tested by the complaint of the Grecian Jews against the Aramaic-speaking Jews concerning the daily distribution of food. The first Gentile converts were a test for Jewish Christians. Was their understanding of the catholicity of the church sufficiently developed to allow them to accept Gentiles into fellowship or was their conditioned prejudice going to turn the church into an exclusivist sect of Judaism? These episodes were to set the pattern of so many future controversies in the church. Personal interest and prejudice were to cloud and antagonize issues of moral and doctrinal understanding. Problems which might have found solution in the atmosphere of goodwill and love were to cause painful divisions in congregations and were later to create warring camps as the constellations of churches vied for the title of the One True Church.

The congregational conflicts such as those at Corinth as well as the presence of Judaizers in the Galatian churches were ample evidence that Jesus' concern for the unity of His followers was well justified. It is a demonstration of the power of the Gospel message that the church could continue to spread in spite of these divisions. And it is a credit to the Apostle Paul and other evangelists that they did not compromise their evangelistic mission in having to deal with divisive factors affecting the life of the churches.

Although there is no question but what division adversely affected and continues to affect the spread of the Gospel and the growth of the church, there is no way to measure the results of this negative factor. Given the remarkable growth of the church in the first three centuries, one can only speculate what the results might have been had not time and effort had to be directed toward problems of division. Yet unity is not a necessary prerequisite to the spread of the Gospel even though disunity surely compromises the efforts of evangelism. The history of the various great revivals testifies to the possibility of significant results from groups of Christians who were actually involved in

separating themselves from a larger body. And today we are
faced with the irony of seeing churches deeply involved in
ecumenical schemes steadily losing members while church
groups who seem never to look beyond their own denominational lines are showing remarkable growth -- not all of which
is at the expense of the ecumenically involved denominations.

The moral of this seems to be that the unity of
believers is an important factor in implementing the mission
of the church, but that the evangelistic mission of the
church is too important to wait upon the achievement of a
united church. And yet the scandal of division cannot be
ignored.

Recently I had the occasion to be the guest of a
Christian family in a European city. The family are members
of a large evangelical church which was established in the
19th. century with great opposition from the state church.
There is still a relatively small evangelical population in
the country. The state church continues to play a significant role in contemporary society. But the twin forces of
traditionalism and the increasingly humanistic worldview of
modern European life have begun to make the inroads which
have brought sterility and decline to so many European
established churches. The evangelical churches find themselves pressed by both forces. Evangelicals still find
themselves subtly discriminated against because of their
free church position. On the other hand they see the forces
of humanism competing for the hearts and minds of their
children.

Because the son of my host had been my student, I was
received with kindness and love. I was invited to teach a
Bible study in his home, and later I preached for a service
at the church where my host is an elder. Our oneness in
Christ was recognized from the outset.

There was a sad note in all of this. Knowing that I
was from the British Churches of Christ, I was asked if I
knew anything about a small, peculiar group in that city who
used the same name. Because of their isolationism and
"strange practices," they were seen as a sect. When I made
specific inquiries about this peculiar sect it seemed that
little was actually known of what they believed due to their
isolationism. It was supposed that they thought themselves
the only Christians. Not only did their separateness seem
to suggest this, but there had been an incident which tended

to confirm this opinion. A man had left the state church where he had been baptized as an infant, and, after confessing Christ as Lord, was baptized (immersed) in an evangelical church. Later he sought to identify with the small group known as "the Church of Christ." He was required to be baptized again!

Some Church of Christ publications had been mailed to my host's home. As we looked over them, he smiled and shook his head. "The articles sound so good, but their practices are so strange." It was almost as though Christian unity had been dropped from the witness of this Church of Christ in favor of a legalistic restorationism. How stranger still it would have seemed to my host to have explained that such a group grew out of a Christian unity movement.

The churches of the Restoration movement have conceived themselves from the outset as a unity movement. Their concern for unity was motivated by the desire to see the Church fulfill its mission: preaching the Gospel. They are certainly not unique in their concern for a powerful evangelical witness, nor are they alone in their call for Christian unity. But they have called attention in a significant way to the need for Christian unity if the church is to fulfill its mission. Today the relationship between unity and mission is taken for granted in most Christian circles, and there is good reason to believe that the witness of the churches of the Restoration movement have contributed substantially to this common understanding. This is not to say that division has ceased to be a problem in the church at large. It is to say that the scandal of a divided church has been recognized for what it is -- sin. We may be forced to recognize the reality of a divided church, but there is little inclination to justify it, let alone portray it as a desirable state of affairs.

The way to Christian unity was seen to be through the restoration of the New Testament order. There was a mission to be fulfilled, and the mission called for the unity of the church. The best prospect for unity, they early leaders argued, was through reclaiming what had been set out in the New Testament.

In many respects it might be said that the Restoration movement was at one with the Christian world in its concern that the church fulfill its mission. Although there were those groups whose efforts were less than enthusiastic, few would have denied that such a mission existed. And even though Protestant groups may not have been giving much attention to a plea for Christian unity in the early 19th. century, the Roman Catholic Church still called for a united church, even if the terms for that unity were hardly attractive to non-Catholics. Furthermore Protestant groups, by and large, already saw themselves as "reformed" churches, and hence were not easily convinced that another reformation was called for. It is understandable why the early leaders did not want to call themselves Protestants. They wanted a unity that Protestantism did not have. On the other hand their call for an apostolicity which did not recognize the Roman Catholic doctrine of apostolic succession separated them from any Catholic tradition which adhered to that doctrine, whether Roman, Orthodox or Anglo-Catholic.

Hence the Restoration plea called for a church that was **both** catholic and apostolic. But it was these very two features that the Christian world had not been able to synthesize. The very division between the Catholic and Protestant worlds represents what seems to be the mutual exclusiveness of these two characteristics. As the authoritarian unity of the medieval church began to disintegrate, numerous Protestant groups attempted to reform the church using the newly available Bible as their authority. The diversity of these groups and the subsequent contention between them seem to confirm the Roman Catholic opinion that unity must be expressed in the authority of the bishops of the church who are the heirs to the authority of the original apostles and who speak today with the same direction of the Holy Spirit.

Anyone who reads church history or even reflects upon his own experience of church life will readily recognize that division among Christians cannot be explained simply by the variety of opinions as to what the Bible is saying about the nature of the church. Nor can certain forms of Christian unity be explained by supposing that a consensus of interpretation has been reached. Ultimately it is neither the ambiguity of Scripture nor the limitations of human understanding that is the primary source of division in the church. Pride, stubbornness and similar human vices must surely head the list of the causes for division. It has been suggested that Alexander Campbell's "Enlightenment optimism" led him to believe that reasonable men of goodwill interpreting a Book inspired by a rational God would surely be led to a common understanding of that Book. Obviously this is an oversimplification of Campbell's view. He was quite aware of man's capacity for sinful behavior. But there is adequate evidence to indicate that there has always been a certain form of that optimism in the Restoration movement which at least sounded as though one could have such confidence in the efficacy of reason. We may have argued strenuously against a doctrine of "faith only" but we ourselves were dangerously close to a "reason only" faith. The problems with this is not so much the insufficiency of reason, even though it does have its limitations. Rather, the problem is to ignore how much we obscure our own spiritual and moral inadequacies under the cloak of a rational approach to Scripture. Even the most objective laboratory scientist can develop a curious line of reasoning when his departmental budget is at stake!

There is a sense in which the conflict between the Roman Catholic appeal for unity and the Protestant appeal for apostolicity was brought within the body of a single movement in the Restoration movement. Perhaps it is even a part of our mission as a movement to act as a crucible to test whether these diverging elements will synthesize. And it is readily admitted that some of the vapors arising from this crucible have not been promising.

One must find the vapors unpleasant indeed if his view of the history of the movement is that of an imagined Golden Age prior to controversies concerning missionary societies and the musical instrument. Not only is this a mistaken notion of the early history of the movement, it leaves one with a pessimistic view of subsequent history. From an exclusivist view only one group has kept the faith and there has been an enormous falling away. From an inclusivist view the movement is a scandal, a unity movement with numerous factions. Since there is an inclination for all groups today to see themselves as the true heirs of the Campbell-Stone movement, the Golden Age syndrome is more widespread than assumed.

The vapors are equally unpleasant if one sees the movement as broken by time and now faltering in old age. From the perspective of church history a movement less than 200 years old cannot be seen as old unless it has come to conceive of itself as that way. When the United States celebrated its bicentennial it struck many Europeans as strange that Americans would make such a fuss in view of the fact that we were **only** 200 years old. The year following, the city of Mainz celebrated celebrated the 1,000th. anniversary of its cathedral. Given the continuing growth of the

Restoration movement in its various manifestations during the 20th. century, it does not seem to be an aging and faltering church.

Consistent with the possibility that the Restoration movement is a crucible testing how catholicity and apostolicity might be synthesized, I am inclined to view the history of the movement as having both linear and lateral movement. Ideally we would like to see a linear movement which progresses from success to success and which carries with it everyone in the same direction. But few things in life have that kind of unhindered forward movement. For example if one gives a brief account of the victory over Nazi Germany in World War II, the inclination is to start from the dark days of Nazi supremacy and trace a progressive string of victories which eventually led to Hitler's defeat. A closer look at the success of the Allies reveals considerable lateral movement as well, such as the dark uncertainties of the time, efforts that ended in disaster, sordid acts which shock the human conscience even in times of World War.

There have been times in the Restoration movement when lateral movement was made due simply to some lack of Christian virtue. Stubbornness or pride was mistaken for strong faith. Or conversely sentimentalism or fear was confused with Christian love. There were other times when the intent was sound enough, but the methodology or theology was unsound. Granted, lateral movement may well have serious consequences for oneself and those affected by it, but there is a redemptive force at work in the Christian life and hence the church takes account of such mistakes. The Holy Spirit has a remarkable way of working in the most distressing situation, sending the prophetic voice, redirecting the movement and healing the injured. And hopefully a stronger, wiser church emerges from such lateral movements and with a better sense of linear direction.

The reformers of the 19th. century envisioned a church which was both catholic and apostolic. It would have to be catholic if it were to have that kind of visible unity for which Jesus prayed and upon which so much of the success of the evangelistic mission of the church depends. It would have to be apostolic if it were to have an authoritative base upon which Christians could unite in the confidence that they were being faithful to God's call. Integrating the concern for unity as well as faithfulness to the apostolic record has been no small task. It should not be surprising that a concern for the restoration of New Testament

Christianity should have resulted in some lateral movements which became characterized by biblical literalism, legalism and intolerance. Nor should it be surprising that a passionate concern for Christian unity should cause an opposing lateral movement which despairs of finding in scripture any authoritative norm for the nature of the church.

It is encouraging that the lateral movements have rarely separated themselves completely. There have usually been some channels left through which movement takes place between the lateral and the linear even when the lateral movement has taken the shape of a balloon rather than a simple probe. It is to the credit of gatherings such as the World Convention of the Churches of Christ that efforts are made to view the heirs of the Restoration movement as still sharing in a common vision.

Hence we might better understand our past and serve our future by developing an historical perspective which recognizes the Restoration movement as a relatively young phenomenon in the history of the church. It has not fallen from the perfection of an early 19th. century Golden Age. Rather it was born in turbulent times with a robust constitution and of good parentage. It has promise but it also suffered from the sins of its youth. Yet something is to be learned from sin through repentance. Not only is forgiveness and reconciliation available, but so is direction for the future in submission to God.

The very topic of this chapter, "Unity and Mission in the Restoration Movement," may seem to embody a contradiction. The mission enterprise of the churches of the movement has been a source of numerous divisive controversies. At the beginning of the movement many were still influenced by the "Comfortable Doctrine of the 18th. Century Moderates" which questioned the need for a missions consciousness. The hyper-Calvinistic understanding of the sovereignty of God led many to judge enthusiasm for mission as presumptuous. When William Carey expressed a concern for the salvation of those in non-Christian lands he was told, "You are a miserable enthusiast for asking that question. Nothing can be done before another Pentecost" (Drewery, 1978:31).

Those who did take the Great Commission as directive for the church throughout the ages and not just for the Apostles had their attention focused on the American South and the Western frontier. The first, and most successful thrust, was "home missions" as the early evangelists moved with the frontier. It would be a mistake not to see this effort as evangelistic or missionary. These were preachers and teachers being sponsored by Christians in one place to preach the Gospel in another place. In some respects, the American frontier was as "foreign" as some other countries. The dangers were as great, sponsorship was needed, and it often meant separation from family and loved ones. Considerable diversity was found -- after all, in some respects the frontier was a melting pot.

Those perennial voices in the church who do not want to send missionaries to foreign countries "when there are plenty of heathens to convert at home," never had a more persuasive case than when they could point to both the need for mission work and the visible successes of those evangelists who moved with the American frontier. Garrett gives fascinating sketches of some of these successful evangelists such as Samuel Rogers, Tolbert Fanning, B. F. Hall and Pardee Butler (Garrett, 1981).

Butler was one of the first successful home missionaries of the movement. He was sent to Kansas by the short-lived Christian Missionary Society where he proved to be an effective but controversial evangelist (Filbeck, 1980:11). He was a restorationist who wanted to establish churches of the "primitive faith." He was also a social activist who fought the spread of slavery. Garrett finds Butler's approach to Christian unity both engaging and practical. Butler said:

> The protestant denominations will all become one yet, not by other churches coming to any one church, but their differences will almost imperceptibly disappear, and they will melt into one, and not one will be able to tell how it was done (Garrett, 1981:327).

There is some hope to believe that his words were prophetic as well. The Restoration movement was surely not the only means that God had in the nineteenth century to remind the church of the normative nature of what the New Testament has to say about the nature of the church. The church must always be reforming itself. It is too easy to judge the Campbell-Stone movement on its statistical growth alone. Those hearing the call for Christian unity by the 19th. century reformers may or may not have identified with the movement. But it became increasingly difficult for anyone to rest easily with a divided Christendom. Those who had come to accept denominationalism as the normal state of modern Christianity had now to come to terms with the prayer of Jesus in Jn. 17. And as DeGroot rightly observes, it was no accident the Disciples played a significant role in the rise of the ecumenical movement (DeGroot, 1965).

Were modern church growth specialists to compare the receptivity along the American frontier with the situation Dr. Barclay, the first foreign missionary of the Restoration movement, found in Jerusalem, it is doubtful they would consider the frontier efforts of the early reformers misdirected. The fact that foreign mission work came later is understandable enough, and is not, as some have argued, an indication that all the evangelists from the movement were concerned about was proselytizing. There undoubtedly was plenty of that, depending on the vision of the evangelist. But generally the work was approached with the same zeal as the early Christians who realized they had been given a great treasure by God and with it were given the responsibility of sharing it. That opposition and divisions did occur cannot be laid entirely at their feet, no more than one can fault the Apostle Paul for the division that occurred among Jews because of their varying responses to the claim that Jesus was the Son of God. Furthermore, we might think of our contemporaries who, in all Christian conscience have been gripped with the vision of a united church through the forms of ecumenicity being proposed through the World Council of Churches. There is a certain wake of division and controversy behind them as well. But this is not to deny that there were many among them who have done all possible to prevent the divisions that have taken place at congregational level because of the program of the World Council of Churches. There is always the tendency by those caught up in the promoting of a vision to see the negative results as being the responsibility of those small minds who, because they could not grasp the vision, must sow seeds of enmity and division.

Osborn overstates the case when he supposes that the core of the plea was "Ho, everyone who thirsts, come to the waters" (1967:45). He takes this passage in Isaiah and characterizes what he thinks was a "come join me" attitude in the movement. He may be correct in portraying the legalists, but he does so at the expense of abandoning the original plea. Although small-minded legalism was present at an early point in the movement, it was given a considerable boost in the reaction to the advent of Protestant liberalism. Likewise it can be argued that liberalism was given a boost by the presence of legalism. This is a case of the two affecting each other in tandem. Moderates often find themselves being forced to take positions because a vacuum has been left in the center. In the latter part of the 19th. century people like McGarvey and Errett, with their differing views on the nature of inspiration, could remain in fellowship and serve as a model of liberty of opinion (Van Buren, 1978:128-134). In the 20th. century the gap becomes too wide. Robinson characterized the modern dilemma:

> Those who have proclaimed Union and forgotten Restoration have denounced the Restorationists as conservative and reactionary; whilst those who have proclaimed Restoration and forgotten Union have rightly feared that their brethren of the 'left' were ready to sacrifice all that their forefathers had contended for, and have labelled them 'liberal,' 'modernist' and what not. Unfortunately neither 'right' nor 'left' seem to have understood those who have had some glimpse into the splendor of the insight which the pioneers had, and who have proclaimed both watchwords, 'Union' and 'Restoration.' (Robinson, 1945:81).

Both the evangelistic thrust on the frontier and later the foreign mission thrust were expressed in terms of evangelism, not proselytizing: Barclay's purpose was to "engage in teaching, preaching and the practice of medicine among Jews at Jerusalem" (Murch, 1962:149). The plea of unity on the mission field was all the more poignant. The scandal of a divided church among non-Christians was indeed a compromising of the evangelistic effort. Furthermore, as any missionary knows, division and denominationalism is the luxury of a Christian society, just as gluttony is the sin of a state of plenty. It is easier to overlook the differences between yourself and another Christian when the multitudes around you do not even know the name of Christ. The need for fellowship in Christ calls for a broader view.

It was the formation of a missionary society which exposed some serious differences of understanding concerning the nature of the New Testament Church, and more importantly, the hermeneutic to be employed in identifying that nature. There are those who see the formation of the American Christian Missionary Society as the first significant departure from the restored primitive Christianity brought about by the movement. It is more likely that the initial debate over missionary societies reveals that not as much synthesis of thought had taken place as was supposed when the various strains of the movement had come together.[1]

There had been opposition to extra-congregational organizations since D. S. Burnet had led in the organization of the American Christian Bible Society in 1845. But Alexander Campbell had given his blessing to the American Christian Missionary Society by accepting its presidency when it was organized in 1849. Although controversy hardly came to an end, Campbell's aura did lend credibility to this expedient as a means of addressing a neglected task. The American Christian Missionary Society could hardly be regarded as successful. As later observers noted, "The explanation of the discontinuance of the work abroad (through ACMS) was stated over and over again -- "an empty treasury" (UCMS, 1944:2). By 1875 receipts for the ACMS were only $4,671.10 and no foreign work was being sponsored (Warren, 1923:91). But the little it had done in foreign missions was more than was being done otherwise. While there was a lively argument concerning the question of scriptural justification for missionary societies, little interest was being shown in those passages of scripture which called for a universal mission effort. Hence the Christian Women's Board of Missions was formed in 1874 and in 1875 the Foreign Christian Missionary Society was organized to supplement the efforts of the ACMS. The CWBM and the FCMS were not seen as rivals to the ACMS nor did anyone of them claim to be the exclusive or normative channel for brotherhood mission effort. The 1876 convention of the ACMS welcomed their formation with the the following resolution:

> That we welcome as co-workers in the cause of missions the 'Foreign Christian Missionary Society' and the 'Christian Women's Board of Missions,' both of which propose to occupy the foreign field, and bid them Godspeed, rejoicing with them in the work already accomplished, and believing that under God there is a brighter future before them (UCMS, 1944:3).

Archibald McLean did as much as anyone in the 19th. century to develop a mission consciousness in the churches. When he became secretary of the FCMS in 1882 the task before him was enormous. He had to create a mission consciousness in a body of churches who had been preoccupied with the novelty of their witness and with their success on the

American frontier. McLean, an unmarried man, travelled incessantly among the churches promoting the cause of missions. He recruited missionaries and he served them with a sensitive pastoral concern.

The development of foreign missionary endeavors among the heirs of the Restoration movement can be found in a number of histories currently available. Granted all history must be written from the point of view of the author/ historian, but it is unfortunate that most of these histories can be faulted on two points: 1) they do tend to propagandize on behalf of that section of the brotherhood in which the writer finds himself at home; 2) and hence, they tend to concentrate on the problems which give rise to division. These problems are certainly a part of the history but they are hardly all of it. Editors and administrators through their debates may have left historians with an ample supply of source materials. But hundreds of missionaries, both from missionary societies and direct-support churches, have simply gone on about the work of preaching Christ, establishing churches and witnessing to the need for oneness among other Christians. This is a history that needs to be written.

The mission experience forces one to reconsider one's own understanding of Christian unity and commitment to it. As noted earlier, it is often the very isolation of the missionary which causes him to reach out to other believers. Furthermore the awareness of the scandal of division increases in proportion to the percentage of unbelievers in the society which the missionary finds himself. Often, the things which led to a division in one country have no meaning in another country.[2] And what a tragedy it is when these divisive factors are introduced not so much for the supposed good of the mission church, but so that the home folk can be assured of the missionary's loyalty!

There is a freedom in Christian faith which breaks down barriers. The finest minds and hearts of the Restoration movement have appealed to that freedom and exercised it. All sections of the movement are producing capable biblical scholars who readily accept the New Testament as normative for the faith and practice of the Church. These scholars are increasingly working in broader Christian circles where they will have an opportunity to share not only the original plea of catholicity through apostolicity, but also what has been learned through our 180 year attempt to synthesize the two.

Furthermore there are dynamics at work in the Christian world today which make the Restoration plea as relevant as ever. For example, both the evangelical and charismatic renewals have tended to minimize denominationalism. The claim of being "non-denominational" is hardly restricted to heirs of the Campbell-Stone movement. And we are certainly not the only ones calling for a platform which involves unity in faith, diversity in opinions and love in all things.[3]

From my British experience I could tell how questions of national organizations, charismatic gifts, pacifism, the moderate use of alcohol, and so on are left in the realm of opinion -- not that there are not some strong opinions on these matters. People seem better able to accept diversity of opinion when the diversity reflects a difference in culture.[4] And this may be the very demonstration that the mission experience can offer as a commentary on the possibility of making liberty of opinions a working reality. An American congregation which has experienced a division in the past due to the introduction of pentecostalism will have difficulty seeing some of the teachings of modern charismatics as simply differences of opinion which ought not to lead to division. But perhaps a British congregation which has successfully synthesized the charismatic and non-charismatic elements can act as a demonstration of that possibility. And Britain is far enough away that the synthesis can take place without being seen as a threat.

When one considers the total number of foreign missionaries coming from all churches that are heirs of the Restoration movement there is reason for rejoicing that a mission consciousness that was slow in developing has so blossomed. Would that there were many more! And if some of the motivation has grown out of competition among fellow heirs I can only say with Paul, "What then? Only that in every way, whether in pretense or in truth, Christ is proclaimed; and in that I rejoice" (Phil. 1:18). On the other hand there are many cases in which lines which may seem so rigid in the United States can be blurred, if not completely erased in the mission experience.

It was a concern for the evangelistic mission of the church that brought about the call for unity in the Body of Christ. Those involved in the evangelistic mission have both a unique opportunity and an ominous obligation to continue the quest for a united church.

NOTES

[1] Richard G. Phillips deals with this problem in his doctoral thesis, "Differences in the Theological and Philosophical Backgrounds of Alexander Campbell and Barton W. Stone and Resulting Differences of Thrust in Their Theological Formulations." This excellent study should be published.

[2] One of the reasons for the early success of the Restoration movement in the United States was that many European Christians who had migrated to the States had left behind religious issues which had grown out of European political history and hence had no meaning in the new world.

[3] For example see Billheimer's book (1978).

[4] As an illustration, if one were to question an American congregation about the display of the American flag in its building, the question itself might be taken as unAmerican and unChristian. But when Americans hear the reason why British Churches of Christ do not and would not display the Union Jack in their buildings, it is likely to cause them to reflect more objectively on the practice in the United States.

BIBLIOGRAPHY

Billheimer, Paul E.
   1978   Love Covers: A Viable Platform for Christian Unity. Grand Rapids: Wm. B. Eerdmans Pub. Co.

DeGroot, A. T.
   1965   Disciple Thought: A History. Ft. Worth: Texas Christian University.

Drewery, Mary
   1978   William Carey. London: Hodder and Stoughton, Ltd.

Filbeck, David
   1980   The First Fifty Years. Joplin: College Press Publishing Co.

Garrett, Leroy
   1981   The Stone-Campbell Movement: An Anecdotal History of Three Churches. Joplin: College Press Pub. Co.

Murch, James DeForest
   1962   Christians Only: A History of the Restoration Movement. Cincinnati: Standard Pub. Co.

Osborn, R. E.
   1967   "Witness and Receptivity: The Christian Church (Disciples of Christ) and the Body of Christ at Large," in Disciples and the Church Universal. Nashville: Disciples of Christ Historical Society.

Robinson, William
   1945   The Shattered Cross. Birmingham: Berean Press. (reprinted).

United Christian Missionary Society
   1944   Twenty-Five Years of Kingdom Building Through the UCMS, 1919-1944. Indianapolis: United Christian Missionary Society.

Van Buren, James G.
   1978   "Isaac Errett's View of Biblical Inspiration," in Essays on New Testament Christianity, edited by C. Robert Wetzel. Cincinnati: Standard Pub. Co. 128-134.

Warren, W. R.
   1923   The Life and Labors of Archibald McLean. St. Louis: The Bethany Press.

Part Three

MISSIONARY ANTHROPOLOGY

"I have become all things to all men."

I Cor. 9:22

8

Culture, Ideology and Christian Mission

by Charles R. Taber

Human beings do not live as isolated individuals, but in groups whose internal and external social and ecological relationships are clearly defined. Human beings do not hear any message, including the gospel, with a blank slate for a mind, but with minds full of existing ideas -- knowledge, beliefs, values, attitudes -- which unavoidably condition how they understand and react to the message. All of these functions: to order social life, to enable humans to make a living out of the environment and to encode and decode messages are fulfilled by **culture.** It is its culture that gives a group its solidarity based on shared ideas and customs, that makes it feel like "us" as distinct from a miscellaneous assortment of persons and from "them." Because culture so powerfully shapes people's mind and lives, it is crucial that missionaries understand what it is and how it works.

But a culture is not merely an ethically neutral way of life. Along with its essential positive functions of coordinating the God-given abilities of humans for orderly social existence, culture is also the means by which humans express and justify their rebellion against God and their conflicts with each other. I will use the term **ideology** to designate that core aspect of a culture's worldview which explains and justifies a group's self-serving impulses. At its deepest level, the modern term ideology is surely close in meaning to the biblical term "world" in such Johannine passages as Jn. 12:31 and 15:18-26 and I Jn. 2:15-17. It is also close to Paul's use of "this world" in Rm. 12:2.

Therefore, a missionary needs to be especially aware of the profoundly evil and even demonic character of ideologies, including those of his or her own society and culture, in order both to be freed and to contribute to the freeing of others.

In this paper, I will explore the nature of culture, the nature of ideology, and finally note some implications for mission.

WHAT IS CULTURE?

What is culture? Edward B. Tylor was the first to attempt, over a century ago, to define this foundational concept of cultural anthropology (Tylor, 1891). Some decades ago, two of the giants of American anthropology collected well over one-hundred definitions of culture before concluding that this concept, like that of energy in physics, is one of those prime concepts which can be understood, described and used, but not defined (Kroeber and Kluckhohn, 1952).

But the profusion of quasi-definitions did not vary in a totally unlimited way; there are a number of agreed-upon properties and functions of culture which we can usefully spell out. I begin with a general description: culture comprises everything that people need to learn in order to cope successfully with their natural and social environment. Alternatively, culture is a set of patterns for thinking, for understanding and evaluating, and for acting. Again, culture is that socially prescribed and transmitted set of knowledges and competencies by means of which people satisfy their cultural requirements for survival and well-being. Finally, culture can be said to define the goals of human existence and appropriate strategy and tactics for attaining those goals.

Properties of Culture

A very helpful approach to culture is to list some of its central properties. I mention here only ten.

1. Culture is **learned.** The young of every other species are born with a great many biologically necessary behavior patterns already programmed in their genes. An oriole does not take lessons in nest building, but automatically builds the same kind of nest that orioles have always built. Of course, animals are able to learn some things;

certain species are very flexible and capable of learning many new behaviors. But most species have the patterns which are most essential to survival well safeguarded by having them programmed into the genes. Human beings, though, are born extremely helpless, ignorant and incapable of surviving more than a short time without the care of adults; and they spend an inordinate proportion of their total life span learning how one survives and thrives as a human being. A human baby at birth knows virtually nothing, but it is capable of learning the most complex and diverse skills. The animal pattern makes for greater security but greater rigidity. The human pattern makes for high risk but extreme flexibility. All animals of a species over the world behave in essentially the same way, and they are able to thrive only in those environments in which their predetermined behaviors work. Humans behave in many different ways, in accordance with the demands and possibilities of their environments and the culture they have learned. Any child will learn the culture to which he or she is exposed in the formative years, and genes only play one role: to provide the raw material of human potential which a culture will shape in particular ways.

2. Culture is **mental.** That is to say, it exists only in people's minds, not "out there" in some observable place. Culture is given expression in the ways in which people think and act, in the objects they make and use, in the institutions they conceive and operate; but these things are the products of culture, not culture itself. Culture itself is that system of ideas -- patterns, rules and designs -- which govern what people do and make. Culture includes not only the design of a tool, but its total meaning and significance in relation to tasks to be done, to other tools in the kit, to techniques for its use, and so on; the tool itself is a mere artifact.

Similarly, culture is not a particular **objet d'art** (say, Picasso's **Guernica**), but the complex of ideas, values, style and taste that made Picasso's protest against war take just that form. Finally, the tables of descent of the twelve clans of ancient Israel were not culture, but the idea of patrilineality was.

One might be tempted to say from this that culture is a kind of Platonic "ideal," floating far above the sordid real world. This misconception might seem to be reinforced by the correct insistence of anthropologists today that no society actually lives up to its own professed ideals, that there is always a gap between the real and the ideal. But what I have in mind is different from this because the ideals themselves can be open to question on the grounds that they fall short in ways that Plato's ideas did not. The mental structures which constitute culture and which underlie the concrete manifestations of culture -- specific behaviors, objects and the like -- are not self-existent, eternal or perfect. On the contrary, they have particular historical antecedents and they give expression to particular social, economic and political realities. In other words, the cultural ideals themselves are not ideologically neutral.

3. Culture is **adaptive.** That is to say that culture plays the same role for us as specialized physical equipment does for animals. We do not have a thick coat of fur to protect us against the cold, but we are able to design clothes and houses. We do not have strong teeth, claws or hands, but we can make tools and weapons more powerful than those of any animal. It is the adaptive nature of culture that enables humans to live in such a diversity of habitats, including the most forbidding -- the Arctic, the Sahara and New York City. Human beings differ remarkably little in their physical constitution despite the propaganda of racists. We are in many ways very generalized biological specimens. It is culture which permits us to live in such widely different ways.

4. Culture is **shared** by a human group. It is the common creation and property of the group, and it is what makes the group a group rather than a random assortment of individuals. The fact that I share with certain others a set of beliefs, of values, of conventional ways of acting, of speaking, makes us feel like "us" in distinction from all other human beings who have different cultures, and are consequently "them." Culture is also socially transmitted and maintained. The adult members of society are at pains to pass on the culture to each new generation so that the group can perpetuate itself socially as well as biologically. And members mutually reinforce their conviction that their culture is the best one, the right one. History is full of examples of groups which have fought, sometimes suicidally, rather than surrender the culture that gives them their identity and psychic security.

5. Culture is **selective.** This goes beyond mere adaptiveness into the realm of the arbitrary and conventional. Among all the things which human beings are potentially able

to do, each culture selects a subset which is, generally speaking, that subset which works best in the given environment. But even within that subset, it further selects a sub-subset. Out of the abundance of natural products of the habitat which would be chemically nutritious, each group selects some and calls them "food." Out of the two sides of the road on which one might drive, each group which knows of cars selects one. In some cases, as with foods, the range of possibilities is very wide; in other cases, as with the two sides of the road, it is narrow. The point is that whether among many options or few, each group selects one or a small set of options which are "our" way of doing things.

6. Culture is **integrated.** Culture is not a mere inventory of customs and rules. The various domains of a culture -- technology and subsistence, social and political organization, art, play, religion, language and so on -- tend to fit together and to be mutually supportive. I do not mean to say that a culture is a perfectly functioning machine in which every bit works together ideally; on the contrary, every culture has its internal inconsistencies, its tensions and malfunctions, its novelties and its anachronisms. But the point is that one cannot introduce a change at one point without setting off a ripple effect that works its way throughout the culture. Henry Ford had no idea, when he introduced the mass production of inexpensive cars, that he would alter the dating habits of Americans and the design of cities, but he did. Missionaries and national Christians who ban polygamy do not intend to create a new institution -- prostitution -- but they sometimes do. Because things are interconnected, small changes at one place have repercussions at other places. Cultures vary in the degree of their internal cohesiveness; some remain very tightknit, though the number of these is rapidly dwindling in a world where societies impinge on each other; others are at the point of disintegration. Most are somewhere in between.

7. Culture is **heterogeneous.** It is common in some circles to point to the evident internal diversity of complex modern civilizations, and to contrast these with supposedly homogeneous cultures of small, face-to-face, technically simple, socially undifferentiated societies -- the tribal societies of the world. But even in such a group not everyone knows the same things, plays the same roles, or lives the same lives. Even the "simplest" society prescribes sharp differences between men and women and between adults and children. Many have a more elaborate

distinction based on age-grades. In such societies people have vastly different degrees of access to certain kinds of knowledge, play quite distinct roles and do very different things. So even in a tribal society, one can talk of the culture of little boys, that of little girls, that of young men or women and that of old men or old women. And of course, in complex modern societies, multiple differentiations based on education, occupation, income, religion and the like give different people quite different cultures. Ideally the different cultures are a part of a coherent larger system, so that they can be properly called complementary subcultures. In fact, it is rarely the case that such differences are free of tension and even conflict. At best, one can discuss degrees of consensus about certain core values. It may be the case, in some tribal societies, that everyone shares the same beliefs; but it cannot be taken for granted, since differential access to power automatically creates at least a potential conflict of interests.

8. Culture is **normative**. This means that it provides its bearers with rules which it expects them to obey. In the vast majority of the cases, the rules are so deeply internalized during the process of enculturation or socialization that people do what is expected of them almost automatically. Few of us have to reflect consciously on how to hold our forks, or how and when to extend our hands when meeting a new person. Few of us have sharp internal struggles about whether or not to put garbage in the proper kind of containers. Even those prescribed patterns which we find particularly irksome, like paying taxes, we tend to obey, if only because of the penalties consequent to disobedience. Of course the threat of punishment is always in the background: society has ways of punishing its deviants, ranging from ridicule to capital punishment. But those cases where society has to invoke a penalty represent a sort of failure of socialization; and if enough people become deviants, perhaps because the rules are foolish or tyrannical, society finds itself spending more and more of its energy and resources on suppressing dissent and punishing revolt, and less and less on its normal functions.

9. Culture is **cumulative**. Each generation does not have to start from scratch reinventing the wheel, because human beings have retentive memories and make use of language and other symbol systems to pass on the heritage to their cohorts and children.

10. Finally, culture is **adaptable**. In other words it is adaptive in a continuous way. As circumstances alter, culture usually alters to meet the new challenges and the new opportunities. This is true of all cultures, not only modern ones as is sometimes thought. But it is true that some cultures seem in general more open to change than others; or it might be more accurate to say that some cultures are more open to change in some areas than other cultures. American culture, for instance, is not only open to change but demands it for its own sake in such areas as technology and fashion; but it is not at all open to change in its basic political institutions. The cultures of people who live in extremely forbidding environments tend to be resistant to change, on the grounds that you do not tamper with even limited success under such circumstances.

Functions of Culture

What does culture do for its bearers? It is a system which makes provision for all of their requirements for survival and well being as human biological and social organisms. It is possible to list some of the things which we all require and then in a parallel column to lists the ways in which each culture meets these requirements, given the exigencies and possibilities of the environment. The following chart exemplifies what I mean.

UNIVERSAL HUMAN REQUIREMENTS	CULTURAL PROVISIONS
Relating to Ultimate Reality	Religion
Esthetic expression	Art forms
Intellectual activity	Worldview, rules of logic
Physical activity	Work, play
Communication	Languages, signal systems
Belonging	Social structure, kinship
Expressions of sexuality	Rules of mating, marriage
Protection	Clothing, houses, defense
Nutrition and water	Food and beverages

Several things need to be noted about this table:

1. Each term in the left column is stated in universal, culture-free concepts; but each term in the right column is specifically defined and controlled by cultural values and beliefs. Nutrition, for instance, can be defined in purely chemical terms: protein, carbohydrates, vitamins and so on. Food, on the other hand, is always specified by culture. On occasion people have starved in the presence of nutritious substances which their culture did not call food.

2. Apart from the biological urgency of the bottom two items, they are not rank-ordered.

3. The apparent one-to-one correlation between a requirement and a cultural provision, while true, is a great over-simplification. It is the case that almost every cultural trait, pattern and custom is simultaneously connected with a number of requirements. Everywhere, for instance, people eat and drink not only to satisfy animal hunger and thirst; they eat together to express belonging, and they prepare foods in ways that are thought to be attractive to express their esthetic urges. For that matter they often add religious overtones to their eating and drinking, as in the Christian rite of the Eucharist. In other words, one dimension of the integration of culture is that each custom tends to relate to several requirements at the same time.

4. The universal character of the requirements prevents cultures from varying in an unlimited way; but the extreme diversity of environments and of historical experience leads nevertheless to great variety.

Worldview

Nowhere is diversity more striking than in the worldviews by which people explain and legitimate their world. For cultures differ not only in the outward manifestations of technical and social behavior, but also in the ways in which people understand their situation and motivate their behavior. But what do we mean by "worldview?" A worldview is a more or less integrated and comprehensive understanding of what is real and true (reality postulates) and what is good and bad (value postulates). It comprises the concerns which in philosophy are called metaphysics and ontology, epistemology, ethics and esthetics.

1. Cultures differ in their views of what is real:

    a. What is Ultimate Reality like: one, two, or many? personal or impersonal? good, bad, indifferent or capricious?
    b. What is the observable universe made of: matter, spirit or a combination? Is there only one kind of "stuff" or more than one?
    c. What is the nature of humanity, of "us," of personhood? How do humans relate to each other within the group? outside the group? How do humans relate to Ultimate Reality?
    d. What is the disposition of reality to humans: benevolent, hostile, indifferent, capricious?
    e. Is reality harmonious or conflictual?
    f. How is the universe arranged in space? How does it work? Is it predictable or is it unpredictable?
    g. How did things come to exist? What is the nature of causation?
    h. How does one know and test truth? What is the nature of explanation?

In all of these ways and more, people in different cultures pose the questions differently and come up with different answers.

2. Cultures differ in their views of what is good:

    a. What is the highest good?
    b. What is the ideal human like?
    c. What is success?
    d. What are right and wrong?
    e. Are human beings free and responsible, or are they determined by fate, or by Ultimate Reality, or by their genes, or by society?

3. It is important to realize that views in all of these areas are, at the deepest level, taken for granted, not subject to question and verification or falsification. They are assumptions, presuppositions, the Truth. Generally speaking, alternative views from far away are thought to be silly and amusing; but if they are perceived to be making some claim upon us, they are thought to be dangerous and needing to be suppressed. Remember how most Americans reacted a few years ago to the beatniks and the hippies.

4. One last word on this point: though cultures vary profoundly in their worldviews, they do not vary in unlimited ways. With respect to reality postulates, whatever description of reality people give, there is a reality "out there" which is more or less adequately represented by that description. If the description strays too far from the constraints of reality "out there," the worldview ceases to fulfill its function of helping people to cope. Reality postulates are the result of constant interaction between reality "out there" and the social and ideological needs of the group; more specifically, the needs of the powerful and privileged members of the group who are the custodians and beneficiaries of the way things are. This is even more true of value postulates. But even these tend to gravitate toward certain basic principles which turn out to be not unlike the last six commandments of the Decalogue (Ex. 20: 12-17). Why should this be so? Theologically, one is reminded by the existence of these universal principles of the divine image and likeness which are the essence of our being. But even at a purely descriptive level, these are the rules that make society possible; without them, society would self-destruct in short order. As far as I am concerned these two explanations are the same. When the Creator made us, He built into us a sense of those rules which would lead to the successful operation of the human experience. To the extent that groups value and practice these rules they work properly, and to the extent that they ignore or reject or pervert them they break down. One way in which all human groups limit the application of the rules is that they observe them strictly within the group: I must be truthful, I must be honest, I must refrain from seducing my neighbor's wife -- within the group. But the rules may be relaxed or disregarded in dealing with outsiders, especially those who are my enemies. It is because we allow for or even advocate different rules in dealing with outsiders that we pit group against group, nation against nation, to the point where humanity is on the brink of global suicide. Only a small minority of humankind, it seems, has caught the vision that peace and security will never be possible until the same ethical rules apply equally and fairly to the whole human race.

Cultural Relativity

The universal tendency among humans is to consider one's own culture as the correct, natural, sensible way for humans to act, and to judge other cultures and their human bearers by the standards of one's own culture. This spontaneous process of judgment, which makes us look good and others foolish or wicked, is called "ethnocentrism." In a sense, and to the extent that it stops at the point of a strong preference for one's own culture, it is innocuous. But it often goes well beyond this to strong negative judgments which in turn justify aggressive actions against others. If people of other cultures are somehow less than human we are justified in feeling contempt for them and exploiting them. This was exactly the argument used in the past to justify the enslavement of black people, the annihilation of Indians and colonial conquest. In a milder but still virulent form it motivated quite a few missionaries, missionaries who confused evangelization with cultural imperialism, so that native peoples were forced to abandon or change their cultures in favor of the missionaries' cultures which were judged to be "Christian."

Against this arrogant and destructive ethnocentrism among westerners, cultural anthropologists in the early decades of this century began to argue for "cultural relativity" (Herskovits, 1972). As Hoebel said, "The concept of cultural relativity states that standards of rightness and wrongness (values) and of usage and effectiveness (customs) are relative to the given culture of which they are a part" (1972:28). Thus, one must sharply distinguish situation ethics applied at the level of individual conduct from cultural relativity at the societal level. Nevertheless many persons, including anthropologists totally committed to the principle in theory, find it quite difficult to apply it consistently. One could swallow hard and argue that headhunting in Papua New Guinea or infanticide among the ancient Romans was justified by the values of the respective cultures. But could one really say that the slaughter of six million Jews was merely a feature of the culture that spawned Hitler? No anthropologist that I know of is able to say that -- even though the values of racism , of dark romantic excess, and of obedience to authority, which permitted Hitler to do what he did, are deeply embedded in German culture. Cultural relativity apparently has some limits; but why, and on what reasoned moral grounds? It is my conviction that there is and can be no basis for evaluating cultures if we use purely human criteria such as are generated by any culture. Thus it remains out of bounds for us to judge head-hunters or infanticides or even Hitler merely on the grounds that our culture does not countenance such behavior.

How then does a Christian evaluate the profusion of folkways and systems of values? I offer these propositions.

1. Each culture is relatively adequate for its bearers: it permits them to survive under the conditions that gave rise to the culture, it satisfies their basic requirements. In so doing, each culture is an expression of human ingenuity, industry and goodwill, which in turn reflect the divine image. As such, each culture deserves our profound respect.

2. No culture perfectly reflects God's standard for human life. Though some cultures have undergone prolonged and intensive exposure to Christian values, each has through time learned ways of distorting or perverting authentic biblical values. After all, many people in each society are not Christian; and it is the built-in tendency of human systems to deviate from God's design. Thus no culture -- not even that of the United States -- can serve as a criterion for judging others.

3. All cultures, to the extent that they fall short of God's will, are under His judgment. Specifically, to the extent that each culture sets limits on the obligation to love God supremely and to love our neighbor as ourselves, or justifies contrary behavior, it is under God's condemnation. This is all the more true of cultures which have the longest Christian influence, on the biblical principle of proportionality of responsibility (Lk. 12:48). Thus the missionary, reflecting on the way his or her own culture falls short, will be led to be modest about the supposed superiority of things "back home" and respectful of the ways of others.

The Sources of Culture

How does a culture come to be? It is not usually a matter of deliberate planning. What happens is that each generation in a society finds itself with a heritage passed on by the previous generation and a set of contemporary circumstances with which to cope. To the extent that the current situation is like that of the forefathers, culture will remain relatively stable; but to the extent that the situation changes, culture will need to change to fit. We can usefully cluster the situational factors under three headings: 1) changes in the physical environment such as prolonged drought or deforestation; 2) internal social tensions; and 3) the pressures of other groups outside. As each human group struggles to cope, to meet occasional emergencies, to express and defend its interests, it gradually develops new ideas. Such innovations, as Barnett has shown (1953), arise initially in the mind of one person. But given favorable conditions, the innovation can be adopted to the group, either by formal decision or, more often, through the tacit consent represented by imitation.

In some cases -- notably the cases of peoples living in isolated and harsh habitats, such as the Arctic and the desert -- cultures focus largely on wresting a living out of the environment through specific techniques. For such peoples the problem of what to do about foreigners is often of low priority because of the remoteness of such persons. In other cases -- notably groups which live in modern cities -- people's lives are remote from questions of soil and climate but unceasingly involved with the problem of significant but alien people -- people of other "races," ethnic groups, classes, castes or occupations. In such cultures, the techniques for coping are essentially political rather than technical. Each group adopts those political gambits which seem most likely to advance its perceived self-interests in relation to others. But where the groups involved are very unequal in power, it is usually the case that the stronger take advantage of the weaker, unless the even greater power of the state intervenes to defend the powerless.

When the pressure on a society comes from outside -- from a colonial conqueror or a giant neighbor -- the society tries various techniques for self-defense: one thinks of Gandhi's non-violent resistance in India, of small countries calling on bigger ones to help them against big enemies. One thinks also of systematic deception of the conqueror, of continuing traditional practices underground. A powerless society has a surprising number of options for making life difficult for a powerful aggressor society. In the modern world, it seems as though the most difficult aggression to defend against is economic aggression.

Whether the cultures which confront one another coexist within a single nation state or in different states, they mutually influence each other. This is so even when the groups in question hate each other. In the first place, each group constitutes a persistent "problem" for the other, so that group spends time, energy and resources on solving that "problem" rather than on doing something more useful (witness the problem in South Africa). In the second place, each group finds itself adopting bits and pieces of the alien culture, as when one "fights fire with fire" (witness the mutual recriminations between the United States and the Soviet Union over similar involvements in different countries).

The result of all this contact, friction and conflict is that cultures are not closed, self-contained, homogeneous, stable systems; but rather highly permeable, open-ended, heterogeneous, unstable systems. Within each group there will typically be tensions between the advocates of alternative strategies, there will be "conservatives" and "liberals." Bits and pieces of contiguous cultures will float in and out of one's own culture, and some cultural features will rapidly catch on in many cultures. The situation is in perpetual flux; and this flux is a dominant trait of the contemporary world.

Nevertheless, it is in many cases the subjective impression of many people that their culture is and remains unique and that it endures essentially unchanged. It is certainly usually their hope and intention that it should remain so. The culture is uniquely theirs and uniquely right. In the face of any amount of empirical evidence to the contrary, they will deny that their culture in any way resembles that of "those people" or has borrowed from or been influenced by them.

Each culture has a built-in tendency to become totalitarian in its control over the lives of its members; put in political terms, every Caesar wants to become God. Even in the most heterogeneous and tolerant cultures, such as modern American culture, one can easily move across a line beyond which opinion and especially conduct are no longer acceptable. This is the demonic side of culture's normativeness. I call it demonic because it resists accountability to God and rejects the freedom of its members to discern a divine will that countermands culture's rules.

WHAT IS IDEOLOGY?

Apart from a few hints to the contrary, the reader may be tempted so far to think of culture as a matter of arbitrary and ethically neutral choices which people make among available options. That is in fact what a thorough-going application of the principle of cultural relativity leads to. It is indeed impossible from within one's own culture to pass a valid judgment on any other culture, whether a judgment of ethics or of pragmatic efficacy; for success or failure are a function of what one was trying to do, not of what someone else thought one ought to be doing. Not only is this principle valid in general, it is my conviction that it is doubly valid for a Christian who acknowledges that his or her own culture falls short of the divine will. But it seems to me that the Christian can take, with appropriate caution and humility, one extra step: he or she can attempt to apply what can be discovered from Scripture of God's supracultural criteria.

But before such a step is "safe" for someone as arrogantly ethnocentric as a westerner, an intermediate step must be taken. That is the recognition that even from the perspective of social scientists, including many who make no affirmation of faith of any kind, cultures have at their core a biased, not a neutral, point of view. That is, any human group, and in complex societies any subgroup, has at the core of its worldview an **ideology**. The purpose of any ideology, avowed or unavowed, is to present the group, its point of view, its interests and its ambitions in the best light possible. There is no such thing as a disinterested or unbiased worldview. The branch of the social sciences which has highlighted this fact is called the **sociology of knowledge** (Berger and Luckmann, 1966).

The starting point of the sociology of knowledge is the empirical observation that in the real world of human groups and nations, valuables -- wealth, power and prestige -- are distributed very unequally. Even in tribal societies where wealth is limited and cannot be accumulated by individuals, power and prestige are allocated differently on the basis of age and sex, at least. In stratified or competitive societies, the difference between the rich and powerful and the destitute and powerless can be enormous. It is important to note that this difference is not "just in people's minds;" it is an objective fact of daily life. Similarly, in the global relationships between societies and nations there is an almost incredible gap between the haves and the have-nots. And both within each society and between societies, the mechanisms which distribute the valuables work in such a way as to maintain and increase the difference rather than to decrease it. It is true that there are counter-mechanisms, such as social programs of assistance to the needy and foreign aid; but, measured by the net flow of wealth, these are a drop in the bucket in contrast with the mechanisms which move wealth and power from the have-nots to the haves: the allocation of the proceeds of business within each country, and the flow of raw materials and profits from the poor countries to the rich. It is also true that some persons within the competitive societies start out poor and become rich, or vice versa; and these are highly publicized so as to give the impression of a truly open system. But objectively, for every poor person who becomes rich, there are hundreds who start poor and remain poor; and for every rich person who becomes poor, there are hundreds who start rich and become richer. And relative advantage or disadvantage are not merely the lot of each individual, but are passed on to the next generation, so that different people start the race of life at very different starting lines. And all of this operates without regard to the specific merits or efforts of individuals, which only dent the system without modifying it.

But it is not in the interests of maintaining the system for its beneficiaries to admit that it is rigged in this way. And so we have the ideology that wealth and power are allocated by a free, fair, competitive system, and that winners and losers are simply getting what they have earned. The disruptive and unfair effects of inherited privilege or disadvantage are ignored or denied. The multiplying effect of the system on the benefits of initial advantage is also ignored or denied. This ideology is powerfully disseminated, using all the means at their disposal, by the custodians of "the American way of life," those who happen to benefit most from the system. It is disseminated in the literature, in the press and media, in the schools, in advertizing and in the arts. Contrary views are quickly banished or contained as subversive.

What about the ideologies of the disadvantaged and the victims of the system? To an astonishing extent, they tend to accept the ideology which is propounded by the dominant group: in a closed system, the ideology that God or fate has assigned each person a slot in life; in a competitive system, the ideology that everyone gets what he or she deserves. As a result, society's losers and victims tend to have a very low view of themselves, to despise and hate themselves, to see themselves as unworthy and powerless -- which only compounds their plight. It is this fact more than anything else which brings to grief many well-intentioned attempts to rehabilitate the destitute such as training them in job skills. It is relatively easy to teach skills; it is much harder to convince a self-hating person that he or she is worthy and capable, so that they actually show up for the job for which they have been trained.

In saying that the disadvantaged often believe the ideology that consecrates their plight, I do not mean to suggest that they are truly content. It is the report of most people who have managed to gain the confidence of such persons that they are full of a diffuse rage which can explode into undirected destructive behavior, but is usually hidden under a mask of mindless compliance for reasons of prudence. This was certainly the normal state of slaves in the ante-bellum South who were depicted by the official propaganda as loving their masters and being content with their lot. Discontent could also, given a more ordered direction, erupt into revolt, as in the case of Nat Turner. Or, if someone offers a full-scale alternative ideology, such as Marxism, discontent can erupt into revolution, as in France, Russia, China or Cuba. It is true that it is not the majority of the poor who dream up the ideology and launch the revolution; but it is the case that no revolution managed by a few could actually succeed apart from the tacit support of the masses. What happens when the revolutionaries are in power is, of course, something else; since power in turn corrupts them, and they develop modifications of the original ideology which justify their continuing in power. In other words, much more fundamental a feature of any ideology than whether it is, say, capitalistic or Marxist, is where it stands on the question of power as such.

Where does religion stand in all of this? Generally around the world, most religions have supported the ideologies of the classes which wielded power, the "official" ideologies of society and the state. Only occasionally have formal religions played a role in revolt or revolution. But informal prophetic-type religious movements have not infrequently played a more radical role. In ancient Israel during the period of the kingdoms the institutional religion based on temple and priests supported the kings while the prophets denounced injustice and oppression.

What about Christianity? If we take seriously a number of New Testament passages (Lk. 1:51-53; Mt. 19:21; Mk. 10:41-45; Jas. 4:1-6, etc.) we are forced to recognize that Jesus and the apostles: 1) had a very realistic and severe view of the presence of greed, pride and the abuse of power in society; and 2) warned against believers being caught in those traps. In later years a number of Christian leaders, notably John Chrysostom, thundered against the powerful who abused the weak. But from the time of Constantine on the institutional church has usually been on the side of power and the established order, and has exerted its efforts towards dampening and diverting the discontents among the poor by preaching present resignation in light of a future hope. It was this which Karl Marx described in his powerful angry phrase, calling religion "the opiate of the people." Certainly religion and theology were heavily involved in the United States in justifying racism, first in the form of slavery, and then in the form of Jim Crow legislation. As for the international scene, most churches in the United States support the majority line that the United States is a benefactor and protector of small nations rather than the line taken by many of these small nations themselves, that the United States is a part of the problem rather than a part of the solution. It is, of course, the case that there have always been minority voices in the churches who continued in the line of the prophets, apostles and Jesus Himself, defending the weak and denouncing the oppressive strong. But all too often Christians take refuge in simplistic slogans and swallow whole the self-serving ideologies of their society.

How can one be freed from the mental captivity of prevalent myths and ideologies? How can one arrive at a more objective and realistic assessment of the situation? Where can one find a framework for an alternative analysis? I offer the following propositions:

1. The world in the Johannine sense is in rebellion against God. This is as true of its structures and institutions as of individual lives, inasmuch as the meaning of "world" relates to order and system, not simply to the aggregation of individual instances. Having rejected the rule of God and accountability to God, the world is reduced ultimately to a "might makes right" ethic, in any one of dozens of versions. In our society, for example, we emphasize competition in which the strong win and the weak lose.

2. Without the acknowledgement of the rule of God, there is no consistently effective way to avoid the abuse of the weak by the strong. The degree of restraint which is seen in each society -- a varying degree in different times and places -- is usually due either to prudential considerations or to a residual sense of God's justice. As long as either of these considerations dominates people's thinking, it will be seen that order via structures, however imperfect, is preferable to chaos. But every structure needs to be resisted lest it become an idol.

3. Because of the limited good that structures can do Christians are taught to cooperate with them (Rm. 13). But because of their built-in tendencies to idolatry and oppressiveness, Christians are taught to be alert and prophetic, to call the powers to account in the name of God, to denounce injustice, to defend the rights of the weak (Ex. 22:21; Is. 11; Mt. 25:31-46). However much we work with the powers, we must never become their dupes nor allow them to absolutize themselves in our eyes.

4. When Christians work in the realm of the worldly powers, they must avoid the values and motives and methods which characterize the world, which are based on pride and power. This is the true meaning of Jesus' often misunderstood words, "My kingdom is not of this world" (Jn. 18:36).

5. Above and beyond all involvements in the world's affairs, the church must focus on the transcendent, eschatological gospel: transcendent, not in the sense that it is not concerned with the this-worldly plight of people, but that it offers a remedy of a totally different order; eschatological, not in the sense that it has no continuity with life as we know it, but in the sense that it is God's ultimate word and act, the establishment of His eternal kingdom of justice, of security, of abundance -- of love.

IMPLICATIONS FOR MISSION

What does all of this have to say to us in our missionary concern and effort? At least the following seven things:

1. Since each culture is an expression of the ingenuity, the industry and the intelligent goodwill of a group of human beings, and as such an expression of the creative divine image in them, it merits the complete and sincere respect of every missionary and every Christian. No one who is contemptuous of a people's culture has any business being a missionary.

2. Each culture is also the arena in which people express their rebellion against God and erect their idols, together with the demonic ideologies which justify their rebellion. As such, it is under God's judgment and will ultimately be purged by fire in the day of God.

3. It is essential to note that the missionary's home culture is in no better state than the culture of the people

whom he or she is serving. True, the missionary's culture has probably been exposed to Christian influence for a long time, and shows the effects of that influence; but it is not a Christian culture. More light entails more responsibility and more severe judgment for failure (Lk. 12:48).

4. The most dangerous aspect of any culture, the part which is most thoroughly dominated by the "principalities and powers," is the ideology which legitimates and justifies the existing order and which formulates and legitimates a people's pride, greed, ruthlessness and ambition.

5. It follows that for salvation to be complete, it must include liberation from the domination of the world's ideologies in our minds; and indeed it does (Rm. 12:2). But we have to be willing to let God set us free from the devil's lies which are at the foundation of the ideologies.

6. If a missionary is to be able to offer this aspect of salvation to others, he or she must have experienced it personally. This is especially crucial when the devil has woven his lies into a fabric which also includes a great deal of "Christian" rhetoric, as in the West, where the legacy of sixteen centuries of "Christendom" has left its vocabulary but not its power in the ideologies of western civilization. Max Weber has written the classic description of the abuse of religious ideas to buttress an economic ideology (Weber, 1930); others have done similar analyses of the use of Christian terms in support of worldly political ideologies. A missionary needs to do a good bit of critical reading and hard thinking, under the guidance of God's Spirit, to experience liberation from the myths of his own society.

7. To the extent that a missionary has experienced this liberation, he or she can love his or her own society, people and country in a more Christian, less idolatrous way that before; he or she can then love other peoples and preach the authentic gospel which will liberate them from the bondage of their ideologies.

BIBLIOGRAPHY

Barnett, Homer G.
   1953   Innovation: The Basis of Culture Change. Garden
           City: McGraw-Hill Book Company, Inc.

Berger, Peter L. and Thomas Luckmann
   1967   The Social Construction of Reality. Garden City:
           Anchor Books. (2nd. edition).

Herskovits, Melville J.
   1972   Cultural Relativism: Perspectives in Cultural
           Relativity. New York: Random House. (ed. by
           Frances Herskovits).

Hoebel, E. Adamson
   1972   Anthropology: The Study of Man. New York:
           McGraw-Hill Book Company, Inc.

Kroeber, A. L. and Clyde Kluckhohn
   1952   Culture: A Critical Review of Concepts and
           Definitions. Cambridge: Peabody Museum.

Tylor, Edward B.
   1891   Primitive Culture. London: John Murray.
           (3rd. edition).

Weber, Max
   1930   The Protestant Ethic and the Spirit of Capitalism.
           London: Allen & Unwin. (trans. by T. Parsons).

9

The Mexican Middle Class Family

by Rex R. Jones

Mexican family structure is not a unique phenomenon. It is related and similar to the structures found in various parts of Latin America and, in general, to the Mediterranean area. However, to make sense out of its dynamics requires deliberate time and effort.

The writer has a deep appreciation for the Mexican family and earnestly seeks to understand it more fully. The middle class family structure is the chief concern, yet it does not seem to be significantly different than the lower and upper classes. The chief distinction resides in the manner of expression. The lower class does not seek to conceal its motivations and expressions of aggression. The upper class more carefully masks its motivations.

The family structure described in this chapter is most typically found among the middle class people of the provinces and among the middle class Mexico City families of provincial origin. North American influence is strong among the upper and middle classes, particularly in Mexico City. The relationships emphasized here best refer to the nuclear family. The approach used to study the Mexican family is derived from, and placed in the framework of, the culturally accepted axiomatic values -- dominance of males over females and older over younger.

The purpose of this study is to begin the process of getting inside the Mexican family. It is not to provide a comprehensive sociological description of the middle class

Rex R. Jones

but rather to examine pertinent areas of family life that will assist the church planter in presenting the Gospel effectively. Much more in-depth study is needed, and it is hoped that what is said here will stimulate others to pursue the subject.

Of the primary sources used by the writer, that of Mario Ongay is the most comprehensive and helpful (1980:5-81). He writes from inside the family system and tells us the meaning that is given to the family relationships. Many of the deeper interpretations in this article are drawn from his paper.

Keeping these restrictions in mind, the middle class Mexican family will be discussed according to the following scheme. First, the terminology essential to a family perspective will be defined. Then male/female relations, which form the base of the entire system of family relation, are discussed. Each of the role relationships within the family are discussed under the heading of family dynamics. Finally, several insights relevant to church growth will be presented in the context of change confronting the family.

FAMILY PERSPECTIVES

The terms family, system and sub-system need to be defined since they are an intricate part of the Mexican family structure. The term "family" has been defined as networks of people who live together over periods of time, who have ties of marriage and kinship to one another (Galvin and Brommei, 1982:2). The family is a small system in which members are related to each other by reason of strong reciprocal affections and loyalties, including blood ties, comprising a permanent household that persists over years.

Comparing this definition with that of Ongay we get the meaning of a family from the Mexican interpretation. Family to Ongay consists of all those people who live, or have lived, under the same roof for a significant period of time. In its totality family extends to take in friends, maids, and other persons who have stayed together for a long period of time (1980:5).

This part of Ongay's definition is describing the fact that in Mexican society, the **nuclear** family is embedded in an **extended** family network. A nuclear family consists of husband, wife, and unmarried children, and non-biologically related persons such as friends and maids.

The extended family is "any form in which members of several nuclear families defer to the same authority, exchange essential services, and either live together in the same household or close enough to be in daily contact" (Yorburg, 1973:37). Generally the extended family is comprised of at least three generations; that is, grandfather, father, and sons.

Yorburg further introduces the concept of a "much modified" extended family, most commonly found in urban industrial societies. The completely isolated nuclear families, where they exist, are the result of extreme "integrational mobility -- where daughter or son has risen from the working class ... or where children have married across racial or religious barriers" (1973:110). The "much modified" extended family best describes the Mexican middle class family in the changing urban scene.

Extended family ties tend to be much weakened by urban living. However, families may keep in contact in a variety of ways: visiting, letters, telephones, gifts, loans, giving advice in emergencies and coming together at significant life cycle occasions such as baptisms and weddings.

A great deal of social life in cities occurs between pairs of people (dyads) who interact sporadically. Other forms of social life take place in cliques or factions with the interaction focusing on a person or persons. These and other structured social relationships do supply some of the needs formerly provided by the extended family. They certainly point to the growing potential for moving totally nuclear in family form.

Irrespective of what point the family may be on the continuum of nuclear to "much modified" extended, it can be placed into an overall perspective. That leads us to the next basic family term.

A "system" is "a cluster of highly integrated parts, each responding to the others, the entire set somehow maintaining itself as a distinguishable whole in spite of incessant internal change" (Guernsey, 1982). The emphasis in this definition is on the phrase **whole.** The family is doing something together as a system. Minuchin describes the function of the family: "The family is organized around the support, regulation, nurturance, and socialization of its members" (1974:14).

Ongay is essentially in agreement when he uses system to mean "the result of the inner action, quality of relationships, and transactions among the members" (1980:6). This explains why the system, in all its totality, depends on the presence or the absence of each of the members. When a member is absent, for whatever reason, the family system is modified. Modification may be illustrated in the case of the death of the father in the Mexican family. The relationship which the mother previously had with the father will be replaced with a similar relationship. However, that relationship will be with the family as a **whole**. The mother clings to the rest of the family, behaving in maternalistic and paternalistic ways as if the family as a whole represented the characteristics and qualities of the lost mate.

The mother may choose another form of modification. She may focus instead on one of the sons, or another family member as a substitute for a husband. The victim in this case is the substitute who is not allowed to develop personal autonomy or selfhood. These inner dynamics could not be discerned apart from seeing the family in its total context.

The family carries out its functions by "sub-systems." Pairings of individuals within the family make up the sub-systems. Dyads such as husband/wife, mother/child, father/aunt, grandfather/nephew can be sub-systems. Sub-systems may be formed by generation, sex, interest or function. Family functioning requires clear boundaries for the sub-systems. The composition of sub-systems is not clearly so important as the clarity of the sub-system boundaries.

Each family has its own systems and sub-systems, uniquely designed, that makes it different from any other. Every family has its own operational style, identity, values and attitudes that gives it a special life-style. The norms and regulations form a whole that guides the family members. When any member does not follow these regulations the system is threatened. Immediate pressure will be brought by other members with the intent of bringing the deviation into conformity to the system. In this way the family maintains balance and equilibrium by encouraging unity, cohesiveness and loyalty. The family provides a place of security and an atmosphere for developmental growth for its members, but at the same time it acts as a bridge to society as it engages in the process of fitting into society.

A **closed** family system is not flexible. Members handle their problems by the status quo, "We always do it that way." It is highly structured, hierarchical and rule-governed. The individual is subordinate to the group. Movements are closed, regulated, screened and monitored (Kantor and Lehr, 1975:122). Outsiders do not fit. Visitors remain strangers. New ideas are seen with jealousy. The concern of this system is balance without change. This fits some Mexican families.

Where an open system operates, the family has rules but members are direct, clear and appreciative of each other. There is bonding with outsiders and visitors come freely and interact with family members. Members are given a voice in family goals. This form exists, but not in its pure form in the Mexican family.

In the urban setting of Mexico City one is exposed to both modern and traditional families. The traditional tends to be authoritative and father-dominated. The modern family gives its members more equality on a feeling and emotional basis. The open system is worth striving for. Urban families need to be trained and guided in its use. It should be taught because it is the biblical model and is certainly applicable in the Mexican family, in which interdependency and hospitality are strong characteristics. Its practice can make the Bible come alive in family relationships. The practice of open systems will greatly influence the family system as it interacts within other systems, particularly the church.

FAMILY DYNAMICS

Attention is now directed to the dynamics at work within the family. These dynamics are physical, psychological and spiritual (Akpem, 1983:134-135). They are intermingled throughout the remainder of the family study, and are crucial to its understanding. The **physical** sphere includes dynamics such as interactions, relationships and communications among members. This sphere is readily identified in the Mexican family. The **psychological** sphere includes emotions, feelings and other functions which transmit messages, both spoken and unspoken. There are several points where these appear and are crucial to interpreting what is happening within the interpersonal relationships. The **spiritual** dynamics include belief systems and transcendent atmospheres in which the family may be involved. These elements will appear at many levels in family relationships, especially under the heading of religion.

Male/Female Relations

It is important to identify behaviors that can be considered "consistent" and "expected," and thus normative within the Mexican middle class family. In the discussion which follows it should be explicitly understood that many of the traditional family structures are changing. The descriptions given are not intended to be stereotypes. They do not fit all middle class members. Many variables, such as generational status, socio-economic status, upward mobility and social movements are contributing to diversity. The impact of these variables is causing intra-familial stresses and personal conflicts for family members.

One of the characteristics of the literature on the Mexican family is the rigid adherence to gender-appropriate behavior (Carrillo, 1982:255). One Mexican writer believes that these norms are the most rigid in the national culture (Penalosa, 1968:683). The concern here is to describe the way male/female relations are expressed and to understand the rationale behind them.

Dimensions of Sexuality

<u>Male/Female.</u> Carrillo provides us with a working definition of these terms. He defines Mexican males as proud, authoritarian, uncontrolled, vengeful when dishonored, possessive in relationships. The Mexican female is defined as protected, submissive in relation to the male, sexually pure and seen as vulnerable to seduction by the sexually aggressive male (Carrillo, 1982:255).

These sex roles are currently changing to the extent that both men and women are less insistent on the strict separation of these roles. For example, the sex role behavior of the "submissive female" has been impacted by the social movements for greater personal freedom of expression. As the process of urbanization increases more women will have greater opportunity of reaching economic independence from men who have nurtured and encouraged their submissiveness. Nevertheless, the sex roles do maintain a high degree of adherence to appropriate gender behavior expectations.

<u>Authoritarian Father and Male Supremacy.</u> From childhood male virility is encouraged by the stressing of courage to the point of aggressiveness, steadfastness and honor. Boys are taught never to run from a fight and to honor their word. These behaviors in turn are rewarded by compliance to

the father's wishes, nurturance by women and respect from others. From adolescence, and through his entire life, male virility will be measured "primarily, by sexual conquests, and secondarily, in terms of physical prowess in relation to other males" (Carrillo, 1982:256). Beneath the male's undisputed authority in the home, and in all other functions related to the female, is the fact that he is a man and is expected to conquer through his sexual powers.

All that has been said is embodied in the term machismo. Aramoni, a Mexican psychoanalyst, defines machismo as the expression of "exaggerated masculine characteristics ranging from male genital prowess to towering pride and fearlessness. It also is a specific counterphobic attitude toward women and of the anxieties of life and death" (Aramoni, 1972:69). The term macho emphasizes virility, but has a much wider meaning. It depicts a particular orientation to life that has the cult of virility as a central focus. This aspect is expressed by Stevens who observes that virility is characterized by exaggerated aggressiveness and intransigence in male-to-male relationships (Stevens, 1973:90).

Most Mexican males practice machismo to some degree. This is because it is culturally transmitted and practiced as "normative" behavior through the lengthy process of socialization. It must be noted, however, that all Mexican males do not practice machismo. A middle class friend of the writer who lives in Mexico City could not identify at all with this concept, but it is interesting and encouraging to note that he is a third generation Christian. Rincon notes that machismo has both positive and negative results which tend to cancel each other (1973: 17). It is significant that when speaking of machismo the Mexican male identifies with the positive aspects. When the Mexican female talks about machismo she refers to the negative aspects.

Authority and male supremacy are fostered through child rearing practices from birth. In fact the behavior is fostered preceding birth through a set of highly valued expectations of a male child. Female infants have merit in the family following several male infants. The merit in such cases is seen from a utilitarian perspective, in that the girl may assist the mother in serving the fathers and brothers. In turn the girl is protected by male family members. It is not uncommon for a husband, whose wife has given birth only to girls, to seek other sexual partners by which he can fulfill his manhood by having a son.

Role Expectations of the Male. The child must grow up to fill the dignified role of a man. He must refrain from any demonstration of feminine interests. Such would meet with disapproval by older brothers, certainly the father and mother as well. Boys are discouraged from participating in activities which might be interpreted as "submissive" and unmanly, such as helping in the house. Household chores have traditionally been identified as female roles and boys are to be little men, coming and going as they please, accepting responsibilities and preparing to accept their adult roles as authority figures. Therefore they are never to show weakness, and must always strive to keep self-control. They are taught to expect females to attend to most of their physical needs. In short, males are prepared from birth to avoid anything which might undermine their roles as men and the male-supremacy role of father.

The role of the father remains, ideally, sole breadwinner and absolute master of his household. Being the provider requires that he spend long hours outside the home, making him a virtual stranger to the family activities. He is not open to the idea of his wife leaving the house, except for short periods, for work or for education. In spite of his outward bravado, he feels inwardly dependent in ways he cannot express openly, due to cultural expectations. For this reason he wants his wife to be available when he leaves, calls on the phone or returns home. If she is not present he becomes suspicious, feels abandoned or has his needs left unsatisfied. Such role changes threaten him.

Female Role Expectations. The role expectation of the middle class woman is in the home, first that of her father, then in that of her husband. She is expected to care for the household, the educating of the children and in general to make life pleasant for the male. In practice the principle is only partially fulfilled. It is least fully maintained in the modern families at the upper and middle class levels.

In general there is a clear-cut role distinction between the responsibilities of males and females. Otero found that 25% of marriages have an egalitarian approach, while 75% continue traditional separation (1968:146). Presently, it is safe to say that both men and women are less insistent upon strict separation of sex roles. They do, however, seem to agree definitely on respect for authority and relatively strict child rearing practices.

Hembrismo or Marianismo is the female counterpart to machismo. Examination of this phenomenon will greatly illumine our understanding of the role of the woman. Hembrismo or Marianismo means "the dominance of the self-sacrificing mother over the family by a balance of dependence and affection" (Stevens, 1973:91). The roles of machismo and hembrismo are reciprocal roles that call for one role to be matched by the motives and expectations of the other. In this way it is possible to predict with some degree of accuracy the effect of one's behavior on the other.

Stevens believes that marianismo is as prevalent as machismo, but far less understood by Mexicans. She uses the term to mean "the cult of feminine spiritual superiority, which teaches that women are semi-divine, morally superior to and spiritually stronger than men" (1973:91). In essence it is a set of beliefs and practices related to the position of women in society. Hembrismo is an amplification of the characteristics considered to be feminine, that is, semi-divinity, moral superiority and spiritual strength (Stevens, 1973:94). Spiritual strength provides an infinite capacity for humility and sacrifice. No self-denial is too great. She is submissive to the demands of men: husbands, sons, fathers and brothers.

In spite of this high ideal which embodies desirable feminine qualities, this writer believes that in reality the Mexican woman resents her assigned role of submissiveness and sacrifice.

The middle class Mexican woman is seldom troubled, as is her American counterpart, by personal identity. She knows who she is because she retains her individuality after marriage by merely taking her husband's name onto hers and passing both to the children. When the husband indulges in infidelity, as the machismo norm expects him to do, prejudice in favor of the woman guarantees her community support.

In respect to a working mother, marianismo serves notice to her employer that nobody has the right to ask a mother to neglect a sick child. Granting of sick leave to the mother of a sick child is a matter of employer's duty to respect the sacredness of motherhood.

FAMILY ATTITUDES AND BEHAVIORS

Marriage

Marriage is considered to be a religious-legal contract. This implies a special interpersonal and emotional process. The religious-legal contract is a solemn and explicit code. The legal contract is a civil or state requirement. The religious ceremony is held at the church and is the one socially recognized. The personal and emotional agreement made between the two participants may or may not be put into words or shared with one another. Their expectations are really submerged and often unspoken, making it a complex matter to study marriage in this setting. Even here change is occurring.

The legal contract does not change. It remains the same. But the interpersonal and emotional process is constantly being modified and at different stages of the life cycle. One example is the birth of the first child, hopefully a son, which brings a new set of expectations, needs, use of time and energy. The result is fundamental changes in the structure of the marriage relationship. The same is true as other children are born.

The period between the ceremony and the firm establishment of the home is often difficult particularly because of the difficulty of one or both parties to separate physically and emotionally from the family of origin. It is most common that young men and women customarily remain in the family home until marriage, allowing no transitional period of separation from parents. The result is that the couple has divided loyalties as it struggles to adjust in the areas of roles, values, functions, emotions and physical contacts as a basis for their new life together. A great deal of fighting often accompanies this period, in which feelings become intense. Often the fighting is passive, verbalized as one way, but actually acted out in a form of denial. Ongay contends that there needs to be a more democratic and flexible approach to roles and functions during this time to maintain a sense of equilibrium within the system that can be supportive in the working out of the adjustments to married life (Ongay, 1980:16).

Sex in the Family

The traditional education of children includes sexual repression. Sexual curiosity and stimulation are aspects that are not permitted in the family and are punished. The family in Mexico continues this line of thinking and attitude. The underlying reason of this attitude is the supposition that children are sexless creatures (Ongay, 1980:30). Any sexual interest on the child's part will therefore be quickly reprimanded, creating an imprint of repression. In the Mexican family constant pressure is placed on the child to contain himself. This attitude is supported outside the family by the school and other institutions.

Sex at the time of puberty is not only considered dirty and wrong, it is something that must not be discussed. Virginity in the adolescent girl must be protected. To the boy it is something to conquer. Thus, a double standard exists between boys and girls. Sex education is not seriously practiced and contraceptive methods are not fully accepted by the parents as useful and legitimate.

At adulthood and with matrimony the woman is permitted a sexual life, but as the years pass, sex is viewed as dirty, sinful, prohibited and dangerous (Ongay, 1980:33). While it is admitted that sex and attitudes toward it are relative, it does seem to be viewed by some women as a form of torture, or at best of limited pleasure.

The male view of sexual pleasure involves a woman other than his wife, especially after the birth of his children. To a man, sexual life in a woman is associated with a prostitute and is not suitable for the mother of his children. Trust between husband and wife is threatened when the wife is seen by other men as being sexually desirable.

Discipline

The primary form of discipline used by parents is intimidation and shame. This is manifest in the use of insulting language, threatenings, spankings and gesticulations designed to get results. The motive is to produce fear and to keep control. Parents also control by producing shame in the children. If a child's behavior is not as expected, parents shame him by telling him that he is no good or ugly. This inhibits the child from expressing himself freely. Parents, according to Ongay, notice only the wrong behaviors of the child, but seldom express appreciation for right actions (1980:23-24). Certainly it should not go unnoticed that more emphasis needs to be directed to the positive and accomplishment side of behavior than on the negative and non-success of the child. Failure to do so impairs the development of self-worth.

Communication in the Family

Verbalization is not a highly developed art within the Mexican culture (Ongay, 1980:28). Expressions of this are manifest in many different ways within the family life. Early in life the child learns that if his parents suspect he has done something which is prohibited his best recourse is to be untruthful. Truth telling brings punishment, while silence or lying avoids it. The child is severely punished for lying. But if a child catches his parents lying, the parents resort to an irrational affirmation of authority. This contributes to the system of values learned by the child. A priority in life is to avoid being hurt, which is accomplished by silence or lying.

Part of the family tradition is to keep children shielded from family problems. Parents discuss these in the privacy of the bedroom. Exclusion from such talk merely causes the child to be suspicious and to act out his fantasies, never really knowing what is happening.

Secrecy is an institution within the Mexican family (Ongay, 1980:29). It can best be understood as a psychological operation to avoid unpleasant events. It hopes to achieve the magical process of preserving family stability. Its prevalence, though, has many ramifications and in the end may cause emotional instability.

Birth in the Family

There is a great sense of expectation when a child is about to be born. If the child is a girl, parents find consolation by rationalization. Little girls, they reason, are loving and give less problems to their mother. This apparent acceptance is not actual, for in reality the girl is basically rejected.

Boys are of greater importance, especially those with light complexions. It is important to the family and causes a great deal of fantasy in early life. Such expectations are assimilated and internalized by the children. At times these expectations are verbalized in joke form or casual comments by parents, and the child feels that he does not fulfill either his parents or society's ideals.

Following birth, the care and nurture of the baby is delegated to the mother, with the grandmother playing a significant secondary role. The grandmother traditionally teaches the young mother to care for the baby.

The first baby causes internal stresses within the family, creating a distance between husband and wife. During courtship and early marriage the woman was treated as a woman. Before the birth of the first child she had a definite sexual attraction for the male, but at birth that is reduced. The mother begins to lose importance as a woman and is viewed by the husband as the mother of his children, rather than as his wife. Consequently, the mother totally dedicates herself to rearing the children for the rest of her life. The birth of the last child is equally stressful, but for a different reason. It brings frustration and anxiety to the mother because it is the end of all that has exemplified her purpose in life.

When children leave home the mother attempts to remain intimately tied to them. Because of her total dedication to motherhood and lack of formal preparation for other pursuits, she is left at loose ends.

Death in the Family

In the case of both birth and death, the information given to family members, especially to children, is limited. Knowledge about the beginning and ending of life is hidden and mystified. Children see the emotional state of adults at death, but receive little information which would allow them to participate in the event. They are left with torment on the one hand and silence on the other. Any need on the child's part to cry must be done in secret for he is not supposed to know what is happening. To question adults at this time is futile for they evade confrontation, rationalizing their action as protecting the mind of the child. While the adult lives out the hurt and the loss, the child lives in the dark.

Death is especially traumatic if it involves the head of the household. At this time the family system is extremely vulnerable. There exists in the family a delicate balance which makes it possible for husband and wife to function. The father knows little of what goes on in the home, and the wife knows little about what goes on outside it. At death the equilibrium is tipped and a crisis exists. If the husband dies the wife may cease to be aware of what is happening around her and find it difficult to live without her husband. The man finds it equally difficult to function without the wife because his socialization makes it hard for him to express the affection that gives emotional security to the children.

Since life and death are interminable processes within the family, all members need to be knowledgeable and to participate fully in its expression when it occurs. The mother should not be expected to cease being a sexually responsive women, nor should the man who expresses affection to his children be seen as less manly.

Divorce

The attitude of many towards divorce is to deny the possibility or to act as though it did not occur. The 1975 UN Demographic Book declares that the annual divorce rate in Mexico is a mere .024 percent. The 1980 Census of Mexico states only .5 percent of Mexicans have ever obtained a divorce. Reasons for the increase in the rate of divorce might be: 1) an increasing disregard for the church teaching among the middle class; 2) more tolerance found in the urban centers; and 3) women beginning to express their freedom from the subservient roles and double standards imposed by men. The relative small divorce rate does not reveal the whole picture, for there are scores of husbands who leave their wives without benefit of divorce, and there are many more marriages which remain intact in name only. The majority of divorce proceedings are initiated by men, but recently there is an increase in women filing, another indication of the weakening autocratic role of the male.

Social consequences of divorce are severe, often isolating divorcees from social gatherings; but the cosmopolitan attitude of the urban setting may modify such effects. Even though the marriage may not be working, divorce seldom occurs. The woman may refuse it on religious grounds, while the man may not consider divorce because of career ramifications. It is noteworthy that when infidelity of the male occurs, the female maintains family and community respect only if she assumes the posture of martyr. Any attempt to expose the man will bring universal reproach on her.

Professionals

It is well to repeat here that those fitting into the opening vistas permitting work outside the home are the modern families at the upper and middle class levels, and the provincial and metropolitan lower class. The latter encourage women to work out of economic necessity.

Occupations which are found desirable are those which have been traditionally viewed as sex appropriate. The desired occupations for women are those which display the ideal of self-sacrifice and service. On the other hand, men desire the jobs which reward by advancement, assertiveness and hard work.

There is a growing tendency for middle class women to work outside the home. This creates some tensions both professionally and personally. Antoni comments, "There is a confusion with roles. Mexican men are used to being gallant, the conqueror, the seductor. They are not used to dealing with women on a work level, where they have to take them seriously" (1982:18).

One factor contributing to rapid absorption of women into professional ranks is educational advance. The female enrollment in Mexican universities has increased from 19% in 1960 to 26% today. Women university graduates are expected to have higher degrees than men to get equal jobs.

Two conclusions seem apparent: 1) traditional attitudes about work among middle class women are breaking down; and 2) women moving into the work force can expect professional competition both at work and at home. With urbanization a continuing fact, more and more women will enter the professions becoming more economically active and less economically dependent on the male.

THE FAMILY AND INTERPERSONAL RELATIONSHIPS

In Mexican family relationships the key attitude is harmony through cooperation. Competition among its members poses a threat to this harmony. For example, it is unthinkable that brothers should play on opposing soccer teams or that a family member should embrace a non-Catholic tradition within a Catholic family setting.

Strong emphasis is put on the development, maintenance and enrichment of interpersonal relationships. The Mexican does not hesitate to use contacts among his relationships and such use is understood to be reciprocal.

There are a number of ways in which interpersonal relationships are developed. Social gestures such as friendliness, romanticism and sentimentality are common, and there is a deep appreciation for light-heartedness and humor in conversation. The people touch freely, laugh together, sing and assist each other in needs. Closely linked to the appreciation for interpersonal relationships is the respect for affiliation, affection and the need for belonging to a large network of family and friends. This network requires life-long commitment which includes others in a variety of situations. The need for these relationships is expressed in the conversation, contact, caring and presence at times of death, illness or similar difficult life situations.

FAMILY IDEOLOGY

Ideology is a set of more or less systematized beliefs and values. Kraft says, "A people's ideology provides the integrating core of their culture -- the "glue" that holds all the rest together" (1979:305). Ideology embraces the core assumptions, values and allegiances of a people. In regard to the Mexican middle class family three aspects will be discussed: loyalty, values and religion.

Loyalty

Loyalty is an expectation of all family members. A family member must be in basic accord with the values and rules of the group. The family places great emphasis on this process because of its concern for balance. The father expects his son to repeat the expectations imposed upon him by his father. If he does not, he meets with disapproval. Independence, privacy and individuality have little relevance within the family system. Far more important than these is loyalty from all members toward the group for which the family works hard to achieve. Mothers and sons maintain a loyalty which excludes the father. Loyalty to the extended family is also of great importance, but often creates conflict between husband and wife.

While absolute loyalty is expected from the wife in the marriage relationship, the same is not required of the husband. Because his primary loyalty always remains the original family, a betrayal of his wife, in his thinking, is justified. This is a unique dynamic in Mexican culture by which he dismisses guilt feelings.

The woman on the other hand resolves this dilemma by paying **his** generational debt. All her internal values are transferred to the children. In this way she makes up for the needed loyalty to the original family. Loyalty of the mother toward the children is important, almost ritualistic. In many ways it is similar to the unfaithfulness of the husband toward her.

Values[1]

A value is any concept referring to a desirable or undesirable state of affairs (Spradley and McCurdy, 1975:471). Values are mental conceptions, and it is impossible to observe them directly. The importance of learning family values, which is done indirectly, is that they enable us to interpret many specific actions and to fit them into larger patterns of the culture.

Nida gives a general listing of core values applicable to the Mexican family. They are: personal dignity, kinship ties, stratification of society, materialism, spiritual values, emotional expression, fatalism, a decent way of life and opposition to manual labor (1975:9). These values, together with authoritarianism (structured control of society from the "top"), individualism (personal reaction to status quo), and machismo (male dominance versus hembrismo or female dependence) form opposing sets (Nida, 1975:11).

Religion

Knowledge of the aspects of the religious ideology of the middle class affects communication more than any other single factor. Communication does not take place in a vacuum. Kraft has reminded us that "there are always ideological presuppositions, beliefs, understandings and concepts in the minds of the participants which pervade the presentation and the reception of the communication (1979:304).

The 1980 Census lists 89.4% of all Mexicans as religiously affiliated with Catholicism. In terms of the middle class this ought not to lead to the conclusion that religion profoundly affects their lives. Many have rejected Catholicism outright, while others are only nominal adherents.

Noteworthy from the same census is the fact that 6.1% of Mexicans declare no religious preference or claim to be without religion. It is not inconceivable that a partial explanation for this rising percentage of those without religion represents a new movement among the middle class to reject traditional Catholicism. They are included among the "neo-pagan" socio-cultural segment of society.[2] They are persons who have lost all or almost all contact with the Gospel. An increasing number are openly declaring themselves non-Christian. Others continue to call themselves Christian, but their connection with the faith is little more than intellectual acceptance. Their lives, at the deepest levels, are untouched by the Gospel.

Also among the middle class are undoubtedly many who have a profound religious conscience, but it is questionable that this conscience is the result of a meaningful contact with the Gospel. It is not unfair to state that the majority of these have had no experience of the Cross. They represent a special challenge to church planters, yet little study has been directed to them. The task, then, is to find the "neo-pagans" who are totally alienated from God as well as the nominal adherents who are confused about God, and to take them along the road toward new life in Christ and to enthusiastic discipleship.

It would be incorrect to conclude that the Catholic Church has lost all influence among the middle class. While it has experienced a growing exodus, it continues to exercise moderately strong influence. Catholicism maintains its strongest influence in the rural areas and among the more traditionally oriented. Its influence cannot be ignored even among the middle class, many of whom look to the church for important life ceremonies. These rites have traditionally been closely associated with the church but show signs of becoming more social than religious. This is not to deny that the church has no prominent role within the family. The church is still the main instructor of religious, cultural and traditional values. The general population still desires the church's blessing.

According to the 1980 Census over 800,000 in the Mexico City area declared no religious preference or religion. The weakening is most noticeable among the affluent. The primary reason is the result of urbanization accompanied by its undermining of the value system. The middle class is becoming increasingly caught up in the secularization process. The pursuit of wealth and status has, in many cases, become the religion of the family. The media has contributed greatly to this trend. The constant portrayal of elegant lifestyles is aimed at appealing to the materialistic desires of the middle class. Family television programs portray a hedonistic lifestyle that excludes God altogether. These values are echoed by the movies and television shows which come from the United States. Young people are now beginning to mimic the "sacred values" of their neighbors to the north.

NEUROSIS AND THE FAMILY

Neurosis producing factors are related to role expectations within the family. The individual's failure or inability to conform to the sex-role standards is a primary source of neurosis.

Conflicts prevalent among males are: 1) submission/assertion and compliance/rebellion in the area of authority; 2) preoccupation and anxiety regarding sexual potency; 3) conflict and ambivalence regarding the need for role consistency at all times; and 4) isolation and depression because of his inaccessibility as a "man who never breaks or falters." Generally speaking, symptomatic behavior emerges in relation to problems associated with one's sex role and identity.

Female conflicts are related to the double moral and social standard displayed in the male's behavior. Failure to line up to these standards leads to feelings of failure, depression and repressed anger.

THE FAMILY AS A THERAPEUTIC GROUP

At times of emergency reference is first made to the extended family. If a loan is needed, a baby born, a job lost, a divorce secured, the family becomes money lender, job seeker and marriage counselor. Whatever the type of emotional crisis or unbalance, the family comes to the rescue. It immediately intervenes without question. The family tries to get the situation back into equilibrium. The family is concerned with the emotional stability of its members. The primary interest is to maintain that stability within the family and in the outside world.

The Mexican family is group oriented. It does not focus on the individual. Decisions are made in behalf of the group as a whole. The individual is not permitted to impose his will on the group. The group decides collectively where an individual member will study, what friends are acceptable and even the hairstyle that is appropriate. Tension is an expected part of the family system. As tension increases so does the family togetherness. It is only when the tension reaches excess that it is viewed as a disintegrating factor, and thus alerts the family to the need to apply the necessary methods to restore the family cohesiveness. Whatever the crisis, it must be relieved and order restored.

In a system of loyalty and expectation such as exists in the Mexican family it is essential to have equilibrium in the system. The family system is integrative and therapeutic. In the Mexican family education, health and sexual selection are still functions of the family. In such a system there are many aspects that help maintain equilibrium in the lives of its individual members. However, due to its traditional and conservative character that system sometimes restricts the process of individual creativity and autonomy.

A healthy, functioning family is a family that lives in the present yet does not deny its past, but at the same time thinks of the future. It has the capabilities of adapting to and using new information provided by science and technology. It allows for the personal achievement of its members in addition to those of the group. It promotes differences as an acceptable trait and admits and promotes mobility; mixture of races; and customs (Ongay, 1980:69).

There are occasions when the family, in itself, is not able to function in ways that deal with crises and bring about needed change in destructive conduct. Examples of such situations are learning disabilities, delinquency, management of difficult children or marital problems. It is then that an acceptable option is to defer to family therapy in which a psychologist can help the family to help itself. The family as a system has the structure to reach out to family members and help them deal with almost any kind of problem. The new trend is the employment of family therapy as opposed to individual therapy in those cases which are beyond the capability of the family to meet.

THE MEXICAN FAMILY FACING CHANGE

According to Ongay the middle class has the capacity for instituting change, but lacks the will to do so (1980:81). Those who have the education and vision to introduce new forms of family life are not generally men of action. Lacking the motivation to take risks, it is preferable to copy or imitate something else rather than change. This fits the generalization of Carrillo that the typical way the Mexican resolves problems is "by modifying the person rather than modifying the social environment" (1982:261).

Irrespective of whether or not the family is motivated to plan and introduce changes in family norms, there are forces of change relentlessly at work which affect the thinking, acting, values and customs of the family. Like it or not, the contemporary family form is changing, and indeed it must in order to fit the demands of contemporary living. Some of the most obvious changes confronting the middle class family are:

1. A shifting from the extended family to the nuclear family.
2. Increasing mobility, weakening extended family ties.
3. Increasing participation by the family in making choices and carrying out responsibilities.
4. The family now shares many of its functions with other institutions so that it has a more specialized function.
5. The continuing effect of secularization.
6. The changing attitude toward women entering professional roles.
7. The increasing tension focusing on the male/female roles and their functions in the family.

There have been both gains and losses for the family members in the midst of these changes. The urban family cannot provide the individual with his job, protect him from outside pressures, nor propel him into an established set of religious patterns. Yet the family remains the basic institution of society which gives being to the individual, cares for him, gives him an individual personality and teaches him to adjust to the larger society. The home continues to serve as the center for emotional satisfaction, moral guidance and psychological security. The home is not the tightly interlocked network that it traditionally was, and is, therefore, freer to help individuals absorb the stresses and strains produced in the less personalized parts of everyday living.

The changes and their effects on the middle class family also suggest some matters to which the church planter should give careful concern:

1. The Mexican family needs help in re-orienting its value system to meet the complex pressures of the social situation. This means teaching from God's word so that family members can select and implement values and norms as a standard for their behavior.
2. Parents need Bible teaching in parenting and role modeling to help family members live through the stressful life cycle.

3. There is need to be alert constantly to felt needs within the family. When discovered, efforts should be made to give guidance that will strengthen the home and offer help which will enable individuals to meet the points of strain and tension which they face.

NOTES

[1] Diaz-Guerrero, psychiatrist and professor, has provided some practical studies on middle class values (1976). The reader is referred to these studies to more fully understand middle class Mexican values.

[2] I am utilizing Visser't Hooft's term "neo-pagan" (1974:81-86).

BIBLIOGRAPHY

Akpem, Yosev Yima
    1983   A Family Life Education for the Church's Ministry to Urban Migrants in Nigeria. Ann Arbor: University Microfilms.

Antoni, Guadalupe Loazade
    1982   Untitled article in Mexico News, 7-19-82:18.

Aramoni, Aniceto
    1972   "Machismo." Psychology Today. 5:8:69-72.

Carrillo, Carmen
    1982   "Changing Norms of Hispanic Families," in Minority Mental Health, ed. by E. Jones and S. Korchin. New York: Praeger Special Studies.

Diaz-Guerrero, R.
    1975   Psychology of the Mexican: Culture and Personality. Austin: Univ. of Texas Press.

Galvin, Kathleen and Bernard Brommei
    1982   Family Communication: Cohesion and Change. Glenview: Scott, Foresman and Co.

Guernsey, Dennis B.
    1982   Notes from a Class Lecture, 2-16-82. Pasadena: Fuller Theological Seminary.

Kantor, David and William Lehr
    1975   Inside the Family. New York: Harper and Row.

Kraft, Charles H.
    1979   Communicating the Gospel God's Way. Pasadena: William Carey Library.

Minuchin, Salvador
    1974   Family and Family Therapy. Cambridge: Harvard Univ. Press.

Nida, Eugene A.
    1975   Understanding Latin Americans. Pasadena: William Carey Library.

Ongay, Mario
    1980   "La Familia de las Classes Medias en Mexico," in Revista Mexicana de Ciencias Politicos y Sociales. 25-26:98-99:5-81.

Otero, Luis Lenero
    1968   Investigacion De La Familia En Mexico. Mexico City: Instituto Mexicano De Estudios Sociales.

Penalosa, F.
    1968   "Mexican Family Roles." Journal of Marriage and Family. 30:680-689.

Rincon, Bernice
    1973   "La Chicana." Regeneracion. 1:10.

Spradley, James P. and David McCurdy
    1975   Anthropology: The Cultural Perspective. New York: John Wiley and Sons.

Stevens, Evelyn P.
    1973   "Marianismo: The Other Face of Machismo in Latin America," in Female and Male in Latin America, ed. by Ann Pescatello. Pittsburgh: Univ. of Pittsburgh Press. 89-100.

Visser't Hooft, W.
    1974   "Evangelism in the Neo-Pagan Situation." International Review of Mission. 63:249:81-86.

Yorburg, Betty
    1973   The Changing Family. New York: Columbia Univ. Press.

10

A Maasai Purification Ceremony

by Doug Priest Jr.

In the letter to the church at Philippi Paul tells us that Jesus left His home in glory to come to earth "in the likeness of men" (Phil. 2:7). The apostle followed the example of the Master and became as a Jew to the Jews, (so as to win the Jews); as one under the law to those under the law, (that he might win those under the law); as one outside the law to those outside the law, (that he might win those outside the law). He became "all things to all men" that by all means they might be saved (I Cor. 9:20-22).

If we would seek to model our missionary efforts after Jesus and after the Apostle Paul then we too should strive to be at one with those to whom we are sent. Such an attempt is costly; one must in a sense die to one's own culture and way of doing things. One must take the time and the strenuous effort to learn the language and the culture, to eat foreign food, to learn another way of greeting and another people's history and values, as well as myriads of other details. Incarnational evangelism, the embodying of oneself in another culture, is the goal of the missionary. Jesus was so much like the people He sought to reach that most of them did not even realize He was the Son of God.

Setting about to learn the culture of the host society is a missionary imperative. Luzbetak says, "Missionary effectiveness has always gone hand in hand with immersion in local culture" (1970:3). He goes on to add that before the missionary "sets out to change the world he should first study it with detachment" (1970:8). It follows that such a study cannot be completed in a period of weeks or even months, but is a continual process. For these reasons and others the study of cultural anthropology is crucial for those desiring to work in other cultural contexts. Anthropology is simply the study of man -- man in the totality of his activities, thoughts and relationships with others. With the aid of anthropological study one is better equipped to understand man in his various contexts. The missionary who has studied anthropology will have developed a healthy respect for the ways of other peoples. He will better be able to see and deal with his own ethnocentrism. He will have learned techniques for discovering the cohesion of another culture. And most important for missionaries is that the study of anthropology "provides a means of effective communication" (Nida, 1974:310).

To work in another culture without knowing that culture is highly presumptuous. It is not an exaggeration to say that the bulk of missionary heartaches result from an inadequate understanding of the culture of those with whom he or she works. Costly mistakes are made due to an insufficient understanding of the behavior of the people. Luzbetak reminds us that "it would be difficult to find a missionary who would in his right mind claim that he could give adequate spiritual guidance -- without a proper grasp of the mentality of his flock" (1970:8).

Advice is given to those who seek to plant churches in a cross-cultural situation by the veteran missionary-anthropologist Tippett. He says that:

> 1. Those who plant churches across cultures should do so in the terms of those cultures.
>
> 2. Those who engage in cross-cultural church-planting should preserve as many of the indigenous forms as possible.
>
> 3. They should explore the need for functional substitutes.
>
> 4. They need to safeguard the faith against the incorporation of pagan beliefs (Tippett,1969: 146-153).

To fulfill any of these objectives assumes that a thorough knowledge of the host culture has been gained.

Doug Priest Jr.

As one comes to understand another society, he sees that God has not left Himself without a witness in that culture (Acts 14:17). Rather, among every people are those **stepping-stones** upon which the missionary can trod to facilitate Gospel witness and teaching. It behooves all engaged in cross-cultural witness to search for such redemptive analogies. But, to repeat, such can only be discovered through diligent study of the culture.

The paradox of the adoption process, whereby a missionary seeks to identify with another culture, is that complete identification is never possible. Outsiders are limited in their attempts to be all things to all men. Better to admit that one will never be completely Maasai; in my case, among other reasons, because my mother and father are Americans.

WHO ARE THE MAASAI?

On the savanna plains of Kenya and Tanzania in East Africa live the Maasai, a tribe of semi-nomadic cattle herders. Numbering perhaps as many as half a million, the Maasai along with the Samburu, Arusha, Njemps and the Baraguyu all speak the Maa language. Theirs is a life which revolves around their cattle along with smaller herds of sheep and goats. In earlier days the Maasai depended solely on their animals for food and clothing. The main part of the diet was milk supplemented occasionally with meat. Their comfortable homes are simple constructions of woven leaves and branches covered by cow manure with the beds being made of dried cow-hides.

The Maasai tribe is made up some sixteen or seventeen separate sub-tribes. Each sub-tribe has its own geographical area of residence, its own variations in ritual and marriage practices and its own unique style of ornamentation. During the 16th. through the early 20th. centuries the Maasai were a strongly united tribe who plagued her neighbors. The travelogues and missionary journals are full of tales of the ferocity of the Maasai. Their geographical spread was from central Tanzania to southern Sudan. But due to drought, smallpox and inter-tribal warfare their numbers and influence in East Africa began to decrease.

Today in Kenya and Tanzania the Maasai are attempting to come to terms with the modernization process, something that they have cared little for in the past decades. The traditional disdain of education and agriculture has given way to primary schools throughout Maasailand and the beginnings of cultivation efforts. Almost every village has at least one member who has completed primary school or who is employed in the city. Adult literacy, clinics, stores, veterinary medicine, a growing dependence on other foods and small-scale development projects are all part of the scene of present day Maasai culture. All of these innovations reflect an openness to change that was not present even fifteen or twenty years ago.

A Brief Note on Maasai Worldview

The Maasai view the world as being made up of God; the earth which includes plants, trees and inanimate objects; the Maasai people themselves; cattle; sheep and goats; the other animals and all other people. This cosmology is diagrammed in Figure One.

MAASAI WORLDVIEW

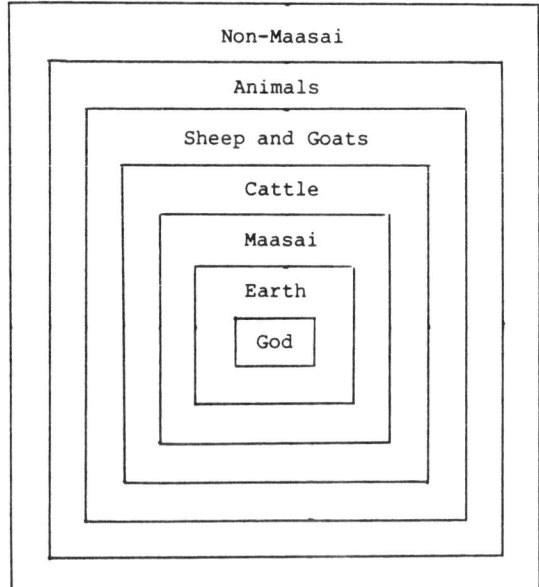

Figure One

God is seen as the Creator of the world. He is Almighty and All-knowing. The Maasai say in a proverb, "There is not anything that God does not know." He is called "The Wide One." God is also termed "He who is both Far and Near." God is associated with good, but He can also display His anger, as especially noted during storms. Healing comes from God. He is the provider who gives life as well as the one who brings death.

The earth is the work of God. Mountains are sacred places where one goes to be near God. The term God, **Enkai**, is synonymous with both "sky" and "rain," though these are God's manifestations and do not limit God to being simply a Sky God. God shows His attributes through the colors of black and red. When the sky is black and rain is soon forthcoming the Maasai say that God is good. But when the sky is red as in the middle of the dry season the Maasai say God is angry and far away.

The world contains grass which is one of God's most precious gifts. God also gives trees and plants to the Maasai. These are used for medicinal purposes, in rituals and in a variety of everyday uses around the village such as in fences and for food storage.

God created the cattle and gave them to the Maasai, who are the real owners of all the cattle in the world. Cattle raiding is seen as rightfully getting back what God gave the Maasai in the beginning. The cattle are used for food in the form of milk, meat and blood. Cows also provide leather, manure, sinews for thread, horns for containers, etc. Cattle are seen as the most important single item in the Maasai worldview.

The Maasai are very close to God. God blessed the Maasai by giving them life and everything they need to live, including sheep and goats for food besides cattle. All other animals are "friends" of the Maasai. It is a sin to be cruel or to kill animals except in cases of self-defense, protection of the herds or to prove the prowess of the warriors.

Maasai myths see the tribe arising out of the valley called Kerio and assuming a pastoral way of life. Those who did not escape had to rely on agriculture to exist. Non-Maasai are called foreigners or "Those who do not know God." A different word describes other people as enemies, that term being defined as "one who does not drink milk."

While the world, the Maasai, cattle, sheep and goats are close to God, the other animals and the non-Maasai are more distant from Him. The relation between the various components of this worldview can also be expressed in the following chain: God -- rain -- grass -- cattle -- milk -- Maasai. God gives the rain which makes the grass grow and become green. This grass is then eaten by the cattle who in turn produce milk to feed the Maasai.

This brief sketch of the Maasai worldview can be seen to include the philosophical categories of self and other, classification and causality, space and time, and to a certain extent values.

THE OLKITENG' LOO LBAA CEREMONY

The Maasai, like any other people, have numerous rites of passage throughout their lives whereby they move from one status to another. One such rite is called the Olkiteng' loo lbaa ceremony. The phrase literally means the "Ox of Wounds," because an ox is sacrificed so that the celebrant may be purified by God. A lengthy account of the ceremony can be found in Voshaar (1979:218-252), while both Mol and Sankan offer brief descriptions; (Mol, 1978:37) and (Sankan, 1971:36-38). The following description of the ritual includes my observations made at several ceremonies I was invited to attend while in Kenya between 1979 and 1983.

The major function of the ceremony is to do away with "the wounds and injuries, possibly sins, which one has caused to society and to individuals" (Mol, 1978:37). In Maasai culture adolescent boys and girls are circumcised, but before a married man is able to perform this important ceremony for his children, he must be purified. The cleansing of the father comes about from the "ox of the wounds" ceremony. Voshaar says,

> The changes a man undergoes during this period of his life are dramatized during this ceremony. There is a mock beating between the man and his wife, a mock-fight between the men and the women present and a beating of the cows by the man. The wounds of olkiteng' loo lbaa refer directly to the "wounds" that result from those beatings (Voshaar, 1979:219).

In order to perform the ceremony several obligations must be met. The celebrant's first wife, who will assist in the ritual activities, must be properly married -- all of the bridewealth must have been delivered to her parents' home. Sankan further notes that, "A man may not perform this ritual before his elder brothers have paid up all their bride-prices and therefore married their wives permanently" (1971:36).

Preparation for the ceremony is made by the celebrant, his family and the other members of the homestead. The man secures a special ox if he does not have an appropriate one in his own herd. The ox to be sacrificed must be holy; it must be either black with white markings on its underside, dark brown, brown, mottled white or whitish gray. The horns of the animal must point upwards rather than out or downwards. The celebrant also sees that honey and sugar are available for brewing into honey-beer which is consumed at the ceremony.

The women of the homestead prepare for the ceremony by brewing beer, washing their clothes, preparing special garments for the celebrant, doing beadwork which will be worn for the occasion, gathering firewood, hauling water and preparing snuff (powdered tobacco) which is given to the visitors.

At the beginning of the three-day event, the village appeals to God to bless the celebration. God is asked to keep troubles away, especially those troubles associated with drunkenness, such as arguing and fighting. Several men of the ritual-expert clan perform this ceremony with the celebrant overseeing their work. A small gourd containing magic powder -- special plants which have been dried and ground into a fine powder -- is brought, along with a pointed branding iron and a calabash of beer. The men performing this ritual pour some powder into their hand and with their fingers draw a line across their forehead with the powder. A small hole is then dug in the celebrant's gateway by pushing the pointed branding iron into the soil. Powder is sprinkled into the hole. Prayers are said as a small plant is put into the hole on top of the powder. Some of the beer is poured into the hole which is then tapped as if planting the small plant. A similar exercise is then performed at each gateway of the village and finally in the entrance of the cattle pen. The prayers offered up at each gateway are given by the ritual-experts with the onlookers responding in agreement at the end of each phrase. The prayers, when translated into English, go something like this:

O God, defeat the words from the mouths of
    trouble-makers.
Give us cows. Give us children. Give us women.
Give us birth in the daytime and at night.
Give us a long life and the blessings of the
    'fertility' tree.
God, give us life.

The celebrant then makes himself a pair of leather sandals to be worn throughout the celebration. The sandals come from a cowhide given to him by his mother. The cow from which the hide came had to be holy, meaning that it had no deformities and was of a certain color.

The final activity of the first day occurs when the men are all brought together to be addressed. Each age-grade is given instructions. They are told where they will receive their beer and asked to behave throughout the ceremony in an orderly fashion. The celebrant tells the participants that he does not want any trouble to occur at the ceremony. The men are then divided up by age-grades and each group shares the honey-beer which it was given.

On the morning of the second day the celebrant is decorated with special attire. His head is smeared with a mixture of fat and red ochre. Ceremonial garments -- sheepskins decorated with intricate beadwork -- are put on as a cape over the man's back. These same skins are worn at weddings and circumcision ceremonies. The celebrant wears his sword as well as a specially made container for snuff. On his back hang a quiver of arrows which also contain the elements for making a fire. He has his bow with him as well.

The celebrant has previously chosen an age-mate to be his partner during the course of the ceremony. This partner has to be well respected and a man who has not slept with the celebrant's wife on any previous occasion. The partner, as well as the celebrants wife, are also attired in ceremonial clothing. The wife's garments are worn as a skirt instead of a cape. She wears many beads and a new cloth which with she wraps herself as a dress. The partner and the wife each have their hair smeared with red ochre. Throughout the celebration the partner does not leave the side of the man being purified. And after the ceremony is completed the partner will be given a heifer by the celebrant. From that day forward they will greet each other affectionately.

When the celebrant and his partner finish these dressing preparations the men are formed into an assembly and all go into the forest. The special ox is driven ahead of the group until all reach a specified area. The site chosen is one situated between two wild olive trees, or if such trees are not found in the area, between two cordia ovalis trees (Mol, 1979:161). The celebrant and his partner sit at the base of one of the trees while the rest of the men prepare for the sacrifice. Branches with leaves need to be gathered and sticks and firewood collected. The celebrant and his partner watch the activities along with some of the men who are too old to do such strenuous work. The older men visit with the celebrant and his partner who pass around their gourds of beer and give out snuff to those who ask.

After the firewood is gathered a fire is kindled by members of the celebrant's father's age-grade, men he refers to as "Father." Cedar bark is shredded and used to catch the sparks from the spinning dowel-shaped piece of wood placed into a small hole on a flat piece of wood.

A gourd of milk with a matted grass stopper is brought and sprinkled onto the back of the ox. A prayer is uttered and the ox is killed. A knife is inserted into the back of the head to paralyze the animal whose throat is then cut. As the meat is removed from the animal it is placed on the branches with leaves to keep it off of the ground. After the bed of coals is ready the meat is roasted, not on the ends of sticks as is normally done, but on a grill made of small poles set over the fire. As the meat is finished it is set into two separate piles; one pile for the men and a smaller one for the women who will eat the meat in a different location. Only a few pieces of meat and fat are not roasted.

When all of the meat is cooked the man to be purified is given a new name. He is first addressed four times by a false name which he refuses to acknowledge. Then he is called four times by the acceptable name which he acknowledges. As he answers to his new name he is blessed:

> May you be blessed by this new name.
> May you be blessed with children and cattle.
> May you be helped.
> O God, bless this meeting. Bless our sub-tribe.
> Bless the Maasai. Bless the earth.
> Give us the blessing of the 'fertility' tree.

Next an enclosure is made by laying branches on the ground in the form of a circle and including the two trees. The name of this enclosure is the same word which is used to refer to the calf pen which is a part of all Maasai homes. Inside of this enclosure sit the celebrant, his partner, men from the celebrant's father's age-grade and those men who meet certain specifications: 1) they must have two good eyes; 2) they must have two testicles; 3) they may not have broken another man's bones; 3) they must have children; 4) they cannot be crippled; 5) they cannot have been cursed by their father; 6) they must not be illegitimate; and 7) they must not have had sex with married women prior to being circumcised.

While the meat is being roasted a kinsman of the celebrant goes into the forest, locates and brings back to the man being purified a stick. The stick will stay in the man's house for a few days and then will be used to beat his cows until the stick breaks. It will then be left in the middle of the cattle pen lying on the ground.

The roasted meat is then brought into the enclosure and placed in front of the man to be purified. Nobody will eat any of the meat until the man has eaten. A man from the celebrant's father's age-grade then holds up the roasted heart of the ox. This piece of meat is run up the bridge of the celebrant's nose and onto his forehead four different times. The celebrant then takes four bites of the meat proffered to him. He may not use his hands to hold the meat for the first bite, but can use them to assist him on the following ones. The ritual is accompanied by a blessing:

> May God help you.
> May you be able to take care of cattle.
> May you able to take care of your family.
> O God, bless the Maasai.
> May you be blessed with the blessing of the
>   'fertility' tree so that you do not die.
> May you be able to stand up like the trees.
> O God, defeat the words from the mouths of
>   trouble-makers and sorcerers.

The partner is also blessed in the same fashion. This rite is done four times, with a different piece of meat being used each time. The four pieces of meat used include the heart, a section of the upper foreleg, a piece from the chest and one from just outside of the rib-cage.

When this ritual feeding and blessing is done, the rest of the meat is divided and eaten by all present. The men eat with other members of their age-grade, each group sitting in a different area. The rites in the forest are open to all men, though some are not allowed to sit inside of the enclosed area.

After all of the appropriate meat is finished the bones are gathered up and thrown onto the fire with the exception of the breast-bone, which is put into the rafters of the celebrant's house. It will be kept there until he leaves that house to move into another one in a different homestead. The leaves that were used to keep the meat off of the ground and the branches used to make the enclosure are thrown onto the fire.

A long stick is split down the middle and a remaining piece of meat is put into the middle area. The two sections are then tied together, thus holding the meat which will be carried back to the homestead to be eaten in the evening. The first bites will again go to the celebrant and his partner before the rest of the piece is eaten by others.

As the fire is smoking from the wet leaves, the men form a procession and dance in a circle around the fire four times. They sing as they dance:

> I pray to the God of this earth, and I pray to the God of the Ilterito.
> I pray to the God of this earth, and I pray to Magilu.
> I pray to the wet season, and I pray to God.
> I pray to the God of this earth, and I pray to Mt. Kirim.
> I pray to the God of this earth, and I pray to the God of the Iltalala.

The song is actually a prayer to God that is sung. The words <u>Ilterito</u> and <u>Iltalala</u> are the names of age-grades of older men; the word <u>Magilu</u> is the name of a famous Maasai ritual-expert; and the word <u>Kirim</u> refers to a still-active volcano in Tanzania which can be translated into English from the Maasai as "the Mountain of God." While the Maasai know only one God, they believe that each age-grade has a unique relationship with Him, that ritual-experts have a special relationship with Him, and that He makes Himself known in the rumblings and the smoke of the active volcano.

After dancing around the fire the procession leaves the place of sacrifice. They walk single-file out into an open area where the married women have gathered and are singing while waiting. The men sing as they walk, and they also break off small slender branches to be used momentarily.

As the procession arrives where the women have gathered the celebrant and his mother sit on the stomach of the ox that was sacrificed. The man is again given his new name. As before, he does not reply to a false name but answers to his real new name, followed by the appropriate blessings. In this way the women can learn of the man's new name since it is inappropriate in Maasai custom to say one's own name. The celebrant's new name will be his for the remainder of his life, though it does not take the place of his other names.

The women are given their share of the roasted meat which has been cut into pieces for them. In a large ceremony each woman may only get a small piece or two of meat. If the women's portion of meat is not all eaten, it is carried back to the village to be eaten later.

The few pieces of meat and fat which were not cooked are brought to the center of the opening. They have been impaled on a stick which is set into the ground. The celebrant then takes a small branch and proceeds to playfully beat his wife. As the crowd sees this all of the men and women grab their slender branches and beat one another. A woman dashes up to the meat that is stuck on a stick in the ground and runs away with it to where other women "protect" her. But a "brave" man rushes into the flailing sticks and recovers the meat for the men's "side." This "stealing" of the meat goes on with each group claiming the meat several times. All the while men are "beating" women and the women are "beating" the men.

After a few minutes of the playful activity which all enjoy, the crowd begins to slowly walk back to the homestead, singing and dancing the entire way. A portion of one of the women's songs which was repeated over and over can be translated as saying:

> I pray to the blessed child of God,
>   who is mine.
> I pray and I praise the blessed child of God,
>   who is mine.[1]

As the group comes within sight of the homestead they are joined in their singing and dancing by the younger unmarried girls and warriors. The assembly is quite large now as it sings and dances.

The celebrant enters the village followed by the other men and women. The men are again divided into their age-grade and given honey-beer to drink. As evening approaches the man who has been purified and his wife stand by the entrance to the cattle-pen and bless the cows. Milk is sprinkled on the back of the cows as they pass through the entrance. The celebrant and his partner eat the piece of meat which has been saved for the evening meal. For the remainder of the night the men drink beer and sing songs of praise in honor of the celebrant.

On the following day the ceremony ends. The celebrant and his partner, who has not left his side throughout the entire ceremony, take off their ritual garments. If any beer is left, it is finished and the celebration comes to an end. The man catches up on his sleep and continues with his normal activities.

A BRIEF ANALYSIS OF THE CEREMONY

A detailed analysis of this ritual and its symbolic elements cannot be attempted here. It is appropriate, though, to discuss the ceremony under the theme of separation and unity. The major function of this ritual is purification. The celebrant seeks to be purified, to be made clean, to be united with God. He knows that his accumulated sins have separated him from his Creator. The "ox of the wounds" rite remedies this separation. The celebrant identifies with and is enjoined with the "holiness" of the ox, the "holiness" of those inside of the circle and the holiness of God. His sins are taken away, not by a slaughtered ox or through strict adherence to ritualistic detail, but by God who created the ox and gave the ceremony.

The purification resulting from the celebration also unites the man with his family. The rite occurs preparatory to a man's circumcising his children. A requirement of sponsoring such circumcision ceremonies is that the father be purified. This unification with the family involves the relationship of the man to his parents if they are still living, the man to his siblings, to his wife or wives, and to his children. There are rituals during the ceremony designed to strengthen each of these primary relationships.

During the ceremony the man is blessed in the center of the forest by members of his father's age-grade. When he comes out of the forest and into the clearing where the women are waiting, he receives a new name while sitting on the bloated stomach of the slaughtered ox with his mother. When the procession arrives back at the homestead he takes his seat in front of one of his wive's houses, sitting on a stool that has been blessed with both milk and beer. Some of his children are brought to him and are blessed as they take a sip form his gourd of honey beer. At dusk he stands at the entrance of the cattle area with his wife and blesses his herd. All of these varied activities serve to unite the celebrant with his family.

The "ox of the wounds" ceremony is also a communal event, in which the man to be purified is united with his society. Members of the community are invited to attend, some with personal invitations, most with the typical hospitality extended to all at Maasai ceremonies. The larger celebrations have hundreds of participants. All are fed, many sing and dance, all of the men are offered beer and many visitors elect to spend the night in the crowded homes. Throughout the night following the second day of the ceremony men sing songs of praise in honor of the celebrant's life, prowess as a warrior, fine herds and respectful character. The celebrant shares his wealth in the form of tobacco, food and beer. His family wear their best clothes and beadwork. The problems of the homestead are forgotten and the celebrant's "sins" fade in the minds of all as he is honored.

Following the ceremony the celebrant's status in the community is changed. He is now seen to be more mature, better suited to fulfill the characteristics of the ideal Maasai man. He is expected to act with wisdom and respect, more so than in the past. He has gone through the purification rites and is now able to circumcise his children, yet another important advance in the life of a Maasai.

THE CEREMONY FROM A CHRISTIAN PERSPECTIVE

An implication of the death and resurrection of Jesus, the Lamb of God, is that "we have been sanctified through the offering of the body of Jesus Christ once for all" (Heb. 10:10). Therefore, "it is impossible that the blood of bulls and goats should take away sin" (Heb. 10:4). For all Christians, including the Maasai Christians, purification for sins comes only from the atoning work of Christ. The "ox of the wounds" ceremony cannot bring about purification -- the forgiveness of sins -- that the Bible mentions. While the ceremony allows the Maasai man, his family and his community to feel that purification has taken place, nevertheless, true forgiveness of sins comes only through Christ.

It does not necessarily follow, though, that there is no place for sacrificial practices for Christians today. To assume that all sacrifices have no merit fails to understand the differing **functions** of sacrifices. The sacrifices performed in the Hebrew religion were primarily to remove sin. But not all Maasai sacrifices have this function. The major function of the "ox of the wounds" ceremony, as noted, is purification. However, some other Maasai sacrifices do not have this function. For example, sacrifices are performed to thank God for a successful cattle raid, to ask God's blessing on a newly circumcised child, and to thank God for the birth of a baby.

Is it possible to see beyond the purificatory view of sacrifices and to view these latter day rituals as acts of adoration, thanksgiving, commemoration and devotion to God? If so, can we perhaps see sacrifices as acts that the Christian Maasai can offer up in remembrance of God? While acknowledging that only Jesus can cleanse sin, must present day people who offer sacrifices for other than purificatory purposes give up those practices when they become Christians? Would continuing such acts detract from the the Lord's Supper which is symbolic of Christ's sacrifice? These are not easy questions, especially if one tries to see them from the Maasai point of view rather than from the American point of view -- that which has no history of offering animal sacrifices to God. In answering them, we would do well to follow the advice of Tippett: "The Church must accomodate itself to the culture as a whole, as a functioning and integrated system, with its own values and goals; and the culture to the requirements of the Gospel" (1969:147).

THE NEED FOR FUNCTIONAL SUBSTITUTES

The consequences of the celebrant's being united with God, his family and his society are positive functions of the "ox of the wounds" ceremony. It would, therefore, likely be a mistake for the Maasai Christians to discard the entire ceremony, even though they know that purification for sins comes only through Jesus Christ. How, then, should they view the ceremony and its continual practice?

While only the Maasai can determine the answer to this dilemma, it would seem that there are two options open for their consideration. On the one hand they can continue with the "ox of the wounds" ceremony as currently practiced, but teach that the forgiveness of sins comes only from Jesus Christ. This option is possible, but there is the strong possibility of syncretism -- the calling by Christian names of what are really pagan practices. Should the Maasai choose to pursue this approach they would hope to keep the form but change its meaning.

A second, and perhaps better, option would be to keep the positive meanings or benefits of the ceremony, but discard or change the forms. This approach calls for the use of "functional substitutes." Tippett explains the term:

> The functional substitute is a corrective mechanism. It covers up the possibility of the creation of cultural voids because of the discarding of forms and customs that cannot be accepted by the Christian faith. We need to remember that everything in a culture has some function, and many of them satisfy felt needs that are basic. When a custom is rejected because it cannot be made Christian we should ask ourselves why it existed in the first place, and find some other way of meeting the felt need which is left unsatisfied by the rejection (Tippett, 1969:149).

For an outsider to suggest such new forms is simply to engage in speculation. The new form would likely be communal in nature and could contain a public declaration of sin which is directed to God, the family and the community. The communal sharing of a meal, similar to the _agape_ love feast, might be appropriate. The honey-beer could either be used sparingly or not at all so that drunkenness would not be a feature of the new Christian celebration. Songs of praise to God could be sung. The celebrant might choose to slaughter an ox and give the meat to the poor of the community as a "sacrifice of praise" so as to "do good and share" what he has (Heb. 13:15-16). Undergirding all of these innovations would be adequate Christian instruction. How much better it is to use the culture -- that which human beings **created in the image of God** have designed -- than to ruthlessly reject it.

Tippett offers what can amount to our prayer and our hope:

> If in our church-planting we preserve the cultural structure and as many as possible of the cultural forms, and see that functional substitutes are discussed when things are discarded, and attend to post-conversion instruction adequately, the indigenous Church should grow in all its dimensions (1969:150).

NOTES

[1] The evidence given by the Maasai is inconclusive as to who the "blessed child of God" refers to. Some suggest that obviously Jesus is the focus of the song. Others say that the song pre-dates any Christian influence. Regardless of the answer, here is yet another form in the Maasai culture that can be used as a stepping-stone for the Gospel.

BIBLIOGRAPHY

Luzbetak, Louis J.
    1970   The Church and Cultures. Techny: Divine Word Publications.

Mol, Frans
    1978   Maa: A Dictionary of the Maasai Language and Folklore. Nairobi: Market and Publishing Ltd.

Nida, Eugene A.
    1974   "The Role of Cultural Anthropology in Christian Missions," in Readings in Missionary Anthropology, ed. by William Smalley. South Pasadena: William Carey Library. (307-313).

Sankan, S. S.
    1971   The Maasai. Nairobi: Kenya Literature Bureau.

Tippett, Alan R.
    1969   Verdict Theology in Missionary Theory. Lincoln: Lincoln Christian College Press.

Voshaar, Jan
    1979   Tracing God's Walking Stick in Maa. Unpublished dissertation, Katholieke Universiteit, Nijmegen.

11

An Eye-Opener for the Rural Javanese

by W. Michael Smith

The multi-faceted story of the liberator-king <u>Aji Saka</u>, when once explained, is a powerful "eye-opener" for an estimated over 60 million unevangelized rural Javanese in Indonesia.[1] Jesus explained to the Apostle Paul that He was sending him to the Gentiles to:

> open their eyes so that they may turn from darkness to light and from the dominion of Satan to God, in order that they may receive forgiveness of sins and an inheritance among those who have been sanctified by faith in Me (Acts 26:18).

A perfectly clear presentation of salvation through faith in Christ is wasted on people whose eyes are closed to the truth. They need an eye-opener. Unless their eyes are opened, there will be no turning, no forgiveness and no inheritance. So Jesus sent Paul to "open their eyes." That commission is as appropriate in modern evangelism among closed-eyed non-Christians as it was when a blinded Saul of Tarsus was commanded to open the eyes of the Gentiles in his age. We will need to look briefly at the rural Javanese setting before we can appreciate the eye-opening value of Aji Saka's story.

The Religious Context in Rural Java Today

The rural Javanese are still an unevangelized people. In spite of notable Christian growth over the past twenty years, an overwhelming majority of the Javanese claim Islam as their faith. The 1980 census figures released by the Central Statistics Office in Jakarta in May, 1981, indicate that 88 per-cent of Indonesia's people are Muslim (Penduduk, 1981:26-27). Almost nine per-cent are Christian; three per-cent Roman Catholic and six per-cent Protestant. But on the island of Java, 96 per-cent are Muslim while only two and a half per-cent constitute the combined Christian population. Clearly, most Javanese would affirm "My people are Muslim."

Effective, non-threatening "eye-openers" can gain an initial hearing for truths that would otherwise be perceived as too un-Javanese to merit consideration. For many Javanese "non-Muslim" is the same as "un-Javanese." Most of those in the 96 per-cent have been taught to acknowledge, "Yes, there are many roads to God, and all of them are good," largely because of the government's sanction of the five religions: Islam; Roman Catholic; Protestant; Hindu; and Buddhism. But the truth of community feeling is that anything outside of Islam merely clings to the fringes of reality. Therefore, on the surface, it appears that Islam is the context that the eye-openers need to address.

However, the appearance of a uniform practice of Islam by the Javanese is deceptive. After the attempted communist coup in 1965, the Indonesian government wanted to build the strongest possible defense against a communist revival. One step in the right direction, they reasoned, was to require every citizen to adhere to one of the five acceptable religions. Communism, being by nature opposed to religion, would theoretically be shut out of Indonesia. Each citizen's identification card has a place to indicate his religion. A "no preference" category is unacceptable. In the years immediately following the attempted coup, large numbers of the unaffiliated chose to simply join their neighbors who were already Muslim. But that is not to say that all Javanese Muslims adhere to pure Islamic belief and practice.

Javanese Syncretism

Clifford Geertz's observation a quarter of a century ago is still accurate in Java today. He said,

> the village religious system commonly consists of a balanced integration of animistic, Hinduistic, and Islamic elements, a basic Javanese syncretism which is the island's true folk tradition, the basic substructure of its civilization (1960:5).

The animism of pre-fifth century Java has remained a major element in the worldview of Javanese villagers through the Hindu period (5th. century to 1500), the subsequent age of Islamic influence (1500-1800), on through the colonial period and into the present. So, we need not assume that an eye-opener for Javanese villagers should relate to a strictly Islamic worldview. In fact, the story of Aji Saka reflects basic Javanese values in a setting typical of the Hinduistic kingdom stories which have molded the popular drama and art forms.

Basic Values of the Rural Javanese Worldview

The pursuit of a state of well-being called slamet is a primary mark of rural Javanese life, thought, belief and religious practice. The sacred/secular dichotomy common in North America is not found in rural Java; thus the desire for slamet is open and pervades all parts of life. One who is slamet is free from problems, accidents, misfortunes, burdens, illnesses, entangled relationships and other negative elements or realities that disturb tranquility of life. One's attainment of well-being both now and in the here-after depends on several factors:

1. His ritual performances, primarily: a) the ritual feasts, slamets, held for a few close neighbors who, before the meal, listen to and say "amen" to the Arabic prayers addressed not only to "The Lord who is All Powerful," but also to a host of spirits going back as far as "Father Adam" and "Mother Eve," and up to the great and small spirits that prowl around the village; and b) the spirit offerings consisting of flowers, water, cigarettes and other efficacious items placed at intersections, bridges and other spots where spirits may lurk.

2. His body of knowledge or scientific insights into the controlling forces of life. A person gains such insight through observation, meditation, study under a teacher and long periods of abstinence from sleep, sex, food, drink, etc. One wins battles not by mere physical strength, but through superior knowledge.

Not everyone can see the deeper truths. Many truths, in fact, have been "wrapped up" or disguised intentionally. The Javanese ancestors who possessed deep knowledge are considered to have been very sparing in imparting it to others. They sometimes wrapped up their knowledge in what I call "historical folk tales,"[2] in such a way that only the truly informed could understand them. The story of Aji Saka is one such historical folk tale. At a later point we will see more of this delight in disguising truths so that only the persistent and the perceptive can unravel them.

Aji Saka, Liberator-King

To begin the story, "Once upon a time ..." would treat this matter too lightly. Many consider historical folktales to be of great significance, especially this one, since Aji Saka is credited with developing both the Javanese alphabet and calendar. The text of the Aji Saka story prepared for school children dates him in the first century A.D. in conjunction with his alleged development of the Javanese or Saka calendar; a calendar which follows the Gregorian calendar by 68 years. Thus, Gregorian 1984 is 1916/1917 according to the Saka calendar (Atmosudjono and Adiwiyoto, 1976:13).

The use of this story as an eye-opener came to my attention through the book Wedaring Tjarakan by Ki K. Tjokrosentono, a Javanese Christian (1970). Tjokrosentono does a masterful job of presenting the story in the setting of a series of typically rural Javanese informal evening "bull sessions."

Permit me to present the story and its unfolded meaning in that format as well -- as if told to a group of fellow Javanese in an evening of informal visiting. In this presentation, we draw from the accounts by Tjokrosentono, Atmosudjono and Adiwiyoto, as well as related insights from Geertz and personal interviews besides general familiarity with the story. We join the conversation under way ...

"I am glad that you asked about that. You know we Javanese do have our own religion; a true Javanese religion. But most people have misunderstood it and misapplied it. Consequently its appearance now is a far cry from the original. I suppose you could say our own ancestors are at fault in not passing it along more clearly and simply. You know how they often preferred to disguise what they meant. But now our people, the Javanese, have failed to understand some very important things that our ancestors knew.

"I suppose it doesn't surprise any of us to see important things wrapped up that way, though. We all still do it. Remember, for example, when we were small boys and would sometimes play on the bamboo sleeping platform? If we sat on a pillow we were scolded by our mothers. But not with clear, direct communication. She would say, 'Hey son, that's rude. Get off the pillow! You will get boils all over you!' What she meant was that pillows are not for sitting but for laying your head on when you sleep, but that is not what she said at all. Her message was wrapped up. That's the Javanese way.

"It seems like we Javanese make a special effort to avoid being direct, especially the refined Javanese. You know, some of the old teachers won't openly correct their students. Rather, they tell a long elaborate story from which the student both gets the point less painfully, and has the discipline of sorting out the meaning from the story (Geertz, 1960:244).

"There are many examples of that sort of thing, but for my purpose, they are just an introduction to a bit of insight that comes from our Javanese ancestors. This insight or truth has proven to be the basis for the well-being of my family since I first understood it a few years ago. I'd like to tell you about it.

"This story will help you recognize how gracious God has been to provide well-being, slamet, for every group of people in the world, even the Javanese people. It is my belief that through this story God has been passing down His grace from generation to generation, but unfortunately, few have recognized it.

"'Long, long ago, the kingdom of Medangkamulan, right here on our island of Java, was ruled by a cruel, murderous king named Dewatacengkar. Every day he demanded the flesh of one of his subjects for his food. Of course, none of his subjects could live in peace. Fear and anxiety dominated their lives. Each morning they awoke dreading the news of who was to be eaten that day.

"'But Dewa Agung, the great high God, took pity on the citizens of that oppressed kingdom and sent a young man from a far country (from India according to our children's school books) to help them. He was a well-educated man with a desire to travel the world to gain wisdom and experience. As per the plan of the high God Dewa Agung his travels brought him to the kingdom of Medangkamulan. Without a moment's hesitation, this young man named Aji Saka, obeyed his calling, pressing on even in the face of danger. As soon as he understood the plight of the citizens of Medangkamulan he formed a plan. One day, with courage and confidence, Aji Saka offered to become the meal of the wicked king. As a final petition before the king, he requested on behalf of his poor foster parents a piece of land the size of the cloth he used for his turban. The king mockingly granted the request but as he unfolded Aji Saka's turban, he was startled to see it expand further and further and further until he found himself backed up to the sea on the south coast of Java. At that point, the clever Aji Saka snatched back his turban cloth with such power that the king was thrown headlong into the sea where he was changed into a white crocodile.

AJI SAKA BEFORE DEWATACENGKAR

Figure One

(borrowed from Atmosudjono and Adiwiyoto, 1976:10).

"'There was great rejoicing in Medangkamulan that day, and Aji Saka was made king. All the citizens who wanted deliverance from the oppression of Dewatacengkar had to be willing to be covered by Aji Saka's turban cloth. As a commemoration of these events, Aji Saka developed the Javanese alphabet that we all know:

JAVANESE ALPHABET WITH EQUIVALENT ROMAN CHARACTERS

ha na ca ra ka
da ta sa wa la
pa dha ja ya nya
ma ga ba tha nga

Figure Two

"Now there is more to this story than meets the eye. As it was passed down from generation to generation, most have forgotten its meaning. It has become just another story. But some of those early ancestors knew the truth it contains. They knew it, but as I said earlier, they didn't portray it in a clear, straight-forward manner. Rather, they disguised it, hiding the meaning as we Javanese like to do. So don't be surprised as we sort out some of the details if we have to rearrange a bit so we can see the true meaning.

"The name of the kingdom was Medangkamulan. Inverted it becomes kemulan pedang, (the m/p switch from medang to pedang, is a common phonetic transition in Javanese), or more clearly kakemulan by pedang, which means "blanketed (kakemulan) by the sword (pedang)." Medangkamulan was a kingdom constantly oppressed by the sword and by fear of death. It was a kingdom filled with anxiety. There was no peace. No one could escape from the shadow of the terrible king.

"Medangkamulan was much like our own world now. After "Father Adam" and "Mother Eve" sinned, we all followed them into the clutches of Setan, the wicked oppressor of this world. Most of our people know no peace.

"The ruler of the kingdom was Dewatacengkar, or cengkar ing dewa, which means "without understanding of God." Setan, from the beginning, has been the enemy of God. His ways are the opposite of godliness. Like Dewatacengkar he enslaves and devours. Setan has always wanted to be God and has used deception and dark power to build a kingdom of shackled subjects. Under his control, we all have the attitude of Dewatacengkar to some extent. We are not able to do good because we do not know God; we are separated from Him.

"Only through the help of Aji Saka who was sent from Dewa Agung were the people of Medangkamulan able to escape the evil sway of Dewatacengkar. Only someone from outside the kingdom could help. No citizen of Medangkamulan could liberate himself from the king's power. And, of course, no one who is himself enslaved can advise others as to how to escape. They needed help from outside.

"Aji Saka was their way of escape. His power and insight were greater than that of Dewatacengkar, and he was able to overthrow him. Anyone who wanted to be covered up by Aji Sawa's turban cloth could be saved, slamet, but whoever came out from under its covering would be eaten by the wicked king.

"The name Aji Saka itself needs to be explained. It means a saka which is aji. Our hero is a saka, a "main support pillar of a house." He is a saka which is aji, or that which is valuable, honored, glorious, powerful and so on. When the saka is strong, the house won't fall. Aji Saka was the pillar that could be trusted to bring well-being to the kingdom of Medangkamulan.

"Dewa Agung is like the creator God Himself who in love has looked on the plight of all His people who are under the power of Setan. He has sent His messenger to break that power and set us all free. His messenger is like the saka which is aji; like the pillar that can be trusted.

"As we continue to unwrap this parcel handed down by our ancestors, I want you to remember that I'm telling you this story because I believe the truth it reveals may bring <u>slamet</u> to your families just as it has to mine. Now, in a moment when I explain the meaning of the alphabet Aji Saka developed, the whole story will be clearer. Have you ever realized that there is a message in the characters of our Javanese alphabet? After Aji Saka became king, he developed our special alphabet with a clear purpose in mind.

"When we were toddlers we memorized and chanted this alphabet -- even those of us who are "blind to letters" or non-literate memorized the alphabet. We chanted:

```
ha   na   ca   ra   ka

ḍa   ta   sa   wa   la

pa   da   ja   ya   nya

ma   ga   ba   ṭa   nga
```

These characters are a part of our lives, but we've failed to see their significance. We've missed what Aji Saka is trying to tell us. To make sense of it we have to put the four lines of the alphabet in the order that discloses their meaning. It is a simple change like this: (the second line is shifted to the bottom position).

```
ha   na   ca   ra   ka

pa   ḍa   ja   ya   nya

ma   ga   ba   ṭa   nga

da   ta   sa   wa   la
```

Now you can see the sentences forming: ha na ca ra ka is <u>hana caraka</u>, or "there was a messenger;" pa ḍa ja ya nya is <u>pada jayanya</u>, which means, "the same in power and might." <u>Hana caraka pada jayanya</u> means "There was a messenger equal in power, might and honor with the one who sent him." Now, that doesn't match our normal experience, does it? Usually a messenger is **not** equal to the sender. For example, if the district government head is sent as an emissary of the king, is he the same in authority and power as the king? Not at all. And think of the prophets of God in the Holy Book like Moses and Abraham. God sent them as

His messengers, but were they equal to God? Of course not. They were sinful men just like us. They were not pada jayanya, or "**not** equal" with the one who sent them.

"But in this alphabet, Aji Saka is telling us that there was a messenger sent from God who was equal to God Himself in everything -- in authority, power, holiness, love, etc. It was not one of the prophets. Who was it? It was a name you have heard but paid little attention to: Jesus the Spirit of God; or Jesus the Messiah; or Jesus Christ. Jesus Christ is God Himself incarnate. He descended into this world in order to rescue sinful men who repent and believe in Him. He gives peace and wholeness; and eternal life in the Kingdom of Heaven to all who believe in Him. He is our source of slamet, the source of our salvation. He is our Savior, our "slamet specialist."

"Remember, in Medangkamulan it was not enough for the citizens to stir up a revolt or to try to break the king's power themselves. They were helpless. They needed help from outside. And Aji Saka couldn't just shout advice and encouragement from abroad. He had to come into the oppressed realm himself. And he didn't hesitate to do so even at great sacrifice and danger to himself.

"That leads us into the last two lines of the alphabet. I'll just put them together: ma ga ba ṭa nga da ta sa wa la becomes maga baṭanga datasawala. Data sawala means "not hesitant." Aji Saka didn't hesitate to be sent by Dewa Agung to rescue the people of Medangkamulan.

"Datan suwala describes Jesus Christ. Though He is God Himself, He was not hesitant to come down into our world and associate with all of us sinful men. It was love for us that made Him datan suwala. We can see the full extent of His willingness in the words maga baṭanga, which mean "to become a dead body." Jesus Christ was willing to die to free us from Satan's power. So here is our alphabet in its intelligible form:

            Hana Caraka

            Paḍa Jayanya

            Maga baṭanga

            Data sawala

Jesus Christ was the messenger (caraka) from God who was equal in all things (pada jayanya) to God Himself, but did not hesitate (datan suwala) to come into the oppressed kingdom and even die (maga batanga) in order to rescue all of us who believe in Him. In the Holy Book Jesus is called the "Lamb of God" because He was sacrificed like a lamb to cleanse our sins, and then broke the power of Setan and rose from the dead.

"I believe our ancestors knew of the slamet or salvation that God has provided and they passed the word along in its wrapped-up version in the story of Aji Saka and in the alphabet that he developed for us. The message is of such importance that they chose to encase it in our alphabet, a symbolic center of all our communications.

"And, by the way, don't you think it is significant that Aji Saka's great rescue marks the beginning of our present Javanese calendar? Men, I think all these factors demand that we seriously study who this Jesus Christ is, and we need to consider if we want to join those who have found slamet, or salvation, under the protection of his turban cloth."

Culturally Appropriate Treatment?

Is this treatment of the Aji Saka story a manipulation, or is it a legitimate, culturally suitable interpretation? We feel it is suitable because, in the first place, the original exposure of the story's meaning was made by a Javanese Christian in Central Java. But even beyond that, it appears to be quite compatible with indigenous forms of oral and written literature.

Javanese people who are considered refined take considerable pride in their ability to speak in such refined language, often utilizing terms from old Javanese so that their meaning is obscure to the untrained. Sometimes the intended meaning is said to be wrapped-up as a treat of meat in sticky rice is wrapped-up in a banana leaf to give it form, to enhance its flavor and to protect it until it is eaten.

Speeches at weddings often contain an intriguing form of speech called jarwo-dosok. A friend who often serves as master of ceremonies for village weddings told me that Javanese speakers like to use the jarwo-dosok because it enables them to convey an important message in a refined but obscure way. Speakers who are able to develop and use this complex form to convey an otherwise simple one-line message are regarded as especially clever and refined.

In one form of jarwo-dosok, the kernel of the intended message is preceded by a key word which either rhymes with it or is a syllabic twin to an important word in the kernel. But that key word is not spoken directly; rather it is hinted at by an often wordy descriptive phrase. It becomes a riddle for the listeners.[3]

Our point in mentioning these traits of Javanese verbal culture is that such indirectness and "cover-ups", and the need to explain them, are very common and highly valued among the rural people of Central Java. Thus, we believe that the story of Aji Saka and its explanation are culturally appropriate. By God's grace they are being used and we believe will be used among the rural Javanese to help to:

> open their eyes so that they may turn from darkness to light and from the dominion of Satan to God, in order that they may receive forgiveness of sins and an inheritance among those who have been sanctified by faith in Me (Acts 26:18).

NOTES

[1] I am indebted to Don Richardson (1981) for the concept of the "eye-opener."

[2] The rural Javanese tend to easily give as much weight to some such folktales that lack historical documentation as to documented historical events. And villager's references to documented accounts often contain unusual and supernatural elements that most westerners would question. Validity and significance here do not depend on empirically based historical accounting to the degree that is true in many western countries. Thus I use the apparently contradictory term, "historical folk tales."

[3] Here is a Javanese example of jarwo-dosok. A speaker wants to apologize for errors in his speaking. He could simply say, "Nyuwun pangapura yen wonten lepat kula." But that would be too direct and unrefined, so instead of the one sentence, "Please forgive the mistakes in my speech," the

speaker uses two lead-in phrases that hint at synonyms which
are key words or parts of words in the "kernel" of his
intended message. So he says it this way:
> Jenang sela
> Wader kalen sesonderan
> Apuranto yen wonten lepat kula.

Even many Javanese would need someone to explain the riddle
in the first two phrases, which would go something like
this:
> Jenang sela is a way of saying "lime dust."
> A synonym is apu. Apu is the first part of the
> word apuranto in the kernel phrase.
> Wader kalen sesonderan literally means "a ditch-
> dwelling fish with a very long tail," or more
> clearly and commonly put, a snake, which is ula in
> Javanese. Ula rhymes with kula in the last part
> of the kernel phrase.

Neither apu nor ula are spoken; they are simply hinted at in
the two lead-in phrases. And of course they have nothing to
do with the speaker's intended message except that by such
hints and riddles the speaker has been able to avoid dis-
tasteful bluntness.

BIBLIOGRAPHY

Atmosudjono, M. and Antonius Adiwiyoto
   1976 Aji Saka dan Naga Baruklinting. Jakarta:
         P. T. Gramedia.

Geertz, Clifford
   1960 The Religion of Java. London: The Free Press
         of Glascoe.

Penduduk Indonesia Menurut Propinsi
   1981 Penduduk Indonesia Menurut Propinsi. Jakarta:
         Biro Pusat Statistik Jakarta.

Richardson, Don
   1981 "Finding the Eye Opener," in Perspectives on the
         World Christian Movement, ed. by Ralph Winter and
         Steven Hawthorne. Pasadena: William Carey
         Library. 421-427.

Tjokrosentono, K.
   1970 Wedaring Tjarakan. Jakarta: Badan Penerbit
         Kristen.

Part Four

THEORY OF MISSIONS

"Go and make disciples."

Mt. 28:19

12

Donald A. McGavran:
The Development of a Legacy

by Herbert M. Works, Jr.

Books abound in our day on the subject of estate planning. They deal with resources, acquiring properties, investments, making the right decisions, timing of moves, and a variety of other elements critical to developing an estate of significance. The goal in providing for a substantial estate is not only to allow one to enjoy its abundance in one's retirement, but to provide a legacy for one's heirs. A legacy, however, need not be thought of only as financial resources. A legacy may consist of ideas, observations and conclusions.

The purpose of this article is neither to describe the legacy of Donald Anderson McGavran, nor to catalog his heirs. Description would be difficult, since that legacy is not yet complete; the one from whom it is received is still living and adding to the wealth of its contents. Furthermore, the most important elements of that legacy are the subject of the article that follows this one, in which McGavran himself lists and describes the major emphases of the "Church Growth School of Thought" as he sees them. The "heirs" -- the recipients of this legacy -- may be described in the words of Rev. 7:9 as "a great multitude which no man could number, from every nation, from all tribes and people and tongues ..." Although the absolutes -- the "every" and the "all" -- in that verse cannot be pressed, it is a matter of record that Donald McGavran's heirs include those from many nations, tribes, peoples and tongues (and those from a wide range of denominations as well!).

Donald A. McGavran has been described as the "father of the Church Growth Movement" and as "the twentieth century's premier missiologist." The category in which he fits most readily, however, is that of mission theorist. Somewhere between theology of mission and mission strategy, there exists a nebulous category that can best be described as missions theory. Earlier missionaries or missiologists who fit into this classification are John Nevius, Roland Allen, Rufus Anderson and Henry Venn. Like some of these men, McGavran was no ivory tower theoretician. His positions on mission theory grew out of the hard realities of his missionary service in India. Furthermore, he has always been ready to travel to the farthest reaches of the globe to help a struggling missionary implement the principles with which one of McGavran's books has confronted him.

That Donald McGavran is a man of prominence in the world of missions today is disputed by no one. Advocates and adversaries alike agree that his writings, lectures and workshops have made an impact on twentieth century missions, the ramifications of which will continue long into the century ahead. The question under consideration in this article is this: what are the most significant **sources in the development** of the legacy Donald Anderson McGavran offers to contemporary missionaries and those of the future? It is to that investigation that we now turn.

FAMILY BACKGROUND

It is no surprise that Donald McGavran would choose a life of missionary service. His maternal grandparents left England on a sailing vessel in July, 1854 as Baptist missionaries destined for Bengal. James H. Anderson's missionary career lasted until 1894, during which for a brief period he served as principal of Serampore College, which William Carey had a part in establishing.

Meanwhile, a young Disciples of Christ missionary from America, John Grafton McGavran, arrived in India in December of 1891. He had recently graduated from Bethany College, intending to enter medical training in order to prepare to be a missionary doctor. However, it happened that Archibald McLean, the president of Bethany, was also the secretary of the Foreign Christian Missionary Society of the Disciples of Christ. Recognizing in J. G. McGavran the qualities that were urgently needed to fill an evangelistic missionary role in India, McLean persuaded him to lay aside plans for medical school and go immediately to India.

In 1892 while J. G. McGavran was in Darjeeling, a hill station north of Calcutta, recuperating from a serious illness, he met Helen Anderson, daughter of the James Andersons. Helen returned to England in the fall, but a "correspondence courtship" developed which eventually led to their engagement. On October 25, 1895 she arrived back in Bombay; the next day, they were married. It was into this home in India that Donald McGavran was born in December 1897.

As a child, Donald McGavran grew up surrounded by missionary activity. The Disciples of Christ work had begun only fifteen years before his birth. It consisted of evangelism, medical work, and -- because of a severe four-year famine -- a heavy emphasis on orphanages. However, when Donald was 12 the family returned to America on furlough and decided to stay there to meet the educational needs of the child. Enroute from India to America, J. G. McGavran attended the International Missionary Conference at Edinburgh in 1910. The emphasis of that Edinburgh conference on the need for more effective preparation for missionaries made an indelible impression on his mind. Upon arrival in the United States, the McGavran family settled for a short time in Ann Arbor where J. G. took a graduate degree at the University of Michigan. Not long afterward, the Christian Churches, responding to the concern of the Edinburgh conference for improved missionary preparation, established the College of Missions in Indianapolis -- the first graduate level missionary training institution in the United States -- and called J. G. McGavran to its faculty. During his impressionable years of adolescence, Donald McGavran was once again surrounded by persons whose first love and commitment was to Christian work on the "foreign field."

Following service with the 139th. Field Artillery in France in World War I, Donald McGavran re-entered Butler College in Indianapolis. Here he met Mary Elizabeth Howard, a young woman whose heart was already set on missionary service. Each of them made application to the United Christian Missionary Society of the Christian Churches. On his application Donald expressed "plans to go to the foreign field as a Preacher or Evangelistic Worker." Mary indicated a desire "to be a teacher on the foreign field." One of the reference letters for McGavran commented, "He will not needlessly give offense, neither will he surrender a principle," and added, "He will stick in the trench to the last man."

In recognizing the contribution of McGavran's family to his sense of direction in life and, ultimately, to his legacy to the world of missions, it is worthwhile to note that in 1922, his parents returned to India and served until health considerations made return to the United States necessary in 1928. Other members of the family also served in India: Dr. Mary McGavran, J. G. McGavran's sister, for 27 years; and Herbert Anderson, brother of Mrs. J. G. McGavran, for 42 years. The Anderson-McGavran family recorded more than 279 years in missionary service in India between 1854 and 1954. Part of the legacy which Donald A. McGavran gives to the Christian world was acquired through his family's commitment to the missionary task.

THE INDIA YEARS: 1923-1954

Donald and Mary McGavran arrived in India in 1923. The India that was to become their home was not the India entered a century earlier by William Carey, Henry Martyn and Alexander Duff. Rather, it was the India of the early twentieth century, with its expectation of increasing independence from Great Britain. It was the India of Mohandas Gandhi; the India of civil disobedience, mass strikes and non-violent resistance. It was also the India in which the caste system still dominated the social structure of the country, the India of ancient and deeply-ingrained religions.

After a year of language study the Donald McGavran family was assigned to Harda, where he supervised primary, middle and high schools, while teaching some Bible and English classes in the middle school and high school. Toward the end of his first term, he was made Director of Religious Education carried on in the missions schools in all fourteen stations of the India mission. In 1930, the McGavrans returned to the United States on furlough and remained there until the fall of 1932 so that he could complete requirements for a Ph.D degree in religious education from Union Theological Seminary and Teachers College of Columbia University.

Their second term of service in India proved to be a pivotal one for the McGavrans in two ways. Shortly after their return to the field, McGavran was elected by his colleagues as executive secretary-treasurer of the India mission. In this capacity he was the general correspondent for the mission and liaison with the home office. In addition, he was responsible for the distribution of monies received for the India work. He became increasingly troubled about the large amount of money that was passing through his hands and the relatively small result it produced. For example, the **Yearbook of the International Convention of the Disciples of Christ** for the year 1932-33 reported total expenditures for the India field as $125,309. The same yearbook reported a net membership gain of 52. The yearbook for the following year showed a similar investment, but with a net membership loss of 29. Much later, McGavran reflected on that experience and said, "It offended my Scotch nature!"

A much more significant event occurred during this second term. For some time, the missionaries in mid-India had been hearing reports of mass movements to Christ among the lower caste and outcaste peoples in the southern part of the Indian sub-continent. Since most of the Indian Christian leaders were of the upper castes, there was deep skepticism that these thousands of untouchable converts could be "real" Christians or whether they were simply "baptized heathens." This concern resulted in a call for a survey to determine the quality of Christian experience of these peoples. A former missionary of the Methodist Episcopal Church, J. Waskom Pickett, was appointed to do the survey. At the conclusion of his work, Pickett published **Christian Mass Movements in India**, a book that clearly validated the viability of people coming to Christ in large numbers. Most surprising was Pickett's conclusion that, in many cases, the turning to Jesus Christ by a large number of persons in one caste together produced a **higher quality** of Christian life than the conversion of men and women, one by one, who were at once outcasted by their family and caste fellows. No one would eat, drink or associate with them.

McGavran was fascinated by Pickett's findings and wrote to the Mission Secretary in Indianapolis indicating his certainty that similar mass movements to Christ were possible in mid-India. Furthermore, the Mid-India Christian Council invited Pickett to meet with them in an attempt to answer the question as to why such similar movements were not happening in mid-India. Following that meeting, the Council appointed a twenty-four person Mass Movement Continuation Committee, of which McGavran was the chairman. This committee proposed a monthly Mass Movement Bulletin and organized a retreat in 1935 with Pickett as primary resource. Of greatest significance was the decision to ask Pickett to conduct a survey of the mid-India regions in 1936 to identify potential mass movement areas and counsel the missionaries of some twenty missions from a half dozen countries in how best to cultivate such movements. In addition to Pickett, the survey team of three was to have a missionary and an Indian national. McGavran was chosen as the missionary. It is no surprise, therefore, that the inscription he wrote inside the cover of his book **How Churches Grow**, nearly thirty years after this India experience, says, "To J. Waskom Pickett, at whose fire I lit my candle."

It was clear to McGavran's colleagues in India that a shift in his responsibilities was appropriate. At the Annual Convention of the Disciples India Mission in 1936, it was proposed that McGavran move from a concentration in education to leadership in evangelism in the Mungeli-Takhatpur area. The proposal carried implications that made the decision difficult. Educational missionaries ranked higher than evangelistic, since they were generally more highly educated, lived in large towns and cities, and were particularly respected by Indian public officials. Evangelistic missionaries, on the other hand, generally had limited graduate education, lived in remote areas, and worked with the uneducated majority of the Indian population. The location proposed involved moving to an area thirty miles off the railroad, working in villages of mud huts, and, occasionally, finding a positive response to the Gospel. However, if a Christward movement was to occur at all, it would occur among **these** people. Finally, in April, 1936 the McGavrans informed the executive committee that if the mission would send two other evangelistically-minded families with them, they would be part of the team.

This decision constituted a major turning point for the McGavrans. For the remaining eighteen years of their missionary service in India, they concentrated on evangelism in this area. Sadly, their work produced neither a sizable people movement nor significant success in persuading colleagues in the mission to prioritize in favor of evangelism and people movements.

Much of the reason for the lack of success lay in the changing mood in India. During this period of time, India was moving toward independence from England. When an autonomous government was set up and members of the depressed classes began to attain a measure of political power, their receptivity to the Gospel diminished sharply. A trend grew among many Indian people to turn toward political and economic reform for the solutions to their problems, rather than to salvation, redemption and personal transformation.

Although it is difficult to characterize the response of McGavran's colleagues to his people movement ideas as either affirming or resistant, it is accurate to say that there was not consistent support for his enthusiasm. He used every means to convince both home office leaders and fellow missionaries on the field to give evangelism of receptive castes priority in funding and personnel. With limited financial resources, however, it is not surprising that some of his colleagues involved in institutional expressions of the mission's work saw the deployment of personnel and allocation of funds to evangelism as reducing that which they would have available for the schools and hospitals. The field missionaries individually seemed to encourage McGavran in his commitments, but not to place the full weight of the mission behind them. The general impression one receives from reading the minutes of the field executive and advisory committees is that little change was made in mission policy as a result of his efforts.

McGavran's growing commitment to people movements was not weakened by his failure to see them emerge from his work, nor by the lukewarm response of those who worked with him. He held occasional symposia for other Indian missionaries on "How Churches Grow." He delivered a series of messages, all directed toward church growth, at the All-Bengal Christian Convention at Serampore. The Christian Endeavor Union of India, Burma and Ceylon invited McGavran to speak at their Golden Jubilee, October 1938 in Rangoon; his subject was "Christ and the Mass Movement Crisis."

McGavran's most important outlet for all his new insights, however, was in his writings. He was an avid correspondent; the home secretary of the mission remembers days on which he would receive several letters from McGavran all at once. Further, he sought to explain and promote his understanding of people movements through periodical articles. He was a frequent contributor to the missions journal of the Disciples, **World Call**, and to their general weekly publication, **Christian Evangelist**. The journal of the International Missionary Council, the **International Review of Missions**, accepted several articles by McGavran during his India years. He also wrote for **World Dominion**, the "voice" of the World Dominion Movement. It was through this association that McGavran became acquainted with the ideas of Roland Allen.

The letters to his board, to the field administrator of his mission, to his colleagues, to editors and to persons of note in the world of missions all focused on one theme: the need of missions to take seriously the new patterns of responsiveness illustrated by the mass movements in India. None of these efforts provided adequate expressions of the burning convictions within him, however. So, early in 1951, he retreated to the hills north of Takhatpur and began a manuscript called "How Peoples Become Christian." This was published in 1955 under the title **Bridges of God.**

This book brought all the insights McGavran had expressed in his previous writings into an integrated whole. But it did more. It attempted to place a biblical foundation under the new concepts, not only validating them from his experience in the field, but from evidence of people movements in the Old and New Testaments as well. In a letter to Don West, India secretary of the Disciples missions board, McGavran stated his purpose in writing the book:

> I have tried to present to the missionary enterprise a base in theory so that it can break the chains of the static Mission Station Approach philosophy and methodology of missions, which at present binds us all to a non-growing concept of missions. We need a **fundamental, dynamic, biblical, philosophy of missions** that will enable us to recognize, welcome, correctly shepherd, and extend all the great opportunities for church growth which God is giving us today and will give us in increasing measure tomorrow -- if we can show we can handle what He gives. Without that philosophy of missions we neither recognize nor welcome these opportunities, and consequently cannot shepherd or extend them, in adequate measure   (McGavran, 1955b).

TESTING THE HYPOTHESIS

The year of 1954 was a furlough year for McGavran, and it was a year of decision as well. During the 1934-1954 period in India, he had examined methods, surveyed fields, written articles, lectured and preached, and barraged the leaders of his mission with pleas for new priorities and new directions. What was the result? Virtually nothing. The prophet had unburdened himself as best as he knew how and it seemed that no one was really listening. In 1957 he would be sixty years old. The policy of the United Christian Missionary Society would require him to retire in seven years. The question with which he struggled was, "Where now, Lord?"

In the spring of 1954, McGavran's board agreed to his request to route his furlough trip to the United States through Africa. For some time he had been eager to compare the people movement conditions on that continent with those he had experienced in India. He felt the need to deal with an urgent issue: were people movements only happening in the cultures and among the peoples of India, or would this phenomenon be found in other parts of the world as well? McGavran found the African missions situation most interesting. He saw scores of people movements, some small, many large, but in most cases the missionaries neither recognized the dynamics involved nor believed that the "group movement" approach to conversion was a valid means of church growth. The African circumstances were different in a number of ways from those in which he worked in India. The Christian school approach had not delivered converts in India; in Africa, schools were frequently effective tools in evangelism. In India, the ruling classes had been universally anti-Christian; McGavran encountered in Africa many tribal chiefs and other leaders who had adopted the Christian faith. As he reflected later on this Africa trip, McGavran said, "... people movements all over and everyone was denying their existence. The missionaries wanted to be doing 'good, sound, solid work' and were afraid of the people movement" (McGavran, 1972). Out of his three-month period in Africa, McGavran saw in greater detail the complexity of church growth, as it existed in cultures radically different from those in India. He could see the need to modify some of his proposals, if they were to be applicable in a variety of circumstances. His basic concepts, however, were reinforced by his observations in Africa.

Upon arrival in the United States, the McGavrans went directly to Yale University where he had been granted a research fellowship for the furlough year. He used the time there to write his second major book, **How Churches Grow**, a volume that attempted to integrate the broadening effects of the Africa observations with the basic stands taken in **Bridges of God**. The theological dimension was much enlarged in the second volume. McGavran dealt with theories or philosophies of missions with greater understanding. By this point in his career, he seemed to have perceived clearly that his position, as articulated in his writings, would likely divide the world of missions. The differences in the two books could be summarized by saying that **Bridges of God** appeared to have been written by a missionary and **How Churches Grow** revealed the touch of a mission theorist.

By the end of his year at Yale, a decision had to be made about the future. Correspondence indicates that at least some of the Disciples missionaries in India were eager for the McGavrans to return to the field at the end of furlough. There was also some talk of his becoming field secretary for Africa for his mission board, the United Christian Missionary Society. Neither of these options materialized. Rather, a need for McGavran's services with the U.C.M.S. emerged that could easily be interpreted as Providential. At the time McGavran arrived home from India, the mission board of the Disciples was deeply involved in the development of a new approach to their strategy of missions. Earlier work in the area had produced, less than six months after McGavran arrived in the United States, a new "Strategy of World Missions," which had been adopted by the Board of Trustees of the U.C.M.S. One step remained in implementing this new strategy -- a series of surveys to obtain a clear, factual understanding of the conditions of the fields in which the society was working. McGavran's time and talents were available; he had experience in field surveys; and he was eager personally to gather information about the growth of the church in various parts of the world. It was an ideal opportunity.

The surveys occupied McGavran from 1955 to 1957 and took him to Puerto Rico, the Philippines, Thailand, Orissa State (India), Formosa, Japan and Jamaica. Their greatest value lay in the broadening influence they had on McGavran's church growth thinking. Just as his Africa trip had served to confirm his basic convictions about how the church grows, these surveys similarly strengthened the foundation on which he was building his church growth principles. It is possible that McGavran's positions could have been dismissed as applicable only to India except for the Africa trip and this series of church growth surveys. While strengthening the fundamental concepts, McGavran's studies in widely divergent cultures and mission policies continually caused him to modify specific elements of his thought, so that the principles might be more and more universally applicable.

THE INSTITUTE OF CHURCH GROWTH: REALIZING THE DREAM

When all the needed surveys had been completed, the question of McGavran's continuing relationship with the United Christian Missionary Society -- and his work assignment -- once again came to the fore. The solution proposed by the administrators of the society was a new position, Professor of Missions and Director of Research with the

Division of World Mission of the U.C.M.S. The title was auspicious, but the position was proposed on only a two-year experimental basis. Furthermore, as details came to light, it appeared that McGavran, technically a part of the faculty of the College of Missions, would be traveling to various institutions of higher learning affiliated with the Disciples of Christ and teaching missions for a quarter or a semester at each one. He would begin July 1, 1957 by which time he was to have completed his reports on the various surveys in which he had been involved.

This period during which McGavran served as visiting lecturer at Disciples of Christ educational institutions was a time of mixed feelings for him. He spent approximately six months at each of six schools, stretching from West Virginia to Oregon. In addition, the McGavrans served as host and hostess during the summer session of the College of Missions at Crystal Lake, Michigan and as hosts for the Missions House there during the summer. The teaching opportunities gave McGavran occasion to contact Disciple seminarians, a small number of whom were preparing for missionary service. Nevertheless he felt that those teaching assignments were a far cry from what he called the "advanced training for missionaries" in which he longed to be involved. His growing sense of "call" was to teach career missionaries of all boards and denominations how to be more effective in carrying out their tasks. The frustration arising from the absence of opportunities to teach career missionaries magnified the petty irritations of the repeated moves, unusual accommodations and rootlessness.

All the while, however, a dream was taking form in McGavran's mind and heart -- an institute of church growth where career missionaries of many denominations could come while on furlough, to share data and insights from their fields with other missionaries. There, they could learn from McGavran and others how they could be more effective in the growth of the church on their fields. Earlier, not long after his return from India, McGavran had shared the idea of a "Church Growth Association" with the India secretary of the U.C.M.S. At that time he envisioned the association as providing a clearing house for people movement information and as publishing a news sheet that would bring together those around the world who were experiencing church growth. His experiences in educational institutions helped broaden that initial concept. Now he was projecting an institute that would function as an arm of an educational institution, with the potential for degree-granting on a graduate level.

McGavran proposed sponsorship of such an institute first to the United Christian Missionary Society, but his idea met a cool reception. So he began exploring the possibilities of such an institute with various Disciples graduate seminaries. Each one responded with encouragement for the idea, but with regret that there were insufficient financial resources and inadequate facilities on its particular campus to attempt the experiment.

With little positive response, McGavran was approaching the conclusion that God's purpose for him was to retire altogether. However, while teaching at Northwest Christian College in Eugene, Oregon he shared his dream with the president of the institution, Ross J. Griffeth, a man who shared McGavran's visionary nature. Northwest Christian College did not meet McGavran's expectations as a home for his Institute; it had no graduate division and was not at that time regionally accredited. Nevertheless, when Griffeth responded positively to McGavran's proposal, the wheels were set in motion to make the dream a reality. Official notification of approval of the Institute of Church Growth came to McGavran in a letter from Griffeth on June 24, 1959. McGavran was invited to join the college faculty as Professor of Church Growth, including "full opportunity to carry on the project in 'New Church Development,' especially with foreign and home missionaries." Because space and finances were limited commodities on the campus, arrangements were made for a large oak table to be installed in the third floor stacks of the library. On January 1, 1961 the Institute of Church Growth opened its doors, with McGavran at one end of the table and Keith Hamilton at the other. Hamilton, McGavran's first research associate, was a furloughing Methodist missionary who had been working with Aymara and Quechua Indians in Bolivia.

The Institute of Church Growth remained on the campus of Northwest Christian College only a short four and one-half years. At the end of that time it became a part of the new School of Mission and Institute of Church Growth at Fuller Theological Seminary in Pasadena, California. However, those few years laid the foundation and provided the initial structures within which McGavran's dream could take shape. In addition, the experiences of those years contributed immeasurably to the development of the legacy McGavran offers to the world of missions.

During those years in Eugene, the Institute of Church Growth saw 61 students sit at that oak table. These were missionaries from 24 different countries and represented 17 different denominations or mission agencies. In addition, several undergraduate students from Northwest Christian College who were preparing for missionary service took courses with McGavran. Some of the Institute students were missionary candidates, but most were furloughees.

As we consider the development of a legacy, we must ask: in what ways did these people and the experiences of the Eugene years add to McGavran's legacy?

1. McGavran's dream became a reality. The Institute of Church Growth proved that the need McGavran perceived was real and was felt by many others. Furthermore, the educational approach and structure McGavran had envisioned was generally successful in providing the opportunity for learning and growth.

2. Through the field information brought by the varied students at the Institute, McGavran acquired a wealth of new information about many people groups. In addition, by interacting with those students, McGavran had opportunity to test his theories against the realities of many fields and people groups which he had never been able to visit. McGavran could also observe and monitor the discussions between those missionaries from different fields. Later McGavran was able to write of "the complex faithfulness which is church growth." His awareness and understanding of that complexity was enlarged in the time he spent with the Institute students.

3. In the Institute of Church Growth, McGavran began developing colleague relationships that reached beyond the Eugene years. Although the catalogue of Northwest Christian College for 1962-63 listed only McGavran as faculty, it included the names of four Research Fellows who would "conduct seminars and teach in their special fields of competence." The catalogue for the following year carried a new category, "Teaching Fellow," with Alan R. Tippett listed. McGavran used Tippett regularly as an instructor while Tippett was completing his doctoral studies in anthropology at the University of Oregon. Furthermore, Tippett accompanied McGavran to Fuller Theological Seminary and became part of the initial faculty there when the School of World Mission opened in the fall of 1965. Tippett made a unique contribution to numerous areas of church growth thinking throughout his association with McGavran.

4. McGavran inaugurated a "hands-on" experiment in church planting during the Eugene years. The McGavrans purchased an abandoned farm southwest of Eugene shortly after their arrival. Before long he and William Siefke, academic dean at the college, were collaborating to begin a house church in the McGavran home, the Fox Hollow Christian Church. This growing congregation now meets in a church building of its own and is known as the Twin Oaks Christian Church in Eugene, Oregon.

SCHOOL OF WORLD MISSION AND INSTITUTE OF CHURCH GROWTH

The decision to move the Institute of Church Growth to Pasadena and integrate it with the new School of World Mission at Fuller Theological Seminary can best be described as the result of a collision -- a collision between McGavran's expansive projections and the severely limited financial resources of Northwest Christian College. In light of the enormously expanded forum for McGavran's ideas that Fuller provided, however, the move could well be evaluated as directed by God.

In many respects the nearly twenty years at Fuller Theological Seminary have been the period of greatest growth for the McGavran legacy. Perhaps most important has been the solidifying, during these years, of McGavran's position as a "world class" missiologist. There is abundant evidence of this fact; illustrative is the invitation to McGavran to be one of the key speakers at the International Congress on World Evangelism, held in Lausanne, Switzerland in 1974. McGavran had never been hesitant to approach (and sometimes to confront) persons with the highest levels of missiological expertise through his correspondence. Now, his growing prestige brought him together, face-to-face, with such persons regularly. His ideas could not be ignored or dismissed as applicable to only one kind of people. He was now a force to be reckoned with in contemporary missiological thinking.

The years at Fuller gave McGavran opportunity to expand his writings greatly. **Bridges of God** and **How Churches Grow** have already been noted as growing out of his India experiences. In many respects these books were to McGavran what the "Ninety-five Theses" were to Luther. The Eugene years were occupied totally with teaching and promotion, although McGavran did edit the **Church Growth Bulletin** and publish during this time a "four way conversation" between himself, Cal Guy, Melvin Hodges and Eugene Nida under the title

Herbert M. Works, Jr.

Church Growth and Christian Mission. But it was in Pasadena that McGavran had the time and the context to formalize in print many of his principles. Perhaps his most notable accomplishment was **Understanding Church Growth**, his comprehensive description of the church growth school of thought. A few of his many other books during this period include his editing of **Crucial Issues in Missions Tomorrow**, and **Eye of the Storm** and his volume **Ethnic Realities and the Church in India**. In addition, McGavran wrote a monumental number of articles for widely diverse periodicals.

To present as his legacy only the published materials that McGavran produced would be inadequate. From the earliest days of the Institute of Church Growth in Eugene, McGavran had been heard saying to his students, "You don't write theses and dissertations; you write books!" By this he meant that the results of the investigations in church growth in many parts of the world all needed to be **published** so that they could be available to help others become more effective. "Disseminate the information!" had been a watchword of the church growth movement from its earliest days. Out of this concern and the problem of scarce funds, McGavran sent the work of a number of research associates at the Institute of Church Growth to India to be printed. In addition to the many church growth studies that have been published by students in Eugene and Pasadena, there are shelves of theses and dissertations that are still unpublished. Each of these represents the gathering and analyzing of information that ultimately is part of McGavran's legacy.

Writings that were stimulated by McGavran from the pens of other significant missiologists must also be included. Some of these represented enlargement of one or more of McGavran's concepts; others wrote to present different perspectives. Many have come from his teaching colleagues at the School of World Mission. Each must be seen as part of the total collection of "church growth materials" that have been precipitated by the ferment of McGavran's challenges.

The rapidly expanding number of missionaries who enrolled in the School of World Mission must also be understood as part of the McGavran legacy. The largest number of students at any one time at the Institute of Church Growth in Eugene was fifteen. By contrast, during the 1983-84 academic year more than 400 students are involved in the School of World Mission. These students are now taught by 10 full-time resident faculty and more than 25 visiting, part-time or adjunct instructors. Between 1965 when the School of World Mission and Institute of Church Growth began and 1984 more than 2,000 students have attended its classes. As of June, 1983 some 606 degrees have been awarded. These figures may seem to be "mere statistics." They are given flesh when one considers that most of these students returned to mission fields to implement there the insights into church growth and other missiological studies they received in Pasadena. When we add to these the uncountable multitude of persons who have been reached with the Gospel message, because of the enhanced effectiveness in evangelism and church planting of the missionaries who have studied McGavran's principles, then, the full size of the McGavran legacy begins to appear.

Long before McGavran's dream of an Institute of Church Growth became a reality, he offered his insights to whomever was ready to listen. Beginning in Eugene, but greatly enlarged in Pasadena, McGavran's travels have taken on almost a legendary quality. Rarely does a summer pass that he is not in various parts of the world, holding workshops and seminars, lecturing at overseas seminaries and colleges, and meeting with groups of isolated missionaries to help them do their jobs with greater effectiveness. Each of these opportunities enables McGavran to share his insights with others, but each also provides him with additional perspective on the complex world of peoples to whom missionaries go.

The scope of the McGavran legacy must also include his influence on his colleagues -- those with whom he taught. Certainly, not everyone who was associated with McGavran on a faculty was in full harmony with all of his perspectives. Still, all were enriched by the give-and-take of those faculty sessions. One illustration will suffice: McGavran called Ralph Winter to be the third member of his faculty in the early days of the School of World Mission. He was frequently stimulated by McGavran's vision. Ultimately, he became instrumental in the founding of the U. S. Center for World Mission, with its several educational dimensions and the interaction it provides for mission agencies located on its campus. Winter frequently credits McGavran with a significant part in challenging and encouraging him to launch into this new venture.

When one sets out to build an estate or a legacy, when is it built? When is it complete? In the financial realm the majority of persons attempting to develop a legacy find themselves never quite satisfied. There is always something more that could be added. Rarely does one stop building a legacy until the time when one is no longer able to function in a productive capacity. How many times during his lifetime did Donald Anderson McGavran reach a point where he could have retired and withdrawn from a productive role? It could have been when he returned from India. Or he could have chosen to retire in 1960 just before Ross Griffeth offered the opportunity at Northwest Christian College. It would have been logical for him to step back when the Institute moved from Eugene to Pasadena. At each of these points in McGavran's life he could see only the tremendous openings with which God was confronting him in the days ahead. In his life he has embodied the challenge he has always flung at missionaries: **Press on to tackle every new opportunity!** His life has been a model of the new opportunities he knew existed in church growth.

McGavran, himself, may have said it best in his first major book:

> The missionary enterprise has not yet experienced the degree of growth which is possible. The magnitude of opportunities for church growth would be considered by most Christian leaders as beyond the bounds of possibility. Yet the world teems with unsuspected opportunity.
>
> As concentration of resources on growing points comes to the strategy of missions, we shall find ourselves in a new era of advance (1955a:112).

BIBLIOGRAPHY

McGavran, Donald Anderson
 1955a *Bridges of God*. New York: Friendship Press.

 1955b Personal letter to Don West, July 7.

 1972 Personal interview with the author.

13

Ten Emphases in the Church Growth Movement

by Donald A. McGavran

First, the Church Growth School of Thought is Deeply Theological.

Church growth is born in theology. It arises in a certain view of God and man, sin and salvation, brotherhood and justice, heaven and hell, revelation and inspiration. The tremendous labor involved in Christian mission, the selfless outpouring of prayer and life that others may enjoy the benefits of right relationships with God as revealed in His Word, would never be undertaken for human reasons. As one looks at the history of Christian missions he sees how closely the fortunes of the apostolate have waxed and waned with the rise and fall of spiritual vitality and biblical conviction in the sending congregations and denominations.

Only those who believe that God wants church growth, continue to send their sons and daughters abroad. Only an unshakeable conviction that God wants His lost children found produces or long maintains biblical mission. Of course, when endeavor becomes institutionalized, it can continue for years on the momentum of the machine. The freight train coasts down the track for twenty miles after the boiler explodes. What we are seeing in some missionary societies today is momentum without theological steam. Long continued mission, however, demands a hot fire and a full head of steam.

A few years ago Winburn Thomas wrote an article for the **International Review of Missions**, entitled "Growth: Test of a Church's Faithfulness." Church growth men agree with that. In responsive populations, (note the condition), faithfulness to the God and Father of our Lord Jesus Christ results in church growth. It is unfaithful to come out of ripe harvest fields empty-handed.

If you would understand the church growth position at all, you must see it cradled in theological concepts -- doctrines -- which have been common to all denominations from Baptist to Roman Catholic.

The vigorous response of the Church Growth School of Thought to the deviations from these doctrines which have been built into the mode of mission being prompted by the World Council of Churches need surprise no one. We are not against the Council. But we believe that the Council, as concerns the world mission of the Church, is seriously in error, that the Commission on World Mission and Evangelism has been captured by a view of mission both wrong and disastrous.

Church growth thinking is poles apart from the theological rationale of mission which the ecumenical movement has promulgated during the last fifteen years and which found such clear expression in the Uppsala document "Renewal in Mission." The distress we voiced in the May 1968 issue of the **Church Growth Bulletin** which asked "Will Uppsala Betray the Two Billion?" rises out of the heart of the Church Growth school of Thought.

Second, The Church Growth School of Thought Advocates Proportion in Mission.

It holds that men have multitudinous needs of body, mind and soul to meet which is thoroughly Christian. The Church is properly engaged in relief of suffering, pushing back the dark pall of ignorance, and increasing productivity. But such activities must be carried out in proportion. They must never be substituted for finding the lost. Christians must never be guilty of turning from the Spirit to the flesh or of deceiving men by offering them transient betterment as eternal salvation.

In regard to the battle raging today between advocates of evangelism and social service, we say that finding the lost and bringing them back to the Father's house is a chief and irreplaceable purpose of Christian mission. It is not the only purpose. It is not even the chief purpose. It is, however, a chief and irreplaceable purpose. Finding the lost is not simply "a chief purpose." That opens the door to a very minor emphasis on what was a major emphasis in the New Testament Church. That allows men to slight our Lord's Great Commission. Bringing the lost home is a chief and irreplaceable purpose.

We plead with any who are so ardent about social justice that they define evangelism exclusively in terms of changing social structures to enable more worldly justice, saying, "Press ahead with social justice. Our ancestors were abolitionists and prohibitionists and we honor their memories. But lay at least equal stress on winning men and women to Christ and multiplying churches. Remember the two billion, shortly to be three billion, who are living and dying without any chance to become disciples of Christ, without any opportunity to sit down to the communion table and partake of the medicine of immortality. How shall they hear without a preacher, and how shall they preach unless they be sent?" We also plead with any who may be so devoted to vertical reconciliation that they tolerate horrible injustices which they have the power to correct, saying, "Press on with evangelism. But remember that the Bible straightly charges Christians to do good to all men, to love mercy, to do justice. Let your light so shine before men that they may see your good works and glorify your Father. Inasmuch as you do it to one of these least, you do it to our Savior Himself."

Third, the Church Growth School of Thought Seeks to See the Actual Situation in Mission.

It advocates action in view of true facts. It deplores the vast discrepancy between theory and practice. It seeks to bring performances into line with promise. For example, the positions set forth in Sections One and Two above are generally accepted by Christian missions and denominations and written into their constitutions. Practically, however, both liberals and conservatives,

> faced with many human needs,
> often limiting themselves to resistant populations,
> always bound by previous patterns of action,
> cumbered by institutionalism in advance of the Church,

burdened with cultural overhang, which leads
   them to evangelize and serve in Western
   ways,
committed to a non-biblical individualism,
not understanding multi-individual accession as
   a normal way men and women come to Christ,
and deceived by their own promotional efforts
   (whatever our missionaries do is wonderful!),

constantly under-emphasize and betray the truths voiced in Section One and Two. Liberals and conservatives too frequently are content to carry on "splendid mission work whether churches multiply or not." Bitter experience teaches them to entertain small expectations of church growth and they spend most of their budget, time, men and women for other things.

Perhaps it is this realistic appreciation of the true situation which sets Church Growth thought apart so decisively. We are resolved not to kid ourselves. We do a great deal of promotion, but we never inhale. We spend much time digging out the truth concerning "the amount of Church" actually there. Teaching constantly that church growth is more than number of members, that it includes growth in grace and in organic complexity, we nevertheless insist that numbers of the redeemed are never "mere." We deride the cheap scorn with which some churchmen always view church statistics and show it up for what it is -- defensive thinking afraid to face its own defeats. We preach that most worthwhile human efforts draw heavily on exact quantitative analysis and that the Church should do the same. The Church consists of countable men and women and there is nothing particularly spiritual or meritorious in not counting them.

To be sure, no one was ever saved by accurate membership counting; but then, no one was ever cured by a thermometer. Yet the physician always puts it in the patient's mouth. Statistics do not cure, but they, like the thermometer, tell a great deal about the conditions of the patient. They enable correct diagnosis. They are indispensable to responsive churchmanship. They help dispel the fog of good intentions, promotional inaccuracies, hoped for outcomes, vast generalizations and general ignorance which hide the real situation from ministers, mission boards and professors of mission. Since hard facts enable us to be better stewards of God's grace, men with church growth eyes try to be vividly aware of actual situations.

Let me give you one illustration. Professor Peter Wagner, digging into church growth in Bolivia, unearthed the fact that a two year program of Evangelism-in-Depth which held large numbers of Bible studies, multiplied preaching of the Word, dramatized the Christian cause, secured thousands of decisions for Christ, and drew Evangelicals together in a wonderful way, had, despite all this, made no significant difference to church growth. In seven denominations, church growth continued through the Evangelism-in-Depth years at the same speed it manifested before and after. As a result of Wagner's work, Evangelism-in-Depth programs are up for revision toward making them more effective.

Fourth, the Church Growth School of Thought Believes We Live in a Most Responsive World.

Searching for truth, no matter where it may lead us, we have been pressured by the weight of evidence into accepting the revolutionary idea that during these decades, the world is much more receptive to the Gospel that it has been in 1900 years. This idea is enhanced when mankind is viewed as a vast mosaic of ethnic, linguistic and cultural units. Citizens of India, for example, are not just Indians. They are members of several thousand ethnic units called castes. They are further divided by languages and dialects, and by educational and economic levels. Urban units are very different from rural units.

In almost every land some pieces of the mosaic are receptive to the Gospel. People after people, tribe after tribe, caste after caste, is now winnable. Urban segment after urban segment can now be discipled. After a professor in Hindustan Bible Institute, which enrolls 140 men training for the ministry, had studied at Fuller Seminary's School of World Missions and after a Church Growth Seminar in Madras, the faculty of the Hindustan Bible Institute decided that it was feasible to plant 100 new congregations in Madras City in receptive units of that huge metropolis.

Again, after Dr. E. C. Smith got his Master in Arts in Missiology at the Pasadena school and returned to Java, the Southern Baptist Mission there had an extraordinary spiritual revival, in the course of which it embarked on a deliberate policy of starting -- to use its words -- "thousands of house and hamlet churches" among the receptive Muslims and Chinese of East Java. The mission had started looking at East Java as a mosaic, some parts of which are receptive. It has discovered a degree of receptivity so large that only a goal such as the mission adopted would match the opportunity.

A few years ago I often said that in Africa by the year 2000 there would be a hundred-million Christians. Dr. David Barrett told me he thought my estimate far too conservative. I asked him to make one of his own and let me print it. He kindly proceeded to do the demographic calculation necessary and his estimate appeared in the May 1969 issue of the **Church Growth Bulletin.** He judged that by 2000 A.D. there would be 357 million Christians in Africa! Later, the **International Review of Missions** picked up the story and then **Time Magazine, Inc.** and other newspapers broadcast it, and it has now become part of much Christian thinking.

Church growth men keep pointing out that we live in a responsive world. This fourth characteristic of the Church Growth School of Thought is serving a useful corrective to the deep depression which so discouraged missions following World War II and the liquidation of the European Empires.

Fifth, Despite this Widespread Receptivity, Enough Discipling is not Happening.

This is partly because mission suffers from a paucity of knowledge about finding lost men and building them into the Church. For example, many missionaries and ministers are propagating the Gospel solely along the individualistic lines which in the West have been so successful in building Gathered Churches out of Culture Churches or State Churches. Ministers and missionaries simply do not know the people movement -- the mode of discipling so often used by God to bring strong and enduring Churches into being.

Paucity of knowledge concerning people movements, receptive populations, arrested Christian movements, the effects of revivals, the real outcome of the school approach in Africa, and a hundred other aspects of mission keeps the church-mission organism working in the dark, going it blind concerning its God-given task. All kinds of theories as to the desirability of methods, such as dialogue with non-Christian religions, industrial evangelism, and accomodation to culture, are propounded without adequate knowledge as to the effect these have on bringing **ta ethne** to faith and obedience.

Enough discipling is not happening -- this is typical church growth thinking. Traditional missions take offense at the word "enough" and like to consider lack of discipling as inevitable in view of the hardness of the world or the lack of funds. Church growth men recognize, of course, that some fields are so resistant that no Church grows; but they also recognize that often appeal to the difficulty of the field simply masks the fact that the Church concerned is not seeking lost sheep or is resolutely looking for them in ravines where they are not grazing. In Chile, for example, all the old-line missions are getting very little growth in a country where several hundred-thousand have become Evangelical Christians in Pentecostal Churches.

Granting quite that God is sovereign and men can neither make the Church grow nor convert anyone, the Church Growth School of Thought continually asks, "How can we be better stewards of the grace of God?" It continually turns up cases where lack of growth is clearly the result of preventable human factors. For example, several cases have come to light recently where a whole population became suddenly responsive; but because the old-line Churches were accustomed to working in highly resistant populations and did not change their ways of working, the population became Christian in new-line Churches. And it did this while the old-line Churches were bitterly criticizing "sectarian competition." They might better have been asking themselves whether, seeing their dullness of heart, God had not sent in other laborers to reap the ripened grain.

Church growth thinking insists that our goals for the next thirty years must not be set in view of the long slow exploratory periods in Christian mission. Defeats of the past are not to be our guide in estimating the future. In view of the tremendous growth of the new religions of Japan and other lands, we must give up the concept, canonized in many quarters, that the great ethnic religions of the world will continue to reject the Gospel.

An interesting thing is happening in South India. The dominant party, the DMK (Dravidian) is aggressively atheistic. It makes fun of idols. It ridicules Hinduism. It taunts the Brahmans. It has turned great numbers of Dravidians into atheists. Dr. V. B. Subbamma, the Lutheran, when doing her thesis with me some years ago, repeatedly said, "Indians are becoming Christian not from Hinduism but from atheism. Christians will make a great mistake if they fail to speak convincingly to the vacuum which the atheistic movement is creating. True, some hard-core atheists are violently against Christianity also; but tens of thousands of others have lost their faith in the monkey-tailed, elephant-headed, big-bellied gods of Hinduism and are religiously hungry. Christians must feed them." Yet in these very years some misguided missiologists limit the task in India to quiet Christian presence or patient dialogue with a Hinduism which will not listen to the Gospel.

Church growth men never tire of urging that enough church growth is not going on and suggesting that more would if God's special messengers would work at it assiduously.

Sixth, Emphasis on Research in Church Growth.

Convinced that hundreds of millions who have yet to believe are diverted from knowing Christ through a paucity of knowledge concerning discipling, the Church Growth School of Thought lays great emphasis on scientific research to ascertain the factors which affect reconciling men to God in the Church of Jesus Christ. We believe that tremendous discoveries await us there. Where have denominations grown? Where have congregations multiplied? Where have they not grown? How much -- or how little -- have they grown? Above all, why have they grown? This last question may be asked in an exact way by saying, "Why has each segment of the Church grown?" We must know accurately the growth patterns characteristic of thousands of pieces of the mosaic.

Seventh, Publishing Church Growth Studies.

Church growth men believe that the hard facts about church growth once discovered should be published, taught to ministers and missionaries, read by seriously-minded Christians and used in all evangelistic labors whether in the local churches or in nations.

We encourage those who write master's theses and doctor's dissertations to publish them. We believe that, far from withholding publication until a highly polished research has been done, it is desirable to publish "research in progress." We live in the midst of an explosion of information. Mission must discover more and more about its field and disseminate what it discovers. We hope our convictions on these matters will commend themselves to fellow professors of missions, mission executives and leaders of younger Churches and older Churches. A firm foundation of facts needs to be placed under the missionary enterprise. To do it, large scale cooperation among the Christians of many lands and many cultures is urgently required.

Eighth, Using the Sciences to Further Discipling.

The Church Growth School of Thought lays great emphasis on using the social sciences -- anthropology, sociology, psychology -- to aid Churches and missions in bringing the nations to faith and obedience. It is not merely that we use the social sciences. Every state university and almost every college does that. We use them to further discipling. The state universities often use them to further the spread of a religion of relativism. The sciences themselves, of course, are neutral. They can be used to almost any end. They can be used to prove man is the sum and substance of all things, or that he is merely a highly developed animal, or to help build the Church of Jesus Christ.

Missionary education has used anthropology for many years. When I was as student in the College of Missions in 1922-23 we studied Fraser's **Golden Bough,** Crawford's **Thinking Black, Tribes and Castes of Central Provinces,** and other similar books. Ethnological studies were undertaken to help missionary candidates know the peoples to whom they went and thus to aid discipling. After World War II, however, anthropology was taught in missionary training schools very largely for the purpose of breaking down the missionary's ethnocentricity, of destroying his race pride, of making him able to see values in other cultures. Church growth men, while not denigrating this use of anthropology, emphasize that the more we know about cultures and social structures, the better we can communicate Christ, establish churches in harmony with their surroundings and train leaders who conform to indigenous leadership patterns. Urban sociology is emphasized because the Church will disciple urban populations faster and better if it knows how these are put together, what makes them function, how they are going to develop in the decades ahead and what characteristics urban congregations and denominations are likely to exhibit.

Most of the theses which have been written at Fuller Seminary's School of World Missions and Institute of Church Growth have explored at length the anthropological nature of the people being claimed for Christ. Thus their researches provide ethnological insight for other workers in these fields. The extensive bibliographies, which form part of each research, list the books and articles available on each population concerned.

Ninth, the Church Growth School of Thought Emphasizes Classical Evangelism.

We believe every form of evangelism should be greatly increased. Personal evangelism, good deed evangelism, newspaper evangelism, radio evangelism, Evangelism-in-Depth and saturation evangelism -- all are good. Circumstances dictate which form should be used.

Evangelism is, of course, by word and deed. If the intent is to proclaim Christ and encourage men to become His disciples, then almost any activity of voice, pen, hands or feet is evangelism.

Its effectiveness is to be measured by the degree to which it does in fact communicate the faith. In judging whether evangelism is effective or not, the field must be considered. Some fields are ripe; others have yet to be bought. Evangelistic methods will be different in each.

Church growth thinking holds that when God sends men into ripe fields, He wants sheaves brought to His barn. If evangelism is not delivering them, something is the matter. Looked at from God's side, it is not faithful enough. Looked at from man's side, it is not effective enough.

For example, if thousands of decisions for Christ are obtained, but church membership remains the same, we recommend careful attention to folding and feeding the newly found sheep. If thousands become secret disciples and gradually disappear, it may be because to them existent congregations are too distant, too culturally uncomfortable, or linguistically confusing. If this is the case, we recommend not that secret discipleship be lauded as correct but that congregations be formed within the natural homogeneous units from which the secret disciples came.

Tenth, Revamping Theological Education.

The final emphasis to which I call attention is that theological education in the lands of the younger Churches should be revamped so that Bible schools and seminaries graduate men and women experienced in multiplying churches. Younger Churches cannot afford the static patterns of theological education used in the West where the Church exists in discipled populations.

Yorke Allen a few years ago surveyed the whole world and published his findings under the title **A Seminary Survey**. It showed literally hundreds of schools training leaders of Third World denominations. These institutions absorb large numbers of missionaries. Often they go out straight from seminary and begin teaching immediately. They know nothing of communicating the Gospel in that particular piece of the mosaic. They take no part in church planting evangelism. Yet they teach the oncoming ministers of the Church. Church growth theory, appalled at this, maintains that a seminary is not a place where men learn subjects. It is a place where men learn how to nurture and multiply churches.

Some years ago Clark Scanlon, while studying in the Southwestern Baptist Theological Seminary, wrote a thesis which took my eye. I encouraged him to publish it under the title **Church Growth Through Theological Education**. It has been widely read. Scanlon maintains that theological professors should themselves be competent church planters as well as historians, exegetes, theologians or what not. Seminaries should engage their students and faculties in multiplying churches. Theological education should be revamped so that passing through a seminary turns out men accustomed so to present the Good News that churches do eventuate and proliferate.

This tenth emphasis underlies theological education by extension, which has played such a prominent part in missions during the past few years. Dr. Ralph Winter first proposed extension after he had been greatly influenced by the Pentecostal Churches and their leadership training. He noted that while the Pentecostals produced church leaders who identified with their members and operated in a natural indigenous manner, Pentecostals gave their pastors inadequate biblical instruction. Winter said that theological education by extension would train the actual leaders of the congregations, those laymen who actually carry on the work of the church, and it will also give them systematic theological training. It will therefore turn out better church planters than the Pentecostal laymen preachers.

Conclusion.

I hope that something of the length and breadth of the Church Growth School of Thought is becoming apparent. As we look forward to a fuller understanding, we should avoid a small concept of the movement. Please do not identify church growth thinking with **The Bridges of God.** That book launched the movement and is still influential. But it dealt with only one aspect of church growth. The whole concept has been widened and enriched since 1955. When one speaks of church growth today he or she is talking about a way of looking at missions to which a multitude of practitioners and theorists have made contributions.

A final word. We stand at the beginning of church growth thinking. The biblical base will not change much; but we are only beginning to see the many ways in which discipling and perfecting are carried on. I invite all of you to contribute to church growth from where you stand. You have to start from your own churches, mission organizations and ecclesiologies, and work forward in your own way bringing your **ethne**, your peoples, to the obedience of the faith. To the degree that you do this, you will be engaged in church growth. We need you. In fact, we all need each other.

14

Toward the Symbiotic Ministry

by Tetsunao Yamamori

A book recently off the press is entitled **Division in the Protestant House** and has the subtitle "The Basic Reasons Behind Intra-Church Conflicts" (Hoge, 1976). It is intriguing because the author challenges many of the earlier theories concerning the sources of division in Protestantism. The relevance the book has for my immediate purpose is its demonstration that mainline Protestant churches are divided primarily over the theological issues surrounding evangelism and social action. During the last couple of decades a wide chasm has been erected and battles fought between the evangelicals and the conciliars, and among themselves, not only in this country but throughout the world, over the issue of evangelism vs. social action in the Church's mission. The phenomenon, though tragic, is significant and is called "The Great Debate in Mission" by one missiologist (McGavran, 1972). Any meaningful assessment of mission today must be couched against this great debate.

At the outset, I wish to make it perfectly clear that, in my view, evangelism and social action are not one and the same. The greatest error in recent theologies of mission is that of equating or blurring these two terms. Some conciliars have cited Jesus' reply to the lawyer (Mt. 22:37-39) to mean that to love one's neighbor, namely, social action, is the same as knowing and loving God, namely being evangelized. If this were what Jesus had intended, he could have simply responded to the lawyer's question: "You shall love your neighbor as yourself." To the contrary, however, what Jesus said was: "You shall love the Lord your God with all your heart, and with all your soul, and with all your mind -- And -- you shall love your neighbor as yourself." Even from our common sense and from our personal experiences, we know that loving our brother does not automatically result in loving our Father, and vice versa. I must articulate my love to my Father as well as to my brother. I must make conscious efforts to maintain a relationship with my Father vertically and a relationship with my brother horizontally. My relationship with my Father is one thing and my relationship with my brother is another. One does not take care of the other automatically.

Within the evangelical circle, evangelism has often been raised to the position of primacy at the expense of social action. This is equally wrong, and the confusion has risen out of a misunderstanding of not only the Great Commission but also the New Testament concept of ministry. Careful analysis of the Great Commission itself reveals to us that social action is an integral part of the Church's ministry inasmuch as in the commission Jesus commands us not only to disciple the nations and baptize them, but also to do all He has commanded; and His commandments and teachings had much to do with social action or ordering horizontal relationships.

DEFINITIONS

Personally, I define evangelism as those efforts devoted to the proclamation of the good news of God's salvation in Jesus Christ and bringing men and women under the Lordship of Christ, resulting in a vertical relationship with God; and I define social action as those efforts devoted to the liberation of man in social, political and economic shackles and to the establishment of peace, order and harmony on the horizontal plane.

Furthermore, I propose to define evangelism and social action as functionally separate, relationally inseparable and essential to the total ministry of the Church. Having thus defined the relationship between evangelism and social action, I contend as my primary theme that God's mandate for the Church today, as always, is to buttress the **symbiotic ministry** both at home and abroad.

The term "symbiotic" is the adjective of the command symbiosis, made up of a Greek prefix **sym-** meaning interdependence, and a Greek morpheme **bios** meaning life. Derived from the field of biology, it depicts the harmonious living together of two functionally dissimilar organisms in a way beneficial to each other. Linsley Gressit, in an article on the subject of symbiosis in nature, says, "The term symbiosis actually covers many levels of ecological relationships, but generally implies a distinct interdependence of two quite different living organisms" (1977:136). He goes on to say that "symbiosis may be more strictly applied to relationships that are obligatory in some sense; one partner being unable to live without the other, or each depending heavily on the other" (1977:138).

On the basis on this definition, the symbiotic ministry implies that both evangelism and social action, though separate in function, are inseparable in relation and essential to the total ministry of the Church. In other words, when there are two or more concerns or two or more forms of ministry, which, though functionally separate, are inseparable in relation and essential for the ongoing of total life, we have essentially a symbiotic ministry.

In what follows, I shall argue that the concept of symbiotic ministry is: 1) biblical; 2) historically discernible; and 3) strategically operational.

SYMBIOTIC MINISTRY IS BIBLICAL

If we take the Old Testament traditions seriously, we note that in the earliest stage of Israel's life as God's people there emerged two distinct forms of ministry: the judicio-prophetic ministry represented by Moses; and the priestly ministry represented by Aaron. These two ministries were functionally separate, but they were inseparably related to each other and essential to the ongoing process of Israel's total life as a covenant community. Next, the Deuteronomic history recognized three distinct forms of ministry in the person of Samuel: Samuel as a judge; Samuel as a prophet; and Samuel as a priest. These three offices were functionally separate, and yet form the perspective in Israel's life; they were in symbiotic relationship, with each office functioning separately but at the same time in unison with the others for the enhancement of Israel's total life as God's covenant community.

Later, the prophetic tradition, especially beginning with Amos, bears witness to the dynamic vitality of symbiotic ministry in the twofold concerns of Israel's prophets: on the one hand, concern for man's vertical, personal relationship with God (or the knowledge of God, to borrow

Hosea's phrase); and on the other hand, concern for man's horizontal relationship -- "Do justice, correct oppression, plead for the widow and defend the fatherless" -- (to borrow Isaiah's words). From the perspective of the prophets, to have an intimate, personal, loving relationship vertically with Yahweh and with Him alone, in the Hoseanic sense of knowledge of God, was one facet of Israel's covenant responsibility; and to "let justice roll down like waters and righteousness like an overflowing stream" in one's horizontal relationships was another. To the prophets, the two were neither identical nor exclusive. They viewed the two relationships as involving two distinctly separate objects but at the same time as mutually inseparable and essential for the full realization of God's kingdom. In the prophet's view, one could not live without the other; one without the other was a "vain offering" in the words of Isaiah. Hence, the prophetic ministry at its heart was symbiotic because, while recognizing the distinctiveness of the two concerns, it aimed at relating the two inseparably together for the total life of God's kingdom.

Turning to the New Testament, first we see in the very life of Jesus a symbiotic ministry in action. Throughout the Gospels we find Jesus teaching, preaching and healing. Matthew describes Jesus' ministry in this way: "And He went about all Galilee, teaching in their synagogues and preaching the gospel of the kingdom and healing every disease and every infirmity of the people" (Mt. 4:23). Teaching, preaching and healing are treated as separate functions but are understood as essential to the ministry of Jesus. The text does not allow us to equate evangelism with social action.

Secondly, the very nature of the Church defined as the body of Christ attests to the unavoidability of the symbiotic ministry. In his epistles to the Romans and to the Corinthians, the apostle Paul defines the Church as the body of Christ, consisting of diverse members, each member with its own function, but all working symbiotically. In Paul's own words: "as in one body we have many members, and all members do not have the same function, so we, though many, are one body in Christ, and individually members of one another" (Rm. 12:4-5). Elsewhere, speaking of the Church's ministry, Paul says: "And His gifts were that some should be apostles, some evangelists, some pastors and teachers, to equip the saints for the work of ministry, for building up the body of Christ, until we all attain to the unity of faith and of the knowledge of the Son of God, to mature manhood, to the measure of the stature of the fullness of Christ" (Eph. 4:11-13).

Thirdly, the very life of the early Church as attested in the Book of Acts was the symbiotic ministry in action. In the early stages of the Church's life following Pentecost the Christians were engaged in both proclaiming the good news, or evangelism, and meeting each other's needs, that is, social action.

As seen in these examples in the life of the Old Testament community, in the personal ministry of Jesus Himself, in the teaching of the apostle Paul and in the life of the early Church, the concept of symbiotic ministry is biblical.

SYMBIOTIC MINISTRY CAN BE SEEN HISTORICALLY

Amidst the missiological debates and concerns in recent years, the trend has been one of movement towards the symbiotic ministry. The Uppsala Assembly of the World Council of Churches in 1968 was the occasion that triggered the current "great debate." The section entitled "Renewal in Mission" was openly challenged by some notable evangelical leaders. The document defined the goal of mission not in terms of proclaiming the good news of personal salvation in Christ and persuading men and women to become His disciples and responsible members of His Church, but rather in terms of humanization with an emphasis on the Church's sociopolitico-economic involvement in the world.

If the fuel of the debate was ignited at the time of Uppsala, the debate between the conciliars and the evangelicals was reaching its combustive state by the time of the Bangkok conference of the Commission for World Evangelism and Mission in 1973. The conference dealt with the topic of "Salvation Today." Philip Potter, General Secretary of the World Council of Churches, defined salvation in terms of "liberation of persons and societies from all that prevents them from living an authentic existence in justice and shared community" (Hoke, 1973:84). In these conferences, there were, to be sure, statements acknowledging man's need to be saved from sin and all its consequences, but the main thrust remained in the direction of equating evangelism with social action.

In the meantime, the Lausanne Congress on World Evangelism was convened in 1974 and it issued the Lausanne

Covenant which collaborated the divergent views within the evangelical circle on evangelism and social action. It expresses concern for Christian social responsibility and ties that concern to evangelism. In it we see an incipient concept of the symbiotic ministry. In the words of the Covenant, "... we express penitence both for our neglect and for having sometimes regarded evangelism and social concern as mutually exclusive. Although reconciliation with man is not reconciliation with God, nor is social action evangelism, nor is political liberation salvation, nevertheless we affirm that evangelism and socio-political involvement are both part of our Christian duty" (Douglas, 1975:4-5).

In 1975 the Nairobi Assembly of the World Council of Churches met with much anticipation and anxiety under the main theme "Jesus Christ Frees and Unites." The much debated issue at Nairobi was over evangelism vs. social action. Bishop Mortimer Arias of the Evangelical Methodist Church in Bolivia, in his keynote speech on evangelism, emphasized the "holistic approach" in which he failed to clearly distinguish between evangelism and social action. For example, after enumerating fourteen kinds of activities -- some in the category of evangelism and others in the category of social action -- in which the World Council of Churches has been engaged since its inception, he declared: "All this is mission, and it can be an integral part of true evangelism in the world today" (Arias, 1976:16).

When Bishop Arias said, "All this (namely, all these fourteen kinds of activities) is an integral part of true evangelism in the world today," he was implying that evangelism and social action are one and the same. I personally find it difficult to accept such an uncritical equation in view of my own definition of evangelism and social action. This failure to make the distinction between evangelism and social action was apparent not only in the keynote address of Bishop Arias but also in the Council's study documents. This generated dissatisfaction on the part of the evangelically oriented segment within the Council. Consequently, in its final report, the Nairobi Assembly opted to include the following compromise statement: "As our high priest, Christ mediates God's new covenant through both salvation and service. Through the power of the cross, Christ promises God's righteousness and commands true justice. As the royal priesthood, Christians are therefore **called to engage in both evangelism and social action**" (Paton, 1976:43, emphasis mine). This, like the Lausanne Covenant, expresses a concept of symbiotic ministry. Since Lausanne and Nairobi there have been three world conferences involving both evangelicals and conciliars: Melbourne (1980), Pattaya (1980), and Vancouver (1983). Each of these conferences continued to uphold the concept of the symbiotic ministry. History alone, however, will prove the genuineness of the evangelicals' commitment to social action and the conciliars' commitment to evangelism.

SYMBIOTIC MINISTRY IS STRATEGICALLY OPERATIONAL

My final thesis is that the Church can successfully fulfill its commitment both to evangelism and to social action in symbiotic relations. The key question is how we maintain a system of vital balance in the ongoing symbiosis, as within a natural ecological system.

One of the most dangerous phenomena within the ecological system is the development of parasitism. Parasitism occurs when "one organism appears to have all the advantage while the other is harmed, as with barnacles on whales or fleas on dogs" (Gressit, 1977:136). Danger of such a parasitism is always present in the Church's ministry for the same reason, namely, one particular activity having all the advantage or being given priority over the other aspects of Christian concern. When constant care and self-examination are not exercised, the Church's ministry, instead of becoming symbiotic, may degenerate into a parasitism. I am afraid that too much parasitic ministry is already present in the Church, sometimes deliberately and sometimes inadvertently; and this is the real issue in the evangelical vs. social action debate today.

Another missiological danger, as equally self-defeating as parasitism, is artificial parallelism which adheres to the principle of a 50-50 proportion in every situation. This is too mechanical and may result in the wastefulness of resources as well as opportunities.

I propose that the only way we can prevent the Church's ministry from degenerating into an inadvertent parasitism and/or mechanical parallelism is by applying what I call the principle of **contextual symbiosis.** By this I mean that the strategy of viable symbiotic ministry which aims at the total ministry of God's kingdom must be determined by contextual factors. In other words, the nature of needs, problems, opportunities, receptivity to the Gospel and available resources within a given context of the Church's ministry must determine which aspect of the ministry be underscored at any given time in order that God's work can be accomplished as fully as possible. The principle of contextual symbiosis is not only sensible, practical and necessary, but also Biblical.

In the Old Testament, the moral and spiritual crises that prevailed in pre-exilic Israel and Judah gave birth to the unique phenomenon of the prophetic movement. After the exile, in the absence of the temple and its cultic activities, there emerged within the diaspora Jewish community a movement which sought to relate members of a covenant community vertically and horizontally in terms of **torah**-centered life.

In the New Testament we note the principle of contextual symbiosis, first of all in the life of Jesus who determined the nature and type of His ministry in accordance with contextual factors. For example, in ministering to members of the upper classes such as Sadducees, Pharisees, lawyers and scribes, His ministry was primarily that of preaching and theological discourses. With them He was rarely involved in healing or feeding. In His ministry to the masses His work included not only preaching and teaching but also healing and feeding. And in still other contexts such as His encounter with a Syro-Phoenecian woman, His ministry was primarily one of healing. In these cases, the nature of needs and audience were the determining factors. In sending forth the twelve into a preaching and healing mission, described in Mt. 10, Jesus instructed them that their movement be guided by the nature of people's receptivity of them.

Then in the early life of the Church, the principle of contextual symbiosis determined the nature of the Church's ministry, the nature of its thrust and the nature of its priorities. For example, in the immediate aftermath of Pentecost, the Church carried out its ministry in terms of preaching, teaching, healing and sharing as illustrated in the Book of Acts. As long as the Church remained predominantly Jewish, it expressed its faith and life largely in terms of traditional Jewish ways such as worshipping in the temple and practicing circumcision. The Church in Jewish context determined such expressions. When the Church moved out into the Gentile world, the new context confronting the Church now called for different expression of faith and life as is well known in Paul's strategy with the Gentiles.

Keeping in mind that contextual factors thus determined the nature of the Church's ministry both in the Old and New

Testament life, we can comfortably apply the same principle to our ministry today.

In our mission today, diverse contextual factors confront the Church in the fulfillment of its ministry. America with its industrial and technological advancement plus its secularizing trend presents one kind of context. The Islamic world with its monotheistic faith and its traditional resistance to the Gospel presents another kind. Africa and Western Oceania, with their continued receptivity to the Gospel, present yet another context; the People's Republic of China, with its hitherto anti-Christian policy, still another; and Latin American, with its Catholic entrenchment and oppressed masses, still another. Different contextual factors exist further within each one of these entities.

It may be that one given context would allow the Church to render only relief ministry in terms of feeding the hungry, healing the sick and educating the uneducated. Or, this may lead to a development ministry whereby people are helped to help themselves. In such a context, the Church, recognizing that such a ministry is valid in itself and integral to God's kingdom, should be faithful to that form of ministry, without feeling guilt, while searching for any possible avenue of evangelistic ministry. By the same token, if another context, such as Indonesia with its extraordinary receptivity to the Gospel, calls for major thrusts of evangelistic ministry, the Church must respond to that call directly or indirectly while doing its very best in providing other needed ministries in the light of its available resources and personnel. In still another context, such as Japan, a major industrial and economic nation, wherein a basic need of people is met, the Church must concentrate its efforts on evangelistic ministry. And in yet another context, such as Brazil, which presents equal opportunity for both evangelism and social action, the Church must thrust itself in evangelistic efforts without neglecting opportunities for social action ministry.

IN SUMMARY

1. Evangelism and social action, though functionally separate, are relationally inseparable and essential to the total ministry of the Church.

2. It is my contention that God's mandate for the Church today, as always, is to buttress the symbiotic

ministry which aims at relating the two to each other inseparably for the total life of God's kingdom.

3. The concept of symbiotic ministry is biblically supported.

4. The missiological trend in recent years has been moving toward the symbiotic ministry as God's mandate for the Church.

5. For strategic operability, the symbiotic ministry must be guided by the principle of contextual symbiosis.

BIBLIOGRAPHY

Arias, Mortimer
   1976 "That the World May Believe." International Review of Mission. 65:13-26.

Douglas, J. D. (ed.)
   1975 Let the Earth Hear His Voice. Minneapolis: World Wide Publications.

Gressit, J. Linsley
   1977 "Symbiosis Runs Wild on the Backs of High-Living Weevils." Smithsonian. 7:11:135-140.

Hoge, Dean R.
   1976 Division in the Protestant House: The Basic Reasons Behind the Intra-Church Conflicts. Philadelphia: Westminster Press.

Hoke, Donald
   1973 "Salvation Isn't the Same Today," in The Evangelical Response to Bangkok. South Pasadena: William Carey Library.

McGavran, Donald A. (ed.)
   1972 Eye of the Storm: The Great Debate in Mission. Waco: Word Books.

Paton, David M. (ed.)
   1976 Breaking Barriers: Nairobi 1975. Grand Rapids: William B. Eerdmans Pub. Co.

15

Inter-Cultural Leadership Development

by Edgar J. Elliston

Churches in the non-Western world are facing serious problems in the area of leadership development and theological education. Two kinds of problems commonly affect both the growing churches and the static or declining ones. In the first place the church has inadequate numbers of trained leaders. The growth of the church in many areas only serves to underscore this problem. Secondly, many training programs educate leaders in inappropriate ways so their graduates are ill prepared to minister in the church contexts to which they are called. In contexts where the church is declining, the decline is often related to the inadequate or inappropriate education of church leaders.

Very often western missionaries or westernized national church leaders simply transplant western Bible institutes, Bible colleges, seminaries or non-contextualized Theological Education by Extension into the non-western contexts with the same curriculum, teaching methods and resource materials as is used in other contexts. For example, note how pleased we are when "our" doctrinal textbooks used in our Bible colleges are translated for use overseas with no thought given to the context of the new readers. What has been learned here or elsewhere in terms of content, form and style is simply transplanted into the new situation.

As curricula planners continue to follow a westernized schooling approach, several predictable problems emerge: a) hierarchically based, status oriented and culturally dislocated leaders; b) educational programs which require heavy foreign subsidies in terms of finances and foreign trained personnel; c) slowed growth in the church as the trained leaders become increasingly dislocated from their local cultural context, values and worldview; d) increasing passivity among the "laity" with increasing dependence upon the trained leaders or "clergy;" e) an intellectual merit system where status is acquired by knowing; f) a leadership structure in which pride and status become self-serving ends; and g) manipulative tactics which is a leadership style characterized by the controlling of others to one's own advantage through playing on guilt, fear, division, gossip or other such means (Elliston, 1982:189).

With these problems facing the church we must more urgently seek to develop leaders who both measure up to the biblical criteria for Christian leaders and who indeed effectively lead the church by enabling every member to serve using his or her gifts. Our concern then in this chapter is the development of theological education which leads to a functioning ministry. We seek to train a ministry which remains true to the Scripture **and** which functions in culturally appropriate ways.

Curricula planners need to make several crucial decisions before any educational program is planned or before and existing curricula are improved. If these decisions are not consciously decided, they will be unconsciously assumed. Such assumptions will be heavily conditioned by the planners own cultural heritage. In inter-cultural contexts such assumptions based on another culture than the target culture nearly always lead to less relevant and less effective educational programs than desired. This chapter then seeks to outline five areas in which decisions must be considered to help in the development of contextualized theological education which functions in the local context: 1) What values will be employed for evaluating the purposes, resources, processes and results? 2) What is the context to be served? 3) What resources are to be utilized? 4) Given the contextual and resource constraints, what kinds of educational processes or structures are appropriate? 5) What should be done about evaluation?

VALUES

The effective educator will identify the values which undergird the whole educational program and which form the bases for evaluation very early in the educational enterprise. One's values shape the way he looks at the context, sets goals, assembles and administers resources, structures educational processes and then evaluates results. In this chapter we will identify only four of many value domains which require attention in formulating Christian leadership development curricula. These value domains include: 1) New Testament values for Christian leadership; 2) Curricular values; 3) Anthropological values; and 4) Developmental values.

New Testament Values for Christian Leaders

Jesus clearly taught and demonstrated the basic leadership values for Christian leaders. The Apostles Paul and Peter further clarified these values both by their actions and teachings. We turn to Jesus Christ as the primary source of instruction for criteria in evaluating "Christian" leaders. While many lessons can be drawn from Old Testament leaders, we turn to Christ as the primary referent for Christian leaders.

Christian leaders should **function as servants.** The key feature of Jesus' leadership was servanthood. He clearly saw Himself as a servant (Mk. 10:45; Lk. 22:27). The Apostle Paul also describes Jesus as a servant in Phil. 2:5-11. The life of Jesus and His disciples clearly demonstrated that "the servant is a person who is among, not over those whom he leads" (Richards, 1975:133).

The goal of theological education and leadership development programs then is to develop mature Christian servants. Ward describes such a leader:

> a leader is one who ministers; a leader serves through the gifts of the Holy Spirit; not in terms of prowess, not in terms of accomplishments or acquired knowledge, but in terms of what God is doing through his or her life. Leadership in the church is servanthood (1978:13).

Christian leaders **should live in ways which are exemplary and above reproach** in their communities. The Apostle Paul made this point very clear to Timothy and Titus (II Tim. 3; Titus 1:6-10). While the specific characteristics of these lists receive much attention, this main point is often missed.

Christian leaders **should be distributed within the church** with different persons "leading" according to the particular gift he or she may have. The Apostle Paul's descriptions of the employment of the gifts of the Spirit in the context of the fruits of the Spirit (I Cor. 12-14; Rom. 12:2-8; Eph. 4:1-13) clearly teach a distributed leadership within the Body of Christ. In each of these references the ideal of mutual ministry or mutual servanthood underlies the means by which the functioning is to be accomplished.

Hans Kung calls for a distributed leadership whereby the total membership of the church is employed in ministry.

> The Church's ministry of leadership is meant essentially not to be an autocratic authority absorbing all other functions, but one ministry in the midst of a multiplicity of other charisms and functions: a stimulating, coordinating and integrating ministry to the congregation and the other ministries... (1972:83).

Christian leaders should not base their leadership on their own rank, status or power. In Matthew 23:1-12 Jesus clearly exposes both the leadership styles to be avoided and by contrast those elements of leadership which should characterize Christian leaders. While the Greeks are not specifically mentioned in this passage, the corrupted aspects of their influence and the misapplication of the teachings and authority of Moses are soundly rebuked. Whether the abuses were due to Hellenizing influences or the misinterpretation and application of Moses' teachings, Jesus thoroughly criticized the religious leaders for any leadership style which relied on power, status or rank.

We sometimes read this passage only noting Jesus' criticism of the Pharisees. We then say to ourselves, "We are not Pharisees, so what He said does not apply to us." However, these teachings most certainly do apply to us because we too have been deeply affected by the Greeks. We also frequently rely on power, status and rank to maintain leadership positions or influence. By our leading in this way we also teach emerging leaders to continue in these unacceptable patterns.

One often reads in books on Christian leadership styles how authority may be ascribed to or employed by Christian leaders. However, the source of these writings very often is the western culture from which they spring. Richards and Hoeldtke state:

The assumption (of secular concepts of authority) is that the goal of one who has authority is to cause others to do his will. But this is never the goal of the Spiritual leader in the Body of Christ. The Christian leader always seeks to bring others, and the whole local body, to a responsive relationship with Jesus Christ. Our goal is to help others seek, come to know and do His will (1980:138).

Christian leaders **should contribute to the purpose, fulness and functioning of the Church.** The Apostle Paul taught this value in Eph. 4:11-13, and in I Cor. 12:7 where he summarized, "but to each one is given the manifestation of the Spirit for the common good." It is the work of all Christian leaders to keep the Body in such a state that every member can minister.

Christian leaders **should reproduce themselves through others.** Jesus' commission to His disciples in Galilee forms the basis for this value (Mt. 28:19-20). His command was to disciple the nations or peoples. One essential part of this discipling is teaching the new disciples to obey all that Christ commanded. Paul's instructions to Timothy to teach others what he had been taught (II Tim. 2:2) remains relevant for us today.

Nicholls summarizes our concern about goals for the leaders who receive the theological education we prepare and then go out as Christian leaders:

> The goals of theological education must focus on the kind of person we expect the student to become. Theological education is to train men and women in Christian discipleship so that they become truly men and women of God (1982:13).

> The goal of training the man of God is to bring to maturity his missiological commitment to the proclamation of the Gospel, to the nurture of believers, and to teaching in truth and righteousness; the goal is as well to inspire compassionate service for the poor and despised and sick of this world, and also for the rich and those with whom we have cultural affinity (1982:15).

Curricular Values

The whole educational process should equip the leaders to function effectively in the community to be served and to continue to develop and grow with that community. The educational process should integrate the learners in the community for effective service, not dislocate them from the target community. This value is primary to the other curricular values which are to be considered.

> Properly understood, theological education facilitates the maturation process in students so that they can in turn facilitate that process in others (Plueddemann, 1982:57).

Without integration in the community one can hardly facilitate the maturing process in others.

The curricular decisions which are to be made in the program development are the "**should decisions** which directly lead to the curriculum activities" (McKean, 1977:4). "Should decisions" are value decisions. When one says, "This **should** be done," he is reflecting a value position.

McKean says that curriculum development is the process of making the decisions about what ought to be taught and why, and then putting those decisions into practice. He further states:

> The decisions in curriculum development are not merely mechanical decisions that can be arrived at by systematically working through a flow chart. They are value decisions (1977:2).

The whole educational enterprise -- planning, implementation and evaluation -- should reflect values which are consistent with other values mentioned in this chapter.

The educational goals ought to be appropriate for both the community to be served and the students to be taught. If, for example, the community to be served is a traditional pastoral society whose average literacy rate is less than 15% and whose economy is just beginning to enter the national monetary economy, a goal of bachelor's degree level or graduate level training for church leaders would not be appropriate educationally. A more appropriate level would be completion of a primary level education plus participation in a theological education process which allows the learners to continue to serve in their local churches. On the other hand, if the community to be served is an urban one with many professional people or college graduates, then graduate level education would be appropriate.

The objectives ought also to be appropriate for the learners. The skills, knowledge and attitudes which are to be brought into a learning focus should relate to the current levels and needs of the learners as well as for the communities to be served. The learning experiences should allow the learners to learn by practicing the use of the knowledge, skills and attitudes in ways that are appropriate in the community to be served.

As the curriculum development continues, the values of continuity, sequence and integration should be employed in shaping the learning experiences. Tyler defines these values by writing:

> Continuity involves the recurring emphasis in the learner's experience...; sequence refers to the increasing breadth and depth of the learner's development; and integration refers to the learner's increased unity of behavior in relating to the elements involved (1949:96).

It is necessary that an educational program should begin from where the learners are. An implication of this value can be employed by beginning the focus of the training of church leaders around indigenous values and attitudes which correspond with biblical values. For example, among the Samburu and Maasai of Kenya the value of "worthiness" or "respect," enkanyit, is very important for any leader. Since this value parallels a key biblical value, it may serve as one beginning point for leadership instruction.

Another value which ought to be considered is the cognitive style of the learners. Through what mental processes, strategies and meditations do they learn? For example, among westerners who have spent many years in a school environment it is expected that one will learn new information from reading. Aural learning sources are generally not the most effective way of learning. However, among many nonliterate peoples the skill to remember verbatim long sections of text which were heard only rather than read is not uncommon. Among some peoples the use of parables and proverbs is a much more effective way to teach than to follow western logical sequences.

Anthropological Values

One's view of his fellow men and their cultures heavily conditions his potential for effective and appropriate teaching in other cultures. An ethnocentric approach to curriculum development is not only deeply offensive, it is also ineffective.

Cultural relativism provides a basic value for approaching cross-cultural interactions. Without mutual acceptance and respect among men of varying cultures, the opportunities for effective education remain remote. Cultural relativism maintains

> that an observer should be careful to evaluate a culture first in terms of its own values, goals and focuses before venturing to compare it (either positively or negatively) with another culture (Kraft, 1979:49).

Anthropologists have generally agreed that

> cultures are to be regarded not as assignable to some level of overall superiority or inferiority with respect to other cultures, but rather as more or less equal to each other in their overall ability to meet the needs felt by their members (Kraft, 1979:49).

Even within scripture the authors treat different cultures in a relativistic way. While God's ideal is clearly seen, the fact that He deals with people from different cultures beginning from within their frames of reference is significant. Nida shows that the Bible

> clearly recognizes that different cultures have different standards and that these differences are recognized by God as having different values. The relativism of the Bible is relative to three principle factors: 1) the endowment and opportunities of people; 2) the extent of revelation; and 3) the cultural patterns of the society in question (Kraft, 1979:52).

One implication of this anthropological value is that one should give serious attention to the indigenous leadership values and learning patterns in any curriculum planning. Both positive and negative values should be noted.

The value of "worthiness" or "respect" was mentioned above as a positive value. An example of a negative value may be seen from the same cultures. The Samburu and the Maasai distrust a leader who has been appointed by someone from outside their own culture or who openly aspires to a leadership position. This distrust is openly evident especially if he has received training from an outsider. If in a training program for those cultures that negative value is not considered, the early leaders in a church situation may be discredited through no fault of their own, but through the ignorance of the curriculum planners or foreign church leaders.

Another implication we ought to consider is the likely outcomes of our actions in the local culture and seek to avoid those outcomes which would be disruptive. For example, it is often possible among some peoples to train young men to become leaders, and then to give them status based on their completion of the training. However, if they are to serve in a community which assigns leadership status on other qualifications, such as age as opposed to youth, then there will be resistance or perhaps even conflict.

God is able and does work in and through the diverse cultures of men. As men turn to Him through Christ, the Holy Spirit does His work of regeneration. We can have confidence in the leaders God raises up for His people among cultures different from our own. If the leaders are committed to Christ and rely on His Word, we can and should have confidence both in them and in the Holy Spirit's leading in their lives.

Developmental Values

We are considering leadership **development**. If we expect the leaders who go out from our educational programs to continue to lead in developmental ways then this whole concern should be approached in a developmental way. Curriculum planners should plan and implement the curriculum in developmental ways. One important way to facilitate a "developmental curriculum" is to prepare it with those to be served rather than just for them.

Miller's definition of development provides a useful way of thinking about leadership development because the same processes apply. He says:

Development is a process by which people gain greater control over themselves, their environment and their future, in order to realize the full potential of life that God has made possible (Sider, 1981:19).

One can observe at least five sequential stages in a developmental process. These stages nearly always follow the same order. However, the overall process may be arrested before its completion. Shortsightedness, pride or a desire to grasp power on the part of the ones teaching in inter-cultural contexts often causes the process to prematurely abort. Ward describes the sequence in this process along with the attendant problems of each stage. He suggests that each subsequent stage should be entered as soon as possible to prevent the problems which occur with each prior stage (Ward, 1977).

DEVELOPMENTAL STAGES AND THEIR RELATED PROBLEMS

RELATIONSHIP	RELATED PROBLEM
Giving	Dependency
Helping	Oppression
Teaching	Hierarchy
Leading	Authoritarianism
Sharing	No associated problem

One may observe this sequence in the whole curriculum development process. In fact, one may expect to see it in the whole leadership development process. As one considers the process of developing leadership in an emerging church, the five key words in the first column of this diagram characterize the sequence of what typically occurs unless it is thwarted along the way and stagnates in the related problems, as shown in column two.

The evangelist or missionary begins by **giving** leadership to the new group. If the group does not grow beyond his giving to the point where some of its own leaders begin to emerge, then they become **dependent** upon him. However, if all he does is help them, they will soon feel **oppressed** and begin to harbor resentment toward him. This problem with oppression may be overcome by **teaching** them to lead and to function in their own context. Teaching, however, can not be the end of the process because it typically leads to a **hierarchical** situation where the teacher is above the student. Students aspire to be like the teacher and to be above others. The teacher can move beyond these problems by effective **leadership**. However, a typical problem associated with leadership -- especially from a western perspective -- is **authoritarianism**. This problem may be overcome by genuine participation and **sharing**. The current concept of "partnership in mission" should then characterize our way of relating and working with the emerging church and her leaders. The primary value then being advocated is that the developmental process should continue until there is genuine sharing and participation by all involved.

In the above discussion only four value domains were listed. Each of these value domains serves to give direction and to condition the leadership education which is to be developed or improved. Rather than assume these values, one is well advised to carefully consider what values he will adopt and then employ them carefully and consistently as he makes other decisions relating to the development of curricula.

CONTEXT TO BE SERVED

It may seem trivial to suggest that one should decide upon which context to serve and then to know that context. However, too often "it has gone without saying..." How often have theological education programs been developed without regard to either the church community to be served or to the learners who ought to be taught?

Leadership is primarily expressed in terms of relationships. All of these relationships exist in a context. Within the concept of leadership are four major variables:

> 1) the characteristics of the leader; 2) the attitudes, needs and other personal characteristics of the followers; 3) characteristics of the organization, such as its purpose, its structure, the nature of the tasks to be performed; and 4) the social, economic and political milieu (McGregor, 1976:19-20).

All four of these variables comprise part of the context which must be understood.

The question of **who** is to be taught remains one of the more difficult contextual and resource questions facing theological educators. Are the older men who are already established as leaders in the community and the church, but who probably do not have advanced educational status the primary target group for the theological education? Or, are the younger men who may have more formal education but no leadership status in the church or community the proper primary target group? While one does not have to completely exclude the other, in practice the answer to this question significantly affects the whole structure of the educational system.

Initially, the purpose of knowing the context is to prepare appropriate goals and objectives for that context. Ultimately, the purpose of knowing and working within that context is to present the gospel in terms that the people can and will hear, and so that they will become responsible and reproducing disciples of Jesus Christ. Knowing the context is an early essential step in the contextualization of Christian leadership.

Curriculum planners may ask several questions to begin to understand the wider context. What is the nature of the community to be served? What language to the people speak? What is the church situation? What do the people know of God? of Jesus? What is the average adult educational level? What other religions are represented in the community and what is their relative strength?

Only when the community to be served and the primary target group who will be taught are known, can one establish appropriate educational goals. The training goals would be vastly different, for example, for a traditional nonliterate animistic society and a modern, educated and partially evangelized Buddhist society. When the context is known the job descriptions or "ministry descriptions" for Christian leaders can be defined. A careful evaluation of the context is needed to enable us to set appropriate goals and more specific objectives.

RESOURCES TO BE UTILIZED

Before structuring any educational program, one must give attention to the **resources** available for that program. One must look at the resources which are available and decide which ones to use and which ones not to use or how to combine them. One might decide, for example, that one constraint for all of the church leadership development programs might be that they would be fully supported by the churches they are designed to serve. If this decision were made, the curriculum planners would certainly seek to limit outside resources, emphasize local resource development and structure the program accordingly. If such a decision were made early in the planning, then appropriate educational structures could be designed with this constraint built in. However, if this kind of decision is made after the program has been structured, it is much more difficult to implement.

The available resources offer opportunities, constraints and dangers for program development and ultimately for the development of leaders. As one begins to decide how to employ the available resources, the temptation often arises to employ resources in ways which will not consistently facilitate a developmental educational system. Often the temptation also emerges to build educational structures which are not primarily based on the resources of those churches and church leaders to be served. For example, since it is generally easy to raise money and personnel from western churches for any well presented appeal, many theological education programs are structured with these resources serving both as initial and sustaining support. However, the provisions of outside resources may in fact debilitate the national church's leadership potential. Administered properly, outside resources may serve to "prime the pump." However, improperly administered they may "flood the well" and effectively shut off any significant local support. Therefore, the constraints of local resources should be considered in program structuring.

We must be careful when we are tempted to say, "All of the other churches are starting graduate seminaries. Therefore, we should also." Or, "I want our national church leaders to have all of the educational opportunities I have had even if I have to raise the money to pay for them." One can easily move outside a developmental mode. The reason for the caution is not to hold back the development of leadership education among the third world churches, but in fact to develop it! The goal is not to stop using outside resources, but to use them (if they are to be used) in ways which will in fact develop the long term potential growth of the church.

A key resource, which often is not considered a resource for planning, is the body of learners-in-training.

They bring to the whole learning situation a wealth of experience which may be employed to enrich the whole program. They also bring their own limitations which will affect the way an educational program ought to be structured.

A curriculum planner, therefore, not only makes decisions about financial inputs, but he also is concerned about personnel, facilities, teaching materials and student resources. One can not build an educational program without each of these crucial inputs. Choices are generally available for each of these resources. As the choices are considered, one should maintain a consistent support of the previously stated values lest the program drift from being responsive to the needs of the community to be served or from being genuinely developmental.

EDUCATIONAL PROCESSES

After one has identified his values, the context in which he is to work and the resources which are to be available, then he can make the key curricular decisions. A variety of options remain open. One often begins with the assumption that an educational system or training program must begin first with a school (Bible institute, Bible college or Graduate Seminary) for theological education. However, many choices are available which enable one to work in contexts where schooling may not be appropriate. Schools have been a dominant part of western culture since before the time of Christ. But they are not always the best choice for educating leaders in non-western cultures. Figure One contrasts the more traditional formal or schooling mode and the nonformal mode of curricular decision-making. Within this set of contrasts one can immediately see a number of choices which broaden one's options for decision-making. While the two different options suggested need not be mutually exclusive, often in practice they overlap very little.

As one begins to weigh the contrasts in Figure One, four questions suggested by Tyler provide a useful base from which to work: 1) What educational purposes are to be attained? 2) How can learning experiences be selected which are likely to be useful in attaining the objectives? 3) How can learning experiences be organized for effective instruction? 4) How can the effectiveness of the learning experiences be evaluated? (1949:1). Answering these four questions will provide new options to the educational problems we face.

IDEAL TYPES OF MODELS OF FORMAL AND NONFORMAL EDUCATION

FORMAL EDUCATION	NONFORMAL EDUCATION
PURPOSES	
Long-Term and General	Short-Term and Specific
Credential-Based	Non-credential based
TIMING	
Long-Cycle	Short-Cycle
Preparatory	Recurrent
Full-Time	Part-Time
CONTENT	
Input-Centered and Standardized	Output-Centered and Individualized
Academic	Practical
Clientele Determined by Entry Requirements	Entry Requirements Determined by Clientele
DELIVERY SYSTEM	
Institution-Based	Environment-Based
Isolated	Community-Related
Rigidly Structured	Flexibly Structured
Teacher-Centered	Learner-Centered
Resource-Intensive	Resource-Saving
CONTROL	
Externally Controlled	Self-Governing
Hierarchical	Democratic

Figure One   (adapted from Simkins, 1977:12-15).

Formal Education

The formal or schooling approach to theological education and leadership development provides a long term means by which input-centered and standardized curricula can be taught. It is characterized by being preparatory rather than practical. Being institution-based it is typically isolated from the "real life" of the community where it is located and from the community where the students will ultimately serve. The formal educational structure generally adheres inflexibly to traditions and institutional rules. It provides an opportunity for advanced theoretical considerations in a teacher-centered hierarchical context. The goal of "academic excellence" is sought sometimes as an end in itself without involvement in the community to be served or in the lives of the students. Many criticisms continue to focus on the lack of practical or immediate relevance of formal educational programs.

Sometimes the needs for facilities, faculties, teaching materials, boarding costs and the salary expectations of the graduates place the total costs of a formal approach far beyond the ability of third world churches.

Administrators of a formal educational system generally accept only those students who can give full time and attention to learning. This kind of structure makes it very difficult for mature settled adults to participate. Men and women who have begun leading and who are settled in their communities find it difficult to go to school. This kind of system then is generally forced to focus on the young, unsettled and inexperienced who are as yet not functioning in adult leadership roles.

Ward lists some of the weaknesses of a schooling approach which debilitate leadership training in formal theological education:

1) All learners are assumed to be similar in terms of needs, interests and abilities.
2) Learners are increasingly made more competitive at the price of cooperation.
3) Learners are expected to be receptors of learning rather than communicators.
4) The learners' part in decision-making is minimal and tends to be steadily reduced.
5) The content to be learned is justified in terms of future needs of the learner.
6) Rewards are symbolic more than real (1978:2).

He further states,

> Schooling has been ... the principle means by which the privileged few within a society can maintain themselves and their kind through an apparently 'just' and unassailable meritocracy (1978:2).

Such problems remain common in traditional formal theological education programs whereby members of a church hierarchy maintain their positions primarily through complex systems which involve schools along the way. Bible School or seminary teachers in cooperation with ordained ministers often control the ordination of new candidates and do so primarily on the basis of academic achievements in formal educational settings. Ordination and licensure are granted on the basis of academic credentials rather than on demonstrations of a functioning ministry. We may see these problems in the West, but even more so in non-western contexts.

Nonformal Education

The need for an alternative to a formal approach to education usually finds expression in one or more of the following goals:

1) To bring education to people who are not being reached by the formal educational establishment.
2) To provide education at a lower cost.
3) To direct educational objectives toward goals that are more practical or more closely related to the learners' needs within their society (Ward, 1974:112).

A nonformal approach nearly always faces two stumbling blocks. In the first place some people who have come through a formal educational system tend to depreciate a nonformal approach as not being educational or equivalent. Secondly, leaders who teach and administer the nonformal programs feel pressure to increasingly formalize the programs, thus depriving them of their effectiveness. While such a system can not be described as "not being educational," the question of equivalence is one which needs more attention. In many cases equivalent programs are not desired because of the results they produce. However, in terms of the quality of the ministry produced, the goal must be higher than equivalence. One may face the temptation to

Edgar J. Elliston 287

increasingly formalize the program by reviewing it in light of the values which he has already set.

A nonformal approach to educating the ministry

> may break down the dichotomy between the clergy and laity by encouraging all kinds of leaders to prepare themselves for ministry. It stimulates the dynamics of ministry at the local level by training those men and women in the context of their own communities and congregations. It enables the congregations to develop their own leadership for ministry so that they do not need to depend on outside highly trained professional clergy (Kinsler, 1978:13).

Through such an approach large numbers of students may be served. These students may at the same time be serving the churches from which they come. Experience has generally shown that students who are trained through nonformal or extension modes continue to serve the church following completion of their studies whether they are paid or not and that they generally do not raise the support level expectation.

Theological education by extension (TEE) has generally fit into the nonformal education mode. TEE has been developed within a wide range between formal and nonformal structures. TEE is often conducted alongside traditional theological schools to supplement and extend their programs geographically and to involve a wider range of students. In many other contexts TEE is the primary means of theological education with no ties to a formal theological program. In many cases where it is linked with evangelism, the churches are experiencing both significant conversions and body growth.

However, one must be careful not to view TEE as a panacea for theological education problems. Simply to say, "We are going to have a TEE approach," does not justify one's bypassing the sometimes difficult decision-making which is being suggested in this chapter.

Rather than evaluating and developing educational programs based on "what has been" or on either of the two approaches suggested in Figure One, we should develop educational processes based on the values which have been developed out of and for the context to be served. We may find that one mode or the other is obviously the more appropriate or perhaps a creative combination would be the more appropriate. By working toward a creative combination we may be able to avoid the truth of Kinsler's criticism of traditional theological education about which he says, "Theological education can in fact be a major obstacle to the growth of the church and the fulfillment of her ministry" (1978:12). Education should not be simply equated with schooling. It has much broader potential structures and processes.

EVALUATION

Through this chapter questions about decision-making have been raised and processes for providing the data for these decisions considered. Early in the chapter a section about values was included. Both the processes of providing data for decision-making and the establishment and employment of values properly fall under the heading of evaluation. Proper use of evaluation may then provide the single most useful set of tools in the development of effective and appropriate curricula for church leadership education.

The process of evaluation need not threaten either those doing the evaluation or those who are being evaluated. Very often when the question of evaluation is raised, one immediately thinks of tests and testing, grades and grading or some other activity carried out by teachers in a classroom situation. However, for the curriculum planner evaluation is much broader and has much wider implications and requirements.

Stufflebeam provides a useful paradigm for understanding the functioning of evaluation and its relationship to decision-making. He defines evaluation by writing, "Evaluation is the process of delineating, obtaining, and providing useful information for judging decision alternatives" (1973:129). He then adds the following notes about evaluation:

1) Evaluation is performed in the service of decision-making, hence, it should provide information which is useful to decision-makers.
2) Evaluation is a cyclic, continuing process and therefore must be implemented through a systematic program.
3) The evaluation process includes three main

steps of delineating, obtaining, and providing. These steps provide the basis for a methodology of evaluation.

4) The delineating and providing steps in the evaluation process are interface activities requiring collaboration between evaluator and decision-maker while the obtaining step is largely a technical activity which is executed mainly by the evaluator (1973: 129-130).

Delineating

The decision-makers and evaluators begin by identifying two sets of information. First, they identify the values, criteria and principles which ought to be applied to the overall process. Secondly, they identify the decisions which are to be made along with the kinds of data which are needed to support these decisions. These decisions can be divided into four categories: 1) Planning decisions which relate to the setting of goals and objectives; 2) Structuring decisions which relate to the selection of sources of support, solution strategies and structuring of the educational program; 3) Implementing decisions which relate to the implementing and refining the program design and procedures; and 4) Recycling decisions which relate to program termination, continuation or modification based on the end results.

Obtaining

The obtaining of data is the second step in the process of evaluation. The primary research questions of validity and reliability provide the essential constraints for this step. Validity is concerned with raising appropriate questions which do in fact treat the problem at hand. Reliability is concerned on the other hand with the consistency of results and responses to the questions which are raised.

The methodologies available for obtaining the needed data for the evaluative process range from descriptive methodologies to the more complex experimental forms. The immediate problem to be served, context, and resources available all join in laying the constraints for determining the most appropriate methodology.

Providing

The third step is to give the information from the obtaining process to the decision-makers in a usable form. One must present the data in a form which is appropriate both to the context and for the decision-makers.

CONCLUSION

No two educational contexts are exactly the same so a cookbook formula for developing curricula would certainly fail. Its failure would be even the more certain in a cross-cultural context. However, while the educational forms may vary widely, the leadership goal functions remain constant. With the value and theological constraints imposed by Scripture on Christian leadership, the functions of Christian leadership are clear. The decision questions which aim at establishing forms to fit the known functions are parallel inter-culturally. The actual decisions, however, must come out of the considerations of the immediate context.

In this chapter we have sought to identify some of the more important decisions which will be made in the process of curricula development or improvement. If these decisions are consciously made, the context may be considered. If they are assumed, the context may have very little influence with the resulting curricula being less relevant than is desired. Curriculum planners should consciously make these decisions in the context **with** those being served not only to assure a developmental curriculum, but also to assure a contextualized curriculum.

Once the foundational values have been identified and a commitment has been made to maintain them, the processes of evaluation may serve the process of contextualized developmental curriculum decision-making. Whether one is concerned about the problems of curriculum improvement or new curriculum development, the processes and decisions identified in this chapter apply. As these decisions are made in the light of the values mentioned in this chapter and in the light of the context to be served, the problems of relevance and having adequate leaders may be treated.

BIBLIOGRAPHY

Elliston, Edgar J.
   1982 Curriculum Foundations for Leadership Education in the Samburu Christian Community. Unpublished Ph.D. dissertation, Michigan State University.

Kinsler, F. Ross
   1978 The Extension Movement in Theological Education. Pasadena: William Carey Library.

Kraft, Charles H.
   1979 Christianity in Culture. Maryknoll: Orbis Books.

Kung, Hans
   1972 Why Priests: A Proposal for a New Church Ministry. Garden City: Doubleday.

McGregor, Douglas
   1976 "An Analysis of Leadership," in Leadership and Social Change, ed. by William Lassey and Richard Fernandez. La Jolla: University Associaltes, Inc.

McKean, Rodney B.
   1977 "Uses of Research in Curriculum Development." Mimeographed paper.

Nicholls, Bruce
   1982 "The Role of Spiritual Development in Theological Education," in Evangelical Theological Education Today: Agenda for Renewal, ed. by Paul Bowers. Nairobi: Evangel Publishing House.

Plueddemann, James
   1982 "Toward a Theology of Theological Education," in Evangelical Theological Education Today: Agenda for Renewal, ed. by Paul Bowers. Nairobi: Evangel Publishing House.

Richards, Lawrence O.
   1975 A Theology of Christian Education. Grand Rapids: Zondervan Pub. House.

Richards, Lawrence O. and Clyde Hoeldtke (eds.)
   1980 A Theology of Christian Leadership. Grand Rapids: Zondervan Pub. House.

Sider, Ron (ed.)
   1981 *Evangelicals and Development: Toward a Theology of of Social Change.* Exeter: The Paternoster Press.

Simkins, Tim
   1977 *Non-Formal Education and Development.* Manchester: Univ. of Manchester Press.

Stufflebeam, Daniel L.
   1973 "Evaluation as Enlightenment for Decision-Making," in *Educational Evaluation: Theory and Practice,* Worthington: Charles A. Jones Pub. Co.

Tyler, Ralph
   1949 *Basic Principles of Curriculum and Instruction.* Chicago: Univ. of Chicago Press.

Ward, Ted
   1977 "Participation of Christians in National Development Projects." Lecture given at Daystar Communications. Nairobi, Kenya.

   1978 "Servants, Leaders and Tyrants." Lecture given at Calvin Theological Seminary. Grand Rapids, Michigan.

Ward, Ted and William Herzog, Jr. (et. al.)
   1974 *Effective Learning in Non-Formal Education.* East Lansing: Michigan State Univ.

Conclusion

To Fulfill the Task

by Ray A. Giles

If Ralph Winter is right, the situation is alarming. Dr. Winter, director of the U.S. Center for World Mission, has projected that within the next ten years 25,000 missionaries from North America will retire or return to their homeland for other reasons. With them will retire most of their donors who contribute 700 million dollars a year. At the present rate, only 5000 new missionaries will be going out during this same period. Many of the retiring missionaries went out in a wave of mission expansion following World War II. They have been faithful during their productive years and are now leaving the task to another generation (Winter, 1983:4).

If this is a trend for the decades ahead, it is occurring at the time of a heightened awareness for the church's responsibility to plant churches among the unreached peoples of our time. Mission research has identified 16,750 unreached people groups so that our efforts may be focused on reaching the unreached now. The Edinburgh II Conference of 1980 echoed the theme: "A Church for Every People by the Year 2000."

In order to complete the task of world evangelization, it has been projected that 200,000 missionaries are needed. But North America is not the only source of these cross-cultural workers. The balance has shifted so that there are now more Christians in the world who are non-Western than there are Western ones. These third world believers have become partners in sending missionaries. Dr. Lawrence Keyes has calculated that now there are fifteen thousand missionaries who are being sent out by third world countries. That is equal to one-third of the total full time missionary force from North America. Non-western missionary recruitment for full time cross cultural evangelism appears to be growing at least five times as fast as recruitment in the traditional home base for sending missionaries. This is good news. Yet, with the urgency of the unfinished task before us, we dare not be a disobedient church. In North America, we have expertise in specialized training and financial resources unequaled anywhere else in the world. We must give of our sons and daughters to bear the glorious message.

If there is a trend toward decline in the total number of missionaries being sent out by churches of the Western world, is this same trend evident among the churches of the Restoration heritage? I have not done a statistical study of the total number of persons being sent out for cross cultural and international service, but I am convinced that, though the percentages may vary, the same trend evident in the church at large will be the same among us unless we pursue a major change in priorities. This change must be evident in what is preached from our pulpits, in the priorities within our colleges and in emphasis in convention life. Exceptions to general trends are realized only be deliberate effort and fervent prayer.

All of this underscores the pivotal urgency of missions in this decade. **People are needed.** The trust that God has given to the church cannot be fulfilled without people who are sent to cross geographical, cultural and language barriers to plant churches that will in turn plant other churches among their own people. The cycle is complete only when these new churches begin to send out missionaries to neighboring peoples who are unevangelized.

Prior to the 1980 Winter Olympics in Moscow, Billy Graham commented that 92.8% of the people of the world would be able to see the competition on television or hear it on the radio. Because of this blessing of technology, the proclamation of the Gospel can be accelerated. True, we should use every means. But our commission cannot be carried out without the investment of life in paying the price of incarnational living with people who are different. We must "disciple" the nations and not only take a stab at them with electronic marvels. Life must be invested. **People are needed.**

Not only that -- **suitable people are needed.** The church is not obligated to send everyone who expresses an interest in going overseas. Nor is it good stewardship. Willingness to go is important, bit it is not the only criterion for sending. According to John Stott, it is a matter of the gift and calling of Christ. "It is clearly impossible for everybody to do everything which needs to be done. Therefore, there must be specialization according to the gifts and calling of Christ" (Stott, 1977:31).

One thing is certain. There is no surer way of raising the level of our work in missions than to have the right person representing the church. The cost in terms of inferior work, premature return and destruction to the lives of those who are sent out is enormous. Every effort must be made to get the right person to the right place. Nations who are in a position to receive missionaries are very sensitive about the ones who come. Government and church leaders feel that those who come to minister among them should have the same credentials to do the same kind of work in their home country.

No one can lay claim to an infallible system of predicting missionary success. However, there should be a thorough process that sends a carefully selected and prepared corps of people to the field. Ten suitable people can be more effective in accomplishing the primary task Christ has given to us than fifty who are ill-prepared and unsuited for cross cultural ministry.

Sometimes there is a kind of triumphalism as we make a head count of the number of missionaries we have. Regardless of what a person is doing, either at home or abroad, that name is added to the list with the great joy that we are thus being more effective in our missionary task. More is not automatically better. It does seem unspiritual to question the call of someone who is willing to go, but the church has a responsibility in the stewardship of life and resources. By some instrumentality, the church must sort through the gifts of those who are sent.

Are there identifiable characteristics which differentiate those missionaries who are judged more successful or less successful? If so, the church has a sober task of examining the gifts of possible candidates so as to send only those with the greatest likelihood of success on the mission field. This will be treated more at length later in this concluding chapter.

The most urgent need today is for the career missionary; the one who prepares specifically to be a missionary, learns the language and the culture well and sinks a chunk of his or her life there. **Suitable people are needed to serve long term.** Kerry Lovering states the need clearly:

> Seeing the church of Christ come to birth and grow to maturity among previously unevangelized people is the greatest of all team efforts. It takes the whole gamut of workers -- old pros, young pros, short-termers, long-termers, specialists, generalists, the works.
>
> But behind it all are the career missionaries. These are the ones who conceive the projects, draw the plans, coordinate the workers, guide the stages of development, and see the job through to completion. These are the ones who know the language, understand the culture, comprehend the problems, have gained acceptance by the people, and in general know which end is up (Lovering, 1979:2).

Without question, our greatest need right now is for the career missionary. By that is not necessarily meant one who stays and dies on the field, but one who at least is involved in multiple terms of service.

SUITABLE PEOPLE ARE NEEDED TO DO PRIORITY THINGS

Underlying what has been said thus far is an assumption that is obvious -- that there is no greater priority in missions today than evangelism and church planting. Mission effort must result in the visual manifestation of the Body of Christ. Samuel Zwemer, the apostle to the Muslims, said, "The church is always both **object and agent** of mission" (Van der Werff, 1982:185). The local church is God's primary agent for evangelizing the world. We must be persistent in this declaration. The world can be won only through the mobilization of the local church. Likewise, the object of the mission is that the church be planted. In addition to salvation, the church provides a new community out of which other aspects of life are elevated. Redemption in Christ lifts the rest of life, too. Feeding the hungry and improving the quality of life can best be done when the infrastructure of the church exists and there is a new humanity. Planting churches is holistic.

Ray A. Giles

FINDING THE WILLING

Recruiting deals with finding those who will at least consider the possibility of serving Christ in a cross cultural setting. Willingness is not the only criterion, but it is the first step.

Prayer and Recruiting

There is a direct correlation between prayer and the number of people who are going as missionaries. Jesus clearly states this relationship when He directed the response of His followers to the fields that were "white unto Harvest." He asked them to do only one thing in response to the overwhelming need and scarcity of reapers. "Pray the Lord of harvest that He send forth laborers into His harvest." He is the Lord of the harvest. Saving the world is His idea. Ask Him and He will raise up the harvesters. His disciples prayed, and then they were the first ones to go.

Today there still exists the relationship between the prayer and the availability of workers. J. Hudson Taylor wrote in the margin of his Bible in 1865, "Prayed for 24 willing workers at Brighton, June 25, 1865. If we are obeying the Lord, the responsibility rests with Him and not with us." God answered that prayer in providing willing workers for the China Inland Mission. Again in November of 1886, eleven men joined Taylor in eight days of prayer, four of which were days of fasting as well. They waited on God and prayed for 100 missionaries to be sent out in 1887. What was the result? God sent offers of service from over 600 men and women during the following year. Those considered ready and suitable were sent to China. A prayer to the Lord of the harvest was answered.

The most impressive evidence of God's faithfulness in answering the prayer for harvesters began over 250 years ago. A remarkable prayer meeting began with the Moravian community of Herrnhut in present day Germany. It continued "without ceasing" for 100 years, twenty-four hours a day. During the summer of 1727, in the wake of a great spiritual revival, 24 men and 24 women of the Moravian Christians pledged themselves to give one hour each day to form a continuous prayer chain that went unbroken for over 100 years. History makes it evident that this prayer had an impact. By 1792, only 65 years after the prayer chain had begun, over 300 missionaries had been sent to many nations around the world. When the prayer chain started, there were only 300 believers. They sent out more missionaries into more countries than all of the Protestant churches had sent in the previous 200 years!

In recruiting, the most important ingredient is not a pep-talk to motivate people to go. Nor is it address lists to whom computerized letters are sent, although these can be used effectively. It all comes back to the basics: Pray the Lord of harvest. Speaking about missions in churches, on Christian college campuses and in conventions is a major part of my schedule, but my most effective means of recruiting is my prayer list. I pray for people and with people about their possible future in reaching unreached people. There are dozens of names. This list changes as some make the definite decision to become missionaries and others conclude that their lives should be invested in other ways. But every Tuesday is devoted to prayer for harvesters.

Every minister should pray that God will raise up harvesters from within his congregation. Rather than a general list, it should include the names of individuals who have potential as missionaries. What a grand day it will be when missions is not composed of volunteers, but those who are drafted in the context of the church. The minister, an elder or a Bible school teacher can observe the gifts of a person and say, "I think you should consider mission service."

Pre-Candidate Crisis

For many it is fascinating to think about being a missionary in some exotic land. But when this fascination comes to the final point of decision that involves separation from relatives and familiar surroundings, a crisis occurs. It is like an invisible wall beyond which many would-be missionaries cannot pass. Better offers of Christian service appear. Sometimes leaders in the local church press the seeker towards some work at home that they say is equally important. "After all," they reason, "it is not more holy just because it is overseas, is it?" These potential missionaries come to feel that they can "multiply themselves" by staying at home. And still the lost stay lost for want of the evangel.

This pre-candidate crisis is very real -- and is engineered by one other than the Holy Spirit. Wycliffe Bible Translators receives over 1,000 new inquiries a month.

Of these, 76% do not follow through beyond the first step. In my work of missionary recruiting I estimate that of every 50 persons who make a preliminary inquiry and indicate serious consideration of being a missionary, only one gets to the field. Obviously, everyone who ever thinks about being a missionary is not suited to serve cross culturally and internationally. But I am convinced that many of those who give up their vision of serving Christ on the missionary frontier are gifted and capable of being effective. The world awareness that brings them to the point of serious consideration is aborted.

What can be done about this pre-candidate crisis? An awareness of this invisible wall should lead us to pray more fervently for an individual going through this process and to continue to provide a flow of information about missions. Furthermore, patience is required to allow them to work through the decision without guilt feelings or pressure.

Alternative Service

Some people are willing and qualified to serve in alternative ways, very often called "tent-making ministries." It is possible for some people to go where church-sponsored full time missionaries cannot go, and with all expenses paid. There are over 400,000 American businessmen with multi-national corporations working and living overseas. Why should not many of these be people of Christian conviction who seek opportunities to share in depth with at least one or two other persons in the area of daily association? In China alone 500,000 teachers of English are needed. There are Christian agencies which will match persons trained in teaching English as a second language with such opportunities.

One word of caution is needed at this point. The fact that a Christian is living overseas with another work assignment does not automatically open wide vistas of evangelistic outreach. There are many restrictions imposed in the foreign setting: by the employer, by the government, limitations of time and lack of facility in the language. One should not expect, therefore, to be conducting well-attended Bible studies and public worship services. In order to avoid frustrated expectations it is best to target a few people, perhaps even one person. Even then, a long time of building trust and understanding is a prerequisite. Furthermore, anyone willing to serve in such vocational service should not short-cut preparation. In-depth Bible study should be complemented by specific studies about the area of the world in which he or she serves. Cultural anthropology from a Christian frame of reference would be extremely valuable.

SELECTING THE SUITABLE

From the reservoir of the willing, we find those suited for mission service. Not everyone who expresses an interest in serving as a missionary is suited for the task. Personality traits, emotional state, spiritual strength and God's gifts to the individual have a bearing on effectiveness. It costs approximately $60,000 by the time the average missionary gets settled on the field. Good stewardship demands discriminating selection so that a select corps of people is sent.

This seems like an invasion into sacred territory. "What right do you have to assume the work of the Holy Spirit? God has called me to be a missionary." For one who feels strongly the call to a particular mission, it seems presumptive for any group or individual to analyze that leading. Yet the call must be subject to confirmation in a thorough process by those expected to sponsor the missionary.

Pre-Field Selection versus Natural Selection

It is not as though there us not a process of selection within the mission outreach of the Christian Churches and Churches of Christ. Some recruits are not able to raise funds and are eliminated even though some of these would be good missionaries. In the first term on the field, others are eliminated, usually after great pain to themselves and to the ones with whom they were expecting to work. This is a process of selection. It could be called "natural selection." However, thoroughness in selection before the time of field service is less destructive to lives, less disruptive on the field and far better stewardship of the resources of the church. The sooner in the process unsuitable persons are counseled to seek other options of service, the less painful it is for everyone.

The Inscrutable Five Percent

In calling for a careful look at the qualifications of the person who presents himself or herself for mission service, I want to be most careful not to make it purely a matter of checking off dimensions of personality on a list or calling on a computer to make that tabulation. In missions there is "that certain something" that often augments natural ability, education and parentage. In describing his scouting for baseball players for the Kansas City Royals, Red Whitsett told me that there is an intangible that determines the player who makes it. It is easy to watch a prospective player hit, pitch and run. But there is something else in the man's spirit that determines his long term success in baseball. There is that same intangible in the effective missionary.

Arthur Matthews, Candidate Secretary of the Overseas Missionary Fellowship, calls it the "inscrutable five-percent" (n.d. 29:1). Many times young persons go with great promise as missionaries and fail within their first year of service. Less likely candidates excel. What is it that has escaped us? Perhaps it is because we have tested the obvious 95% of the candidate's qualifications while the 5% has escaped us.

There is a special, intangible, inscrutable something that often determines success on the mission field. What is it? In addition to the hidden springs within the individual I suggest that this intangible is the missionary gift. This gift is not listed among the spiritual gifts in the writings of the Apostle Paul. Anyone who has the missionary gift also has one or usually more of the spiritual gifts listed in the New Testament. The missionary gift is a specific gift of cross cultural ministry which enables one to use gifts demonstrated in his homeland in another culture. Wagner defines the missionary gift as "the special ability that God gives to certain members of the Body of Christ to minister whatever spiritual gifts they have in a second culture" (1983:65).

These gifts are best discerned in the Body, the Church. This is why one selected to serve in another culture should have experience in some corresponding ministry in his own culture.

Predicting Missionary Success

There is the inscrutable 5% to be sure, but experience teaches us wisdom. We should be able to identify those variables that are most likely to make an effective missionary. There are several thorough studies which help in making a profile of the one most likely to make that adjustment. All admit, though, that predicting success is difficult indeed and is never infallible.

Kenneth Williams looks for identifiable characteristics that differentiate the more successful from the less successful personnel within Wycliffe Bible Translators. Comparing information obtained at the time of selection with subsequent performance on the field, Williams delineates the characteristics of the more successful and less successful missionaries. In letters of reference for the prospective missionary, notation of negative characteristics are more significant in selection than the strong positive characteristics that are stated. Negative characteristics are predictive of failure in missionary work. Throughout the study, four categories of negative characteristics appeared to fairly consistently differentiate between successful and unsuccessful workers: motivation; interpersonal skills; psychological problems; and family problems. Persons who have difficulties in these four areas apparently are not able to cope with the stresses of living and working in the field (Williams, 1973:139).

Over a three-year period, Britt used the screening sample of 111 persons who had served overseas with the Agape Movement of Campus Crusade for Christ. He found that combined methods of assessment, including biographical and psychological data, together with reference and interview data, were found to give the best selection of predictors. He cites as important: flexibility in adjusting to a new culture; a healthy self-concept; good ability with interpersonal relationships; perseverance; and facility with language. Depression and fluctuating mood are significant in adverse effects (Britt, 1980:22).

Of 72 variables that distinguish the more successful from the less successful missionary, Britt points to twelve which he deems the most significant (Britt, 1982). The studies mentioned, based on Wycliffe (which deals primarily with a technical specialty) and Agape (which has short-termers in a support ministry), are not universally applicable. For example, missions that emphasize a career commitment to evangelism and church planting will place more emphasis on in-depth Bible knowledge and graduate missiological training as determining factors in success (Hanscome, 1979:153). Nevertheless, the personal dimensions given are highly accurate.

It is risky to distill what has been presented into the most significant factors, but I will make the attempt:

1. The most significant factor is one's relationship to Jesus Christ. This is a part of the inscrutable 5%, that certain something. A missionary must be content with his or her position in Jesus Christ and be able to sustain that relationship through prayer and meditation on the Word without the usual props and promptings of the church.

2. Second to that is a healthy self-esteem. By that I mean one that does not run roughshod over colleagues or demand center stage. Even more dangerous is a low self-esteem, because there is little on the field to boost self-esteem.

3. A third factor has to do with mood-swings, especially those that shift to depression frequently. Successful candidates, in this survey, were rated by their acquaintances as rarely experiencing moodiness.

How can we of the Restoration heritage let experience teach us wisdom? How can we learn from the past in selecting the best possible candidates for service? We must do our best to select the suitable and then incorporate them into whatever system of sending we are using. The Church, missions agencies and missionaries on the field can all be a part of selecting the suitable.

Whereas the church may delegate some part of the selection process to an agency, it should never relegate its total responsibility to others. More and more churches are taking their responsibility seriously and have application forms which are used by each new mission or missionary desirous of support. In addition to personal qualifications, the nature of ministry and objectives of the mission should be stated clearly.

There are many agencies among us that recruit, screen and recommend persons for support in a particular kind of ministry or in a certain geographical area. These requirements for membership in the mission team can be an asset to the supporting congregations. The agency, therefore, must exercise the greatest care in the selection of missionaries.

The Christian Churches/Church of Christ Missionaries to Indonesia (CCMI) is a loosely organized mission including missionaries directly supported by the churches, those with the Christian Missionary Fellowship and others from the Mission Board of the Australian Churches of Christ. CCMI has a set procedure for the approval of new missionaries, including even a financial credit check! Persons associated with a mission agency are screened the same way. Missionaries on other fields should draw up a list of procedures for new people who intend to work with them in that field. Even the best pre-field selection is not infallible. Neither, though, should it be optional.

TRAINING THE CHOSEN

At the time of their decision for missionary service, few people have all the tools necessary for effective ministry within another land and culture. The rule of thumb is that whatever preparation would fit the person to do a similar job in his homeland is necessary plus some other things. Often it has been assumed that since missionary work often involves preliterate and poorly educated people, we are able to subtract some steps in preparation. However, we must add those things in preparation that enable us to understand another culture, learn the language and present the Gospel in a culturally appropriate manner.

The country that gave the world instant coffee and instant potatoes cannot give the church an instant missionary. Walking down an aisle to declare an intent to serve as a missionary does not perform a miracle of instantly equipping for the task. Such preparation is usually slow and deliberate.

In his study of the Christian and Missionary Alliance, Hanscome concluded that there is a substantial difference in the dropout rate of those without graduate work when compared with those who had at least some graduate training (Hanscome, 1979:153). The dropout factor is not the only reason for graduate work. Those who remain on the field should have the tools to be as effective as possible in ministry.

The mission outreach of the Christian Churches and the Churches of Christ can be greatly multiplied by using the same number of personnel, if additional time in preparation would be taken prior to departure to the field. It is almost inconceivable that one would go as a missionary without at least a rudimentary knowledge of cultural anthropology. Furthermore, why should the missionary be handicapped in language learning or give short shrift to it when excellent options are available for studying the techniques of language learning.

A four year college program, whatever the college or major, is not adequate to give all the essential Bible knowledge, general education **and** special tools needed for a career in missions. Building upon the college degree, graduate missions courses should also be taken.

A Delicate Balance

The right kind of preparation involves a delicate balance in two areas: experience and academics. Whenever the subject of training for missionary service arises, our minds usually race towards schooling and classroom situations. Actual experience in working with people, teaching the Bible and leading people to Christ is an absolute necessity. This is not academic, but experiential. One should go to the field with the confidence that he or she can indeed function within his or her home country in a ministry parallel to what will be done on the field.

Whatever is said about academic requirements must be balanced with education that comes from life experiences. Both are essential and a delay of a few years to fill in missing practical experience is not time wasted, but may likely result in more effective and long term missionary service.

A further ingredient of this needed experience is developing skills in interpersonal relationships. Being able to relate to both nationals and colleagues on the field requires these skills.

Real balance is required in getting needed preparation while not delaying field service past the optimum time for a person to arrive on the field. Facility to learn language and make many adjustments is generally easier when one is younger. When there are children involved, it seems better for them to make the transition to another country while still relatively young. This means that the optimum age would probably be between 25 and 35. Therefore, every work and experience that would be useful has to be balanced so that the path to the field is not so long as to be counterproductive. In reality, when considering this balance, it may be best to require the basic beginning preparation with the understanding that furlough includes additional study which is applied to a graduate degree in missions.

Academic Preparation

The academic requirements that are being set forth do not apply in every situation. For example, a mid-career person who wishes to become a missionary has likely had many experiences both within the church and in business that may be counted as equivalents. The academic requirements should be tailored to the need. Specialized roles in medicine, agriculture or administration require preparation of a different kind. Even then, there should be enough background in mission strategy, cultural differences and language learning to facilitate the transfer of these skills to another country.

The following suggestions in the preparation of missionaries are given in the awareness that there are exceptions:

1. A baccalaureate degree is assumed as the basis upon which other academic training is built. The college degree, regardless of major, represents a certain amount of discipline and provides background for further study. Graduate study in missions is possible only with such a background.

2. If the college degree did not include biblical studies, at least one academic year of Bible is a minimum. An overview of the whole Bible, life of Christ, development of the early church and principles of interpretation should be included.

3. Specialized mission studies should follow with emphasis on the following areas: cultural anthropology; principles of missions and church growth; history of Christian expansion; language learning techniques; area studies; worldview; and leadership training in a cross cultural setting.

Experience on the field usually indicates other areas where additional preparation is needed. In addition to the usual responsibilities of furlough, some amount of time should be used in additional study. Through taped lectures and extensive reading, missiological understanding can be greatly expanded through in-service-training on the field.

CONCLUSION

Change is rapidly altering the face of missions. Many leaders have written in books and periodicals about major scene-changes like nationalism, urbanization, skyrocketing costs, Marxism and a revived Islam. We have come to the end of our era and are standing at the dawn of another. We must find ways to be faithful to our Commander in these changing times.

Although many things change, one thing is constant: the fulfillment of the Great Commission requires the investment of life. Suitable trained people are still needed to concentrate on planting the church **Unto the Uttermost**. Although this challenge was given in 1901, John R. Mott's message is still timely:

> Therefore, friends, in view of the awful need of men who tonight live without Christ; in view of the infinite possibilities of life related to Christ as mighty Saviour and risen Lord; in view of the magnitude of the task which confronts the Church of this generation; in view of the impending crisis and the urgency of the situation; in view of the conditions which favor a great onward movement within the Church of God; in view of the dangers of anything less than a great onward movement; ... yes, in view of the constraining memories of the Cross of Christ and the love wherewith He hath loved us, let us rise and resolve, at whatever cost of self-denial, that live or die, we shall live or die for the evangelism of the world in our day (Mott, 1901:10).

BIBLIOGRAPHY

Britt, William Gordon
1980   The Prediction of Missionary Success Overseas Using Pretraining Variables. Unpublished Ph.D. dissertation, Rosemead Graduate School of Professional Psychology.

1982   "Predicting Mission Success Overseas Prior to Selection." Emissary. 13:1:1-7.

Hanscome, Craig
1979   "Predicting Missionary Drop-Out." Evangelical Missions Quarterly. 15:3:152-155.

Lovering, Kerri
1979   "Career Missionaries: Time for a Comeback." Africa Now. 104:2-5.

Matthews, Arthur
n.d.   "Candidate Letter." Focus. 29.

Mott, John R.
1901   "The Responsibility of Young People for the Evangelization of the World," in Missionary Issues of the Twentieth Century. (Reprinted).

Stott, John
1977   Christian Mission in the Modern World. Downers Grove: InterVarsity Press.

Van Der Werff, Lyle
1982   "Our Muslim Neighbors: The Contribution of Samuel M. Zwemer to Christian Mission." Missiology. 10:2:185-197.

Wagner, C. Peter
1983   On the Crest of the Wave. Ventura: Regal Books.

Williams, Kenneth Lee
1973   Characteristics of the More Successful and Less Successful Missionary. Unpublished Ph.D. dissertation, United States International University.

Winter, Ralph
1983   "Answers to Important Questions." Mission Frontiers. 5:8:4.

Index

accomodation 254
adherent 43
Adiwiyoyo, Antonius 219,220
age-grade 206-209,212
Akpem, Yosev Y. 180
Allen, Roland 15,237
Allen, Yorke 258
Alt, Albrecht 61
American Bible Society 97
American Christian Bible Society 147
American Christian Missionary Society 1-3,101,106,110,146,147
American Indians 4
analogue 62
Anderson, Gerald H. 90
animism 218
anti-missionism 96
Antoni, Guadalupe 190
Apocalypse 70-92
apostolic band 52
apostolicity 140,142,148
Aramoni, Aniceto 182
Argentina 3,8,9
Arias, Mortimer 265
Armenia 4
Arndt, W. F. 6,7
Arusha tribe 201
Asbury, Francis 123
Atmosudjono, M. 219,221
atonement 26,28,30,35
Australia 5,304
Austria 5
Azbill, W. K. 5,9

Baraguyu tribe 201
Barclay, J. T. 2,112,145,146

Barnett, Homer G. 167
Barrett, David 253
Barrett, J. Pressley 123
Baxter, William 118
Beardslee, J. O. 2
Belgian Congo 3,8
Belgium 5
Berger, Peter 169
Bethany College 232
Bethlehem 2
Bible colleges 7,14,15,283,298,305
Billheimer, Paul E. 150
Bishop Provoost 117
Board of Church Extension 8
Board of Ministerial Relief 8
Bolivia 242,252,265
Brazil 268
Brazil Christian Mission 10
Britain 149, 234
British Churches of Christ 138,150
Britt, William 302
Brommei, Bernard 177
Brueggemann, Walter 67
Burma 129,237
Burnet, D. S. 102,112,126,147
Butler, Pardee 144
Butler College 233

California 14,242
Calvin, John 125
Campbell, Alexander 1,2,95-112, 119-123,127,140,147,150
Campbell, Thomas 95,125-126
Campus Crusade for Christ 302
Canada 3,5
Cane Ridge 121,124
Carey, William 143

INDEX

Carr, James B. 2,8,11
Carrillo, Carmen 181-182,195
catholicity 137,140,142,148
Ceylon (Sri Lanka) 237
Chief Justice Marshall 117
Chile 13,254
China 3,8,11,15,65,268,297,299
Christian Baptist 96,99,100-102, 112
Christian Chronicle 5
Christian Evangelist 4,7,237
Christian Military Fellowship 12
Christian Missionary Fellowship 10-12,304
Christian Missionary Society 2,3, 144
Christian presence 106
Christian Restoration Association 11
Christian Standard 3,6,8
Christian Women's Board of Mission 3,8,10,147
Chrysostom, John 171
Church Growth Bulletin 244,249, 253
church growth movement 15,231-232, 248-259
Church of Christ (non-instrumental) 4,5,16
Cincinnati Bible Seminary 14
Coleman, Robert 76
College of Missions 233,241,256
Columbia University 234
Constantine 171
contextual symbiosis 266-269
contextualization 281
Continuing Christian Church of India 10
covenant 21-37,74,82
Cox, F. A. 119
Cranfield, C. E. 68
Creath, Jacob (Jr.) 102
Cross, Alexander 2
Cuba 3,5
cultural imperialism 165
cultural relativity 164-167,277
cultural voids 214
culture 155-174

Daily Courier 119
Davies, Samuel 125
day of atonement 23
DeGroot, A. T. 1,118,145
Deissman, Adolf 59
DeLannay, Jules 4
Denmark 3,5
DeRidder, Richard 74-75
development 278-280,290
dialogue 254
Diaz-Guerrero, F. 197
Dickerson, G. Fay 90
direct support 10,12-14,148
Disciples of Christ 5,7-10,16,232-241

discipling 38-54,253-254,256,274
divine silence 6,17
Division of Overseas Ministries 8
Douglas, J. D. 265
Drewery, Mary 143
DuPreez, James 71,74

Edinburgh II 293
elect 27
Elliston, Edgar J. 271
Ellul, Jacques 82-83,90
enculturation 160
England 3,5
Errett, Isaac 3-4,6,146
ethics 21,24-25,33-35
ethnics 21,28-29
ethnocentrism 165,169,200,256,277
evaluation 288-290
Evangelism-in-Depth 252

faith-promise 12
family 176-197
Fanning, Tolbert 3,144
Fellowship and Association of Medical Evangelists 12
Filbeck, David 10,14,144
Fiorenza, Elisabeth 77
Ford, Henry 159
Foreign Christian Missionary Society 3,8,10,147,232
formal and non-formal education 284-288
Formosa 240
forwarding agents 10
Fuller Theological Seminary 14, 129,242-244,252,256
France 3,4
Fuller, Dr. 125
functional substitutes 200,213-215

Galvin, Kathleen 177
Gandhi, Mohandas 167,234
Garrett, Leroy 144
Garrison, J. H. 7,119
Geertz, Clifford 217,219-220
General Missionary Society 6
Germany 142-297
Gingrich, F. W. 67
Glas, John 122
Glasser, Arthur 56-57,66
Good News Productions 12
Gospel Advocate 3
Graham, Billy 294
Great Commission 9,11,21,25,28,33, 35,38,40,42-43,46,50,130,143, 261,274
Gressit, Linsley 262,266
Griffeth, Ross J. 242,247
Grosvenor, Dr. 125
Guernsey, Dennis B. 178

Haggard, Rice 123-125
Haldane, James 122
Haldane, Robert 122

INDEX

Hall, B. F. 144
Hamilton, Keith 242
Hampden-Sydney College 118
Hanscome, Craig 302-304
Hawaii 3
Haystack prayer meeting 118
hembrismo 184,192
Henrichsen, Walter 39
Hendriksen, William 77
Herskovits, Melville 165
hidden peoples 13
historical folktales 219-227
Hoebel, E. Adamson 165
Hoeldtke, Clyde 273
Hoge, Dean R. 260
Hoke, Donald 264
Holland 5
home missions 143
homogeneous unit principle 76,257
Honk Kong 5
Hughes, Richard T. 102
Hungry Children U.S.A. 12

identification 201
ideology 155,164,168-174,191-193
Illinois 119
incarnational evangelism 199
independency 10,12
independent missions 8-17
India 3,6,8-11,15,128-130,132,
    167,232,234-240,244,245,247,
    252,254
India Bible Society 129
Indiana 13,127
indigenous 200,215,226,256,277
Indonesia 13,216-228,268,303
Institute of Church Growth 14,
    240-246
International Congress on World
    Evangelization 244,264
International Convention 8
International Disaster Emergency
    Service 12
International Missionary Conference
    233
International Review of Missions
    237,249,253
Italy 3,5
inter-denominational cooperation
    8
Ireland 120
Islam 217-218,307

Jamaica 2,3,8,9,240
Jamaica Christian Mission 10
Japan 3,5,8,9,240,254,268
Java 216-228,252
Javanese alphabet 222-226
Johnson Bible College 14

Kantor, David 180
Kasemann, Ernst 67
Kentucky 119,121,127
Kenya ix,13,201,204,276

Keyes, Lawrence 293
Khasi Hills 128
Kinsler, F. Ross 287,288
Kluckhohn, Clyde 156
Korea 5
Kraft, Charles H. 191-192,277
Kroeber, Alfred 156
Kuhn, Gary W. 39
Kuki tribe 129
Kung, Hans 273

Ladd, George E. 74
Lambert, Byron C. 102
Lampe, G. W. 67
Latourette, Kenneth S. 58,132
leadership development 270-290
Lehr, William 180
liberalism 2,6-8
Liberia 2,3
Lincoln Christian College 14,90
Liscomb, William 3
living link 11
Lord, J. A. 8
Lord's Supper 213
Lovering, Kerry 296
Luckman, Thomas 169
Lunger, Harold L. 102
Lunkim, T. 129
Lushai Hills 128
Luther, Martin 125,244
Luzbetak, Louis 199-200

Maasai tribe 201-215,276,278
MacClenny, W. E. 124
machismo 182-184,192
Madison, Bishop James 117,123,125,
    126
Mahoning Association 99-100,102-
    103,118-119
Malan, S. C. 68
Malawi 130-131
Manhattan Christian College 14
marianismo 184
Marx, Karl 172
marxism 171,307
Matthews, Arthur 301
Meitei tribe 129
mere numbers 251
Mexico 3,8-9,176-197
Michigan 233,241
Millennial Harbinger 112,120,127
Milligan College x
Milligan, George 57,59,67
Mills, Samuel J. 118
ministry 32-33,36
Minnesota 119
Minnesota Bible College 14
Minuchin, Salvador 178
missiology x-xii
mission agency 2,4,6,10,96-97,100,
    105,147-148
Mission Services 13-14
mission station approach 112,237,
    238

missionary preparation 293-306
Missouri 3,126-127
Mizo tribe 128
Mol, Frans 204-207
Moore, W. T. 3
Morris, Henry 67
Morse, J. Russell 11
Morse, Laverne 14
Mott, John R. 307
Moulton, James 59
Murch, James D. 122,146

McAllister, Lester G. 132
McCaleb, J. M. 5
McCurdy, David 192
McFarland, Harrold 13
McGarvey, J. W. 146
McGavran, Donald A. 14,76,116,
  120-121,231-247,260
McGavran, Mary 233-234
McGready, James 125
McGregor, Douglas 280
McKane, William 67
McKean, Rodney B. 275
McLean, Archibald 70,147,232
McNemar, Richard 124

Naga Hills 128
Nakari, Toyozo W. 67
names of God 61-62
National Benevolent Association 8
National Missionary Convention 13
National Tract Society 97
Neill, Stephen 56
neo-pagan 192-193,197
Nepal 9
neurosis 194
New Zealand 5
New Zealand Churches of Christ 132
Nicholls, Bruce 274
Nida, Eugene A. 192,200,244
Nigeria 5
Niles, D. T. 76-77,84,90
Njemps tribe 201
North American Christian Convention 13
Northwest Christian College 14,
  242-244,247
Norway 5

oath 23
Officer, R. W. 4
Ohio 3,104,118-119
O'Kelley, James 124
Ongay, Mario 177,179,185-187,195
open-membership 8
Operation Evangelistic Ministries 12
oral literature 226-228
Orr, J. Edwin 117,119,121,127,129,
  130,132
Osborn, R. E. 145
Otero, Luis L. 183
Overseas Missionary Fellowship 301

Owen, Robert 107
Ozark Bible College 14

Panama 3
Papua New Guinea 165
para-church organization 2,4,12
Paraguay 3,8,9
parasitism 266
Paris Evangelical Mission 131
Parker, David 96
partnership in mission 280
Patillo, Henry 125
Paton David M. 265
Paul, Azariah 4
Pearce, Carolyn N. 3
Penalosa, F. 181
Pendleton, W. K. 102,112,127
people groups 13
people movements 235-236,239,241
  254
Philippines 3,5,8,9,11,13,240
Phillips, Richard 150
Phillips, Woodrow 14
Pickett, J. Waskom 235-236
Pioneer Bible Translators 10-12
Plato 158
Plueddemann, James 275
polygamy 159
Potter, Philip 264
power 78-89
power-encounter 89
priesthood 24,30-31,36
publishing 245,255
Puerto Rico 3,8,9,240
purification 211

racism 165,172
Randall, Max Ward 14,121,124,129,
  131
reality postulates 162,164
receptivity 253,268
reconciliation 32-33,36,39
recruitment 14
redemptive analogies 201
research 255
resistant 255
responsiveness 238,253-254
Revelation 70-92
revivals 116-132,137,254
Rhodesia 132
Richards, Lawrence O. 273
Richardson, Don 227
Richardson, Robert 102,112,119,122
Rincon, Bernice 182
ritual-expert 205
Robinson, William 146
Rogers, Samuel 144
Rogers, William 121
Rosenkranz, Gerhard 56
Rothermel, Dr. 11

sacrifice 23-24,28-31,35-36,204-
  214
Samburu tribe 201,276,278

INDEX

Sand Creek Address and Declaration 4
San Jose Bible College 14
Sankan, S. S. 204-205
Scanlon, Clark 258
Schaefer, Harry Sr. 11
school approach 131
School of World Mission 14,129, 242-246,252,256
Scotland 5,122
Scott, R. B. 67
Scott, Walter 99-100,103,118-119, 122
Serampore College 129-232
servants 272
sexuality 181-186
Sider, Ron 279
Siefke, William 244
Simkins, Tim 284
Singapore 5
slavery 144
Smith, Ebbie C. 252
Smith, Elias 124
Smith, Mont W. 74
social action 260-269
sociology of knowledge 169
South Africa 5,9,130,167
South Pacific Evangelizing Fellowship 12
Southwestern Baptist Theological Seminary 258
Soviet Union 168
Specialized Christian Services 12
Spradley, James P. 192
Stevens, Evelyn P. 182
Stewart, James 74
Stone, Barton 118,121-122,150
Stott, John R. 70,295
Strauss, James 90
Stufflebeam, David 288-289
Subbamma, V. B. 254
Sudan 201
Sweden 5
Sweet, William W. 127
Switzerland 244
syllogism 32,36
symbols 76
syncretism 57,64,214,217-218

Tanzania 5,201
Tate, Marvin 67
Taylor, J. Hudson 297
TCM International 10
Tertullian 125
Texas 4,119
Thailand 9,240
Thayer, Joseph H. 43
The Disciple 9
theological education 257-258,270-290
Thomas, Winburn 249
three-selfs 15
Tibet 3
Time Magazine Inc. 253

Tippett, Alan R. 89-90,200,214-215, 243
Tjokrosentono, K. 219
totalitarian 168
Turkey 3
Turner, Nat 171
Tyler, Ralph 276,283
Tylor, Edward B. 156

Union Theological Seminary 234
United Christian Missionary Society 2,7-11,147,233,238,240-242
United Foreign Mission Society 97
unity 95,97,136-150
universalism 29-30
University of Oregon 243
urban 176-197,256
U.S. Center for World Mission 246, 293

value postulates 162,164
Van Buren, James G. 146
Vandergrfit, Eileen 2
Van der Werff, Lyle 296
Virginia 104,118,123,125
Visser't Hooft, W. A. 197
Von Rad, Gerhard 67
Voshaar, Jan 204

Wagner, C. Peter 252
Ward, Ted 279,285-286
Weber, Max 174
Wesley, John 125
West, Don 238
West Germany 5
West, Earl 3,4
West, Frederick 102
Whitefield, George 125
Whitsett, Red 301
Williams College 118
Williams, Kenneth 302
Winter, Ralph 16,71,246,258,293
Wisconsin 119
Wolfe, Leslie 9
World Call 9,237
World Convention of the Churches of Christ 143
World Council of Churches 145,249, 264-265
World Dominion 237
World Vision
World War I 6,10,233
World War II 11,13-15,142,253,256
worldview 162,164,169,202-204,218, 271,306
Wycliffe Bible Translators 298,302

Yale University
Yorburg, Betty 178

Zaire 9
Zambezi Industrial Mission 131
Zambia 130-132
Zimbabwe 5,130-131